What Readers Are Saying About *Being at Ease*

Although he has authored other important writings, this time Jim Hylton has produced a true masterpiece. He has tied together the time-space continuum, molecular biology, human physiology, and neuroscience with God's plan to replace sin, fear, wrong thinking, and disease with gratitude, love, pure thoughts, and true rest and ease—and in a way that is understandable to doctors, scientists, theologians, and laypeople alike. I have been a Christian for many years, but I learned a lot from this book and was blessed with a new level of excitement about what my life can become now, as well as what I will do as an eternal citizen of the new Heaven and the new earth. It's a book to be read by everyone.

R. Michael Siatkowski, MD

I have known and loved Jim Hylton for almost 40 years. He has been a faithful and courageous pioneer in things related to the kingdom of God. He has never blinked in the face of fire. His desire to help people know the God that he knows has enabled him to be relevant no matter his age. Now, he is again challenging us to think beyond our traditional paradigms to discover another facet of the great treasure we already have in Jesus. We will enjoy God fully as we find that we can actually love him with all of our mind as well as our heart and soul. Read and think! We have the mind of Christ.

Dudley Hall
President, Kerygma Ventures
Colleyville, Texas
Author: Grace Works, Incense and Thunder, Orphans No More

In *Being at Ease*, Jim Hylton insightfully weaves together what the Bible and scientific research tell us about our thought processes and their affect on our health and wholeness. In these pages we see how the aspects of our pers⌐   d—which Dallas Willard defined as Thought, Feeling, Will, Body, S⌐   nd Soul—function best when we align our thoughts with ⌐   iven me much to ponder and pursue about my th⌐·   ⌐eives when I embrace the mind of Christ. Thaι   ⌐aging book!

⌐ecca Willard Heatley
⌐ɡhter and Ministry Assistant,
⌐reative Director, www.DWillard.org,
Editor oʃ The Allure of Gentleness *by Dallas Willard*

DISCARL

Every once in a while you read a book that completely changes how you think about the way you think, and how you are living the way you live. This is such a book! Jim Hylton is a wise, experienced, and compassionate guide who will take you on a journey toward Shalom. Through these pages you find keys that allow the dormant power within you to come to life. Drink deeply, growing in the knowledge of who God is and of who you really are. You can experience abundant, refreshing, new life.

Leif Hetland
Author, Seeing Through Heaven's Eyes

These pages will challenge your mind and heart. It leads to a journey to not only hear from God but to learn to think like God thinks. Proverbs tells us that as we think in our hearts so we are! Philippians tells us that our goal is to have the mind and attitude of Christ. These pages will point the way to a new way of thinking. They are grounded in the redemptive work of Christ in the lives of believers, and in the dwelling of the Holy Spirit in the hearts of believers.

Jimmy Draper
President Emeritus, LifeWay

Jim Hylton's new book, *Being At Ease*, is truly a godsend, especially to stressed- out, hurting, and sick people, who really should be the most healed, joyous, and peace-filled people on earth. In a recent time with Jim I reflected on knowing him for more than 30 years. We met as neighbors in the same housing development. We shared a common bond of seeing spiritual awakening. In our recent conversation I was reminded how I know him not from his physical appearance, but from his character and integrity. When I get a call from Jim, I see him not because of a picture in my phone but from the image of knowing his inner spiritual qualities. His book is teaching us to know God by knowing His thoughts, His character, and most of all His nature of love. In knowing God we get to know ourselves. I wholeheartedly recommend this book to you.

Kenneth Copeland
Speaker, author,
Host, The Believer's Voice of Victory

The book you hold was not written without years of thinking and spiritual experience on the part of Jim Hylton. These past few years he has shared with me many of the helpful insights he presents. He states very clearly that America has a thinking crisis that has lead us to a health crisis as well other issues of concern. With careful research and insight from both God's perspective and some of the best minds today, Jim offers counsel on how to hear God's thoughts. In God's thoughts are found the peace God intends for everyone. This is an important book teaching us how to be at ease with God, with ourselves, and with others. You will find help in these important realities as well as find ways to help others.

James Robison, co-host, Life Today
Founder of LIFE Outreach International and The Stream website

Contents

Dedication

I want to honor some who now Know As They Are Known:

T.W. and Laverne Hunt
Ernest and Ruth Byers
Bob and Bea Mauldin

As the first elders of Lake Country Baptist Church, they welcomed me as their pastor to serve and learn with them. That journey continued for 18 years. Honor to whom honor is due is offered with deep gratitude.

Dr. T.W. Hunt, professor at Southwestern Baptist Theological Seminary, taught us what later became a book: *The Mind of Christ.*

Dr. Ernest Byers, MD, a highly respected anesthesiologist, taught us the truth of Christ's healing power in the laboratory of his own healing from cancer.

Bob Mauldin, an engineer, became a student of Christ as well as His companion in prayer, and he taught us devotion to God in all things.

Their lives, knowledge, and faith provided many thought-expanding experiences for me.

A stronger foundation was being laid in my life: knowing the mind of Christ is ours to access; knowing His power is ours for healing of every kind—emotional, physical, and spiritual; and knowing His desire to communicate with us.

These families were people with excellent minds and equally pure hearts. They became part of my spiritual family.

Acknowledgments

It takes very skilled people in a village to raise a book. This one is being read because a village of friends gave me help of many kinds. All who helped have my appreciation though I may not have space to mention you.

Fellow Founders of Trina Health of North Texas – Dr. David Capper, Dr. Phil Fuller, Rusty Mayeux: For sharing your lives and professional skills with me and many people reflecting God's loving ways as well as medical excellence.

Bob Roberts: For being my pastor, my counsel on many issues as well as this book. Your insightful, Christ reflective thinking has spurred me on. Thinking what God thinks as evidenced in Northwood Church as well as being an ambassador/pastor to the world while loving as Jesus loves but at the same time without compromise to His kingdom realities – His way, His truth and His life.

Dudley Hall: For your theological check ups as well as your healthy thoughts that have shaped my life over many years – for being one who is "strong in the Lord."

Carl Copeland: For your ingenious skills in keeping my computer healthy as well as giving me insight in many issues of life and being a model of thinking leading to creative breakthroughs as an inventor.

Dr. Michael Siatkowski: For giving far more than a review of correctness about sight as an ophthalmologist, but for a complete review of the book as a committed knowledgeable Christian.

Kay Moreno: For using your writing skills to find typos and grammar that needed transplants for clarity.

Patients at Trina Health: For your fun loving ways of discussing life, facing challenges with your health in faith applications –- for asking about this book and sharing in the progress with many questions as well as affirmations of the need for the concepts.

Keystone Study Group: For your faithfulness to attend our Thursday bible study across six years and eagerly receiving teaching that made it past our discussion edits into several pages that follow.

Friends of God and Mine: For your prayer participation as you claimed the greatest mind ever to think giving me some of the insights to share in these pages.

Preface

Dear Reader,

It is true a book is not known by its cover. However, the cover of this book suggests the serenity a garden brings. The contents review the meaning of life, which started in a garden setting. Life is intended to continue in that same abundance of beauty and life-giving peace.

I want to make a promise to you, the prospective reader. The contents of this book will guide you to a review of the garden God is offering. But this path of thought to gain garden privileges is not just another walk in the park. Weighty thoughts, along with accounts of various life experiences, will take time to process. Easy reading is not the objective. Easy living, or living with a new ease, is the intended goal.

The initial chapters require some diligence to complete. They can be skipped to get to the "ease of garden reality," but in doing so you will not have a foundation for the deeper thoughts that follow. There will be thoughts about seeing with your brain, thoughts about our body being like a medical clinic where we influence healing and health, thoughts about living eternally described in science and verified in Scripture, and most importantly thoughts from God about us and what He intends for us to have and enjoy, namely "all things pertaining to life."

So I am promising to take you on a journey of thought. If this was a mountain-climbing experience, the first six chapters would call for a climb to get a better view of where we are going. Thinking is our greatest gift, one that leads to all the benefits God intends. Speed-reading that exceeds the speed of good thinking only burns needless mental fuel. Knowing as God knows is our real goal.

My promise is this: if you take the time to read on, you will find some insights well worth your time. God wants us to start enjoying His ease now. Don't save eternity until later. Start enjoying this reality now!

Jim Hylton

Foreword

Jim Hylton is on to something really big. It's so big that if we can apply it to our lives it will change us, our families, our churches, our cities, and our world in profound ways that we haven't even imagined. If applied, this is a truly revolutionary book. Jim has always been a pioneer thinker-practitioner, from the move of the Holy Spirit in his life and ministry, to his understanding of the kingdom of God and what that looks like, to now his understanding of the impact of our thoughts and the mind and how we process information and think about things.

"Do not be conformed to this world, but be transformed by the renewal of your mind, that by testing you may discern what is the will of God, what is good and acceptable and perfect" (Romans 12:2, ESV). We've read that verse a thousand times—but do we know how to apply it? What does it mean to have a transformed mind? How does a transformed mind change everything?

We need both the heart and the head for people to experience a transformed life. The reality is that most pastors focus a tremendous amount on the heart, but very little on the head—and that's the problem! The head has been limited to learning some stuff so you won't be a heretic, to perhaps doing some stuff to try to hold on to what you have spiritually, like reading your Bible and praying everyday. I grew up seeing a lot of "heart" transformation, but it didn't last. Instead of a way to move forward from where you were, it was a bath you would take to clean up every once in a while.

I have experienced this in my own life. That led me to take a step forward, because it involved more than just my heart; my head was included as well. In my desire to learn how to "last" and stay on fire for God when others weren't doing so, I began to read about the prayer life of great men like George Mueller, E.M. Bounds, and many others. So I decided I would pray at least an hour a day just like them. I can still remember being prayed out after 10 minutes!

I learned about different discipleship processes that took me into spiritual disciplines, but they didn't deliver for me. It became rules and regulations of what to do to hear God's voice, and though these brought some good fruit in my life, they were still way lacking in intimacy and transformed thinking. All head and no heart didn't work either. Creating a new law for me to "be good" was not enough—I still hadn't discovered living as a son and enjoying the presence of God versus the idea of simply staying "good."

Something happened to me, however, in 1992 that forever changed me. At the age of 34 I stumbled into the concept and life in the kingdom of God. It redefined following Jesus for me in a profound way. I knew the Gospel of salvation: get saved so you can go to Heaven. I didn't know the Gospel of the kingdom, the transformation and reconciliation of all people and all things. At a point of brokenness, the question "When will Jesus be enough?" permeated me, and forced me to ask why he was not enough. It led me to what it really means to follow Him, which led me to the Sermon on the Mount. For the first time I read the radical call of Jesus beyond sin to a radical lifestyle based on the teaching of Jesus—that changed everything. I began to plunge into the Scriptures, pray, journal, worship, and I began to change dramatically. Disciplines didn't bring me to the kingdom, but came as a result of me *thinking differently* about what God's kingdom, his rule and reign, was all about. Prayer and spiritual disciplines were now not something to make me discover God as much as to hear him, commune with him, and follow him.

Dallas Willard's *The Divine Conspiracy* was a guide for me during this process, one that forever changed me. The Christian life for me moved from being an event or secret to being a lifestyle and a dynamic interactive relationship with Jesus. My thinking was changing, from that of a God who stamps tickets to Heaven, to God my Father who wants me living like a son in confidence and security. That kingdom understanding took me into the world, it revealed the critical practice of following the Holy Spirit, and over time it began to reshape how I thought. I saw the same thing happen to many in our church. Why was this the case? It was all in how they *thought*. Knowing God as Father … following Jesus and seeing the Holy Spirit work was creating a whole new set of sensors to hear and see God present at all times. Sadly, I had very little framework to help someone through this transition.

What Jim has done is take an understanding of how the "mind" is forever alive and how we replant a new way of thinking and brought these concepts to his readers. He has merged the head and heart in a way that allows us to see ourselves different, and this releases the potential of God in doing something very new in us and those around us. I'm convinced this is the next great breakthrough that is going to take us to a new level of knowing, hearing, and following Jesus. Jim has been speaking into my life in this area, as Dallas Willard did on the kingdom of God, and the impact has been profound.

This is not a book you'll read in one sitting. Read it slowly; think about it. Don't view it as a quick read, but as a way to think—and this will require you to process, and it will have incredible value to you. Those books that have had the biggest impact on me required smaller bites at a time and they called for reflection to truly digest the matters of importance. This is that kind of book. Thank you, Jim, for this gift to the body of Christ. We desperately need it.

Bob Roberts Jr.
Author, Senior Pastor, NorthWood Church
Keller, Texas

A Word from Jack Taylor

It has never been more important in the history of the world for us to think properly. Thank God for great thinkers, of whom Jim Hylton is one! Jim and I have been friends for almost half a century. His faith has greatly influenced my walk with God; the way he thinks has influenced my mind. I do not know of a more mature balance between the world of humanity and the world of spirituality than what Jim possesses.

When I began reading this book, my mind was immediately captured and newly awakened to the whole idea of what a remarkable thing God did when He created man with a spirit, a soul, and a body. And the miracle is expanded when God, the creator, planned to establish an organic relationship between Him, the creator, and us, the created. Jim has now ingeniously walked us through the issues of how we think and how *what we think* affects what we do and who we are.

Jim has joined others like himself who desire to teach us how to think of God, toward God, in God, with God in us, and ultimately to think *as God thinks*. We are clearly reminded by God that his ways and thoughts are as vastly different from ours as the distance between Heaven and earth. But he doesn't leave us there. He makes clear that as Heaven visits earth in the rain and snow—and these waterings return with mission accomplished, leaving life and growth and purpose—so it can be with us. The difference between us and God is bridged by His Word and life flowing through us. This book is a major push in breaking through to thinking like God thinks.

Our fore-parents, Adam and Eve, made a mistake in thinking, and God has been seeking to recover us from wrong thinking ever since. The way back in is reflected in the way out. They fell through wrong thinking, and God sent Jesus to redeem us from wrong thinking and give us the way to think right! Jim, in this splendid treatise, gives us serious guidelines on such thinking, with credible witness from those who have walked among us.

The first word of the Gospel of the kingdom was "Repent!" This is a word about thinking that literally means to change one's thinking! It will be works like this that will call us to right thinking as a part of informed faith. We have been given the Christ of God who lives in us, and with Him comes all He is and all He has, and that is enough to live life to the hilt!

Jim Hylton is a credible witness and deserves to be heard and read. I love his methodical direction, his careful documentation, and his practical instruction. I esteem his widening scope of leading-edge information with first person illustrations and relevant conclusions.

I am personally excited about what this book can mean in a culture where thinking has gone askew on a wide scale. Jim has called us again to "repent for the kingdom of God has appeared"—and that we will do as we agree with this rather thorough treatment. I challenge you to adopt this prayer as your own: "Lord, change my thinking on every issue on which You and I do not now see eye to eye, and teach me to think with You!"

Read this book slowly and deliberately, savoring the instructions and evidence with determination toward kingdom of God thinking.

Jack Taylor
Dimensions Ministries
Melbourne, Florida

Thinking with God

The greatest Thinker thinks without a brain. Though a *brain* is not engaged, a *mind* exists—one which is offered to us. It is a way of thinking offered to everyone who is willing to accept it. The One who thinks without a brain came, offering His mind and life to us.

One of life's greatest gifts is the ability to think. Descartes said six centuries ago, "I think, therefore I am." We can legitimately add, "I am, therefore I think." Thinking is a trust conferred by One who thinks as none other. His thoughts occur without the usual engagement of a brain. By contrast, our thoughts occur within our brain and will continue eternally in our mind—we will think forever.

Beyond brainpower is a power of thought that offers us an avenue of being *at ease*. Not being at ease is a state of being *ill at ease*, which can lead to a condition called disease. Lack of ease is the bane of every life in every culture. Some come to know ease, but many live outside this treasured realm of inner peace. Without finding this rest, restlessness characterizes life.

A brand new disease is now apparent in our nation. We are anxious, depressed, and often fearful, many times without good rationale. With lives maxed out in routines leading to chronic fatigue, we have settled into being ill at ease. The new disease could be named Pseudo-Anxiety. I am using *pseudo* to mean beyond reality. Our irrational conclusions have maxed our lives to a current breaking point. America has become one of the most ill at ease people groups on earth.

The Hippocratic Oath taken by medical doctors was named in honor of a doctor in ancient Greece who possessed great insight. His understanding included the fact that what goes on in the mind affects what goes on in the body. Hippocrates said, "It is more important to know what sort of person has a disease than to know what sort of disease a person has."[1]

This wise father of medicine knew that the "sort of person" we are becomes a key for dealing with disease or any other issue. The sort of person we are *can* be changed if changes need to be made. God works in our lives from inside out as well as outside in.

C. S. Lewis, an acclaimed man of remarkable insight, noted in his address *The Inner Ring* that people of every stage of life can exhibit this inner state of being disquieted. "I believe that in all men's lives at certain periods, and in many men's lives at all periods between infancy and extreme old age, one of the most dominant elements of life is to be inside the local Ring and the terror of being left outside."[2]

Lewis, who made his way from atheism to faith in God, found insights that carry life-altering relevance. The importance of his description of "the terror of being left outside" offers insight for much human behavior. He was declaring that everyone is assaulted with terror when they sense they are outside of the circle of ultimate acceptance.

This dominant element of life reflects the desire to be in the "local Ring," or, as we would say, the inner circle. Yet the inner circle is not just any circle, but the circle where the presence of God is enjoyed. That circle is a circle of God's love extended without conditions.

Life is either lived out of a love-conscious frame of thought or a fear-conscious frame. Most fear-based thinking occurs without a rational basis to exist—and yet it does. Why? Is there more to fear than fear itself? Should we not be afraid to be afraid? Is it possible there is no fear to fear?

In these pages we will examine the issue of fear and results that come with it. Living life in a fear-free zone is part of the original design for life. How that was violatedand the attending consequences—is what we will pursue.

Is there more to fear than fear itself? Should we not be afraid to be afraid? Is it possible there is no fear to fear?

The greatest offer ever presented to mankind is found in the statement made by Jesus Christ as reported by a doctor—Doctor Luke.

Fear not, little flock, for it is your Father's good pleasure to give you the kingdom (Luke 12:32 KJV).

Love-based thoughts always lead to thankfulness. Fear-based thoughts always lead to fearfulness. These polar opposites offer us a snapshot of our wide-ranging thoughts. We will pursue the reasons for such a dichotomy of thought, which results in a lack of ease, leading to possible disease.

All of life was first a thought. All of life is determined by thoughts. Thoughts affect us now as well as eternally. Life is altered and improved by correct thoughts. Conversely, life is altered or damaged by flawed thoughts.

Healthy thoughts contribute to health in our bodies. In like manner, unhealthy thoughts lead to bodies that are unhealthy. America has a thinking crisis that is greater than its health crisis. Thoughts become actions. Actions become habits. Habits become character. Character becomes our life—both now and eternally.

Our bodies are houses of thought. Every part of our body, starting with our cells, has knowledge. While most cells do not think, they have knowledge with elaborate encoding that causes them to carry out their intended functions as well as to interact with other parts of the body.

God said, "My people perish for lack of knowledge" (Hosea 4:6). Without adequate knowledge, we are more vulnerable to disease. Through this network of knowledge our body seeks to fight off disease as well as bring healing to needed functions. The interactivity of the human body is one of the wonders of communication.

Organs in the body rally to help one another. We can see this clearly in a new therapy developed to treat the complications of diabetes. Diabetes has reached an alarming frequency in our nation.

A local doctor who has 12,000 patients reports that 45 percent of them have diabetes. Their ages are from 30 to 50, yet they are already diagnosed with Type 2 diabetes. You can do the math. This outstanding doctor treats 5,400 people from the ages of 30 to 50 who incubate a disease that will potentially debilitate and limit their lives.

No wonder he is pleased that a new method has been cleared for treatment by the FDA, one which effectively reduces the complications from diabetes. The therapy results in the pancreas being imitated, leading to a response which sends a message to the liver. As the liver is activated to produce the needed enzymes for the body's proper carbohydrate metabolism, the result is normalized energy production in every cell in the body. That reduces neuropathy, thus increasing feeling in the feet and legs as well hands and arms; retinopathy, or loss of eyesight; nephropathy, or kidney failure; and wounds that won't heal and other complications.

These cells have memory because the One who designed them gave them a memory. God is the One who thinks without a brain. He doesn't need a brain. As a spirit without brainpower, He thinks with mindpower. God offers to guide our brainpower into the realm of mindpower so that our minds think in agreement with His mind.

I am privileged to help found a medical clinic in Fort Worth with three other men. Two are outstanding doctors. The other founder has years of association with medicine while serving in hospital administration. After observing near-miraculous results some patients get from the alternate method of treating the complications of diabetes, I have been motivated to spend blocks of time over three years studying physiology, physics, and other related insights with regard to health.

Our bodies contain their own medical clinic. We bear the image of our creator in the cellular composition that makes our bodies function. Each cell has memory. In that memory is the knowledge of how to respond to the function assigned.

Dr. James P. Gills, MD, has written a helpful book titled *God's Prescription for Healing*. He wisely points out, "….not only is it useful to recognize and understand the natural design of your body to promote your health and healing—it is a *responsibility*. ….. we can gratefully acknowledge our health as our greatest earthly wealth; nothing could be clearer."[3]

Your inner medical clinic is made up of the most remarkable technology created by the most intelligent mind that ever engaged in medical practice. It is yours to manage! Taking responsibility as Dr. Gills instructed is very important. How the most complex instrument ever created, your own brain, is used for better health is your right to decide. You are the manager of the clinic. Here are some quick summaries of the functions:

- Our bodies are composed of between 10 and 100 trillion (some believe 60 trillion) cells.
- Each cell contains approximately a trillion atoms.
- Cells are complex building blocks that form 200 different tissues (such as the brain, pancreatic, muscle, and heart tissues), each with its very different properties and responsibilities in the body.
- Each cell communicates with its neighbors across a cell membrane that is thinner than a spider's web.

- Each cell is filled with extremely tiny energy-burning engines that are 200,000 times smaller than a pinhead.
- Each cell generates an electrical field and possesses an intelligent clock that switches off and on in cycles of two to 26 hours. The length of the cycle depends on the cell type.
- Most importantly of all, each cell contains the molecular code of life, the biochemical blueprint for your height, eye color, liver function, and the sound of your laughter. This is DNA.[4]

To see the most amazing medical clinic ever developed, look in the mirror!

A visit to the clinic contained in our bodies will be an important part of this book. Since we have been given responsibility for the management of our remarkably equipped center for health, we will get an overview of important functions.

To see the most amazing medical clinic ever developed, look in the mirror!

A former teaching doctor at the University of Wisconsin will guide our tour of the clinic. As both a physicist and doctor, Dr. Richard A. Swenson comprehends the genius of the mind of God, which can be found both in the complexity of His vast creation as well as the intricacies of the human body. Here are some of the opening thoughts in his helpful book, *More Than Meets the Eye*.

When God set out to create humanity, He put His genius on display … As a scientist with training in both medicine and physics, it is easily apparent to me that the majesty of God is revealed in the human body. His fingerprints are, in fact, all over … I teach young doctors that the human body is a million times more complex than the universe.[5]

Our tour of the clinic will include some time to review the three-pound organic computer called the brain. With this connection of neurons estimated to number 100 billion, we think. *How* we think with the amazing capacities of thought generated in our organic computer has life-changing importance.

Since we *think* and *will think* forever, wisdom would lead us to think good thoughts that we will want to keep forever. How to attain good thoughts, or thoughts worth keeping forever, will make up most of the content of this book.

◆ ◆ ◆

On a hillside years ago, the most brilliant man who ever thought on this earth led a class in thinking. It was not a class for scholars but for thinkers, and everyone there was a thinker. In many cases, they came with thoughts not worth keeping, but His purpose was not to scold or degrade them. His intent was to offer them thoughts to change their understanding of everything and ultimately lead them to the discovery of the greatest idea ever presented to mankind.

The teacher on the hillside was Jesus Christ. The thoughts He knew as none other could know were the thoughts of His Father, God. God thinks as no one else, but He wants His thoughts known and enjoyed by everyone. I do not offer the idea that God thinks without a brain as a teaser to get you to read on—but rather as a significant principle.

In this important principle, we will see how God transfers His thoughts to us. I will be quoting a thinker with few equals who brings clarity to the idea of God not needing a brain. This same thinker offers transforming understanding about how we can actually hear God. Through hearing God, we come to know the reality of being at ease—at ease with God, at ease with ourselves, and at ease with others.

"If only I had known" may be the most revealing phrase ever spoken. God wants us to know. He likes to talk to us. Knowledge is that realm of understanding from which all of life can be enriched as God's way of thinking becomes our way of thinking.

Our tour of this clinic, where we now live, will be the subject of **the first chapter**. As the primary care doctor of the clinic, you may wonder if you have been off duty too long to catch up. Not so—not at all.

Helpful information about the remarkable functions of the clinic will come from Dr. Swenson, who is still a teaching doctor using his excellent books to assist us. He knows, and I know, a teaching doctor who would like to join you in your clinic to give you counsel for better health.

Before you decide if you want a teaching doctor counseling you (the clinic director), I will offer some important aspects of His thinking, temperament, and skills. Much further into the book, I will discuss how the teaching doctor will relate to you.

In the **second chapter** we will look at the compelling story of a blind man who began to see after 43 years. He became a case study of medical research to verify that we do not see with our eyes but with our brains. Stated another way: we see as we think, interpreting what the physical camera is furnishing our brain—our eyes are really an extension of the brain. In fact, the optic nerve is actually comprised of axions that start in the retina and do not stop until they enter the brain substance itself. Unless we know how to think, we do not know what the eyes have projected from the image before us.

Scripture says it this way: "That the eyes of your understanding may be enlightened that you may know … " (Ephesians 1:18).

Further chapters awaiting us will provide a foundation for sitting down with Jesus on the hillside and hearing Him for ourselves.

A miracle in a doctor's brain will be the story of the **third chapter**. His brain developed a twisted mass of threatening blood vessels. Within that brain, also, were some twisted thoughts. First, he faced his thoughts for what they were: thoughts without good rationale. Those thoughts were removed. A miracle then followed that led to the life-threatening twisted blood vessels being removed as well.

Life is forever. Whether we like it or not, we will live forever. One of the things we will think about in this book is why eternity takes so long. (This will be the subject of the last chapter.)

Life is forever. Whether we like it or not, we will live forever.

In the **fourth chapter**, we will also walk with the thinker to whom I just referred, as he takes his last steps in this journey of life. As a professor of philosophy, he was at ease speaking about hearing God's thoughts as much as—even more than—hearing the thoughts of men. Thought-stoppers often came from his statements.

In the pause they elicit—and elicited, during His time here on earth—it is necessary to think further about the insights composed by his understanding. To try and speed through a reading of his writings would be like speeding through beautifully arranged landscape of thought. If you hurry, you may miss half of what you ought to see.

He said, "I believe that God will let everyone into His Heaven who can stand it." You may quickly think, "Then he is a Universalist who believes everyone goes to Heaven with or without knowing God." Let me quickly assert—if that was your thought, please think again. (Thinking again is what the Teacher on the hillside calls for from all of us. It leads to thinking again about eternal life in the way God thinks.)

We will look at God opening Heaven's doors to anyone "who can stand it" later in the book.

When this gifted thinker—whose humility matched his brainpower—received a diagnosis that his life would soon end, he said, "I think when I die, it may be some time before I know it." He was not saying his mind was losing its ability to process thoughts. He was saying that because he lived in such a consciousness of the presence of God here that the transition called death would change so little he might not know it for some time.

Then we will review his last words before he left his body to join the host already in the presence of God. The last two words Dallas Willard spoke will be the refrain of this book. (I will hold those two words until later.) This refrain rightly belongs to everyone who knows the "eternal kind of life" as he identified it.

Two more chapters that can be called testimonies will follow. The first of these two is about a world-famous neurosurgeon. His thoughts in early life did not include the possibilities that awaited him. Despair, such as most of the people on the hillside knew when Jesus addressed them—this man knew all too well.

Others knew him as the dumbest kid in his class. His mother knew him as one who could do whatever others did and do them even better. She got her thoughts from God because she asked Him. Dr. Ben Carson started tapping into those thoughts as well. From being considered the dumbest kid in the class, he became known as the smartest.

Dangerous thoughts that could have led to him injuring, even killing, others were changed for thoughts that led to countless life-saving surgeries. Thinking again— about nearly everything—led him to a place of prominence in our nation. He now proclaims that God has an answer for all that exists.

The next testimony is God's. Most testimonies we give are about our knowing God. God's testimony is about Him knowing us as well as providing all things for us.

Disease does not come from God. God intended that we experience being at ease. Our bodies may have disease—yet even then we can know what being at ease means. When we are at ease, our minds begin to hear what God thinks, and if we think with Him our bodies begin to get in on God's testimony as well. To save the suspense, let me share the conclusion of His testimony: "All things are yours—life, death, things present, things to come—all are yours" (1 Corinthians 3:22).

One thing is missing here that is not yours. See if you can find it. Read on—and I give you my promise that I will share it later. This is God's testimony to you, that all things are yours. These are all found in Christ. We will sit on the hill with Him as He offers new thoughts for our minds to enjoy. Since before time began we were in God's thoughts, and His thoughts were for our good and not for our harm. Knowing that brings hope regardless of present circumstances.

"'For I know the plans I have for you,' declares the Lord, 'plans to prosper you and not to harm you, plans to give you hope and a future. Then you will call upon me and come and pray to me, and I will listen to you. You will seek me and find me when you seek me with all your heart'" (Jeremiah 29:11-13, NIV).

Jesus made it clear that though God does not hide things from us forever, He may hide them until we are ready for them. To lament, "If only I had known" is to miss the timing element of God sharing what He knows at the right time and place. Here is what Jesus said during His hillside teaching session: "Is a lamp brought in to be put under a basket, or under a bed, and not on a stand? For nothing is hidden except to be made manifest; nor is anything secret [hidden] except to come to light" (Mark 4:21, 22).

Every hidden thing is not permanently hidden. They are hidden only to be revealed at the right time. These thought-starters include the fact that God has always wanted to make everything known and bring everything into the light of knowing.

Throughout Scripture this is called the "mystery of God" or the "secret of God." He has always wanted to share His thoughts with both insiders and outsiders—those who think they know and those who don't have a clue. Note this summary of the statement from The Message version of the Bible: "This mystery has been kept in the dark for a long time, but now it's out in the open. God wanted everyone, not just Jews, to know this rich and glorious secret inside and out, regardless of his or her background, regardless of their religious standing. The mystery in a nutshell is just this: Christ is in you; therefore you can look forward to sharing in God's glory. It's that simple."[6]

◆ ◆ ◆

Jesus is the most enlightened person who ever lived. Being with God in creation, He was part of creating time out of eternity. Through His birth He brought eternity into time and prepares us for eternity. His knowledge was so complete that He referred to Himself as the truth.

The pages that follow were formulated carefully after I spent time each day for many months going over and over again what Jesus said about God's thinking and how we can think *with* Him. His thoughts are intended to be *our* thoughts, not just for the time it takes to read a book, but also for all of life, which means through all of this forever-life He shares with us.

Thinking is at its best when we think with God about both now and eternity. Jesus did that and offers us the opportunity to do it as well.

CHAPTER ONE

The Most Advanced Medical Clinic You Can Visit

You may or may not have taken my suggestion seriously in the introduction that you can look in the mirror to find the most advanced medical clinic known to medicine. If not, you might do it now.

You will see before you the exterior of the clinic we are about to tour as led by Dr. Richard A. Swenson. As both a medical doctor and physicist, Dr. Swenson chose a great title for his book: *More Than Meets the Eye*. Your look in the mirror offers but a tiny glimpse of you because there is so much more of you than meets the eye. That is also true of God and all of His creation.

If you looked in the mirror, you saw the largest organ in the human body, the skin. Our subject of major focus in this book is, simply, "Are we comfortable in our own skin?" My dermatologist shared with me why he chose his field of medicine: "I started out to be a surgeon and then decided to specialize in the skin since everyone has it," he told me. We all have skin—but parts of it for not very long.

I'll let Dr. Swenson explain my comment: "Skin cells are continuously turning over—billions every day. The epidermis is replaced every couple of weeks…. Over a lifetime we each shed forty pounds of dead skin, perhaps explaining why old sofas weigh so much.

"Youthful skin is remarkably elastic. As the skin ages, however, it loses elasticity due to changes in collagen. With the loss of elasticity, facial expressions begin to etch permanent lines. It has been estimated that it takes two-hundred-thousand frowns to make a permanent line."[7]

I am amazed that I must have frowned so much!

Dr. Swenson continues:

Although we seldom think of it as such, the skin is the largest organ of the body. It weighs eight or nine pounds and has a surface area of over two square yards. The skin performs remarkable services. For one, it keeps all the water inside. Our bodies are 60 percent water, and were it not for the skin, we would quickly puddle on the floor.

Yet "keeping the water in" is a much more complex process than it appears. The skin must keep almost all of the water in, while allowing some to escape, through sweating, for temperature control. In addition, it must be waterproof from the outside as well.

The skin also protects against the invasion of harmful agents, including chemicals and microbes. Untold billions of bacteria reside on our skin, most of them benignly, yet a few maliciously. The skin is an unyielding and vigilant guard.

Some segments of skin have thousands of nerve receptors per square inch. The pain communicated through these receptors is in fact an important benefit saving us from repeated traumatic and thermal damage.[8]

Not only should we be comfortable in our own skin, we should also find a new appreciation for our skin's ability to maintain its intended role—and all of this without our giving much thought to this daily process.

Now let's go inside this clinic since we have a better understanding of the exterior.

Meet the Receptionist and the Primary Care Doctor

As we enter the complex, our first stop is at the receptionist's desk. Our will acts as the receptionist. That role is a part-time position since we also double as the most responsible doctor practicing in the clinic.

James P. Gills, MD, really hits that nail on the head—and hopefully on ours as well. "You Are Your Own Best Physician" is the title of a chapter in Gills's book. So may I suggest that, before you take this clinical tour of your body, you accept your role as the physician who most influences your health? You will not be able to remove your responsibility, but you can change your primary care doctor by changing your thinking.

A guide to good thinking can be found in Dr. Gills's book, *God's Prescription for Healing*:

There is much you can do for yourself—and must do. For example, if you buy a new $250,000 Ferrari, I believe you would certainly take care of it. You would read the manuals about its proper operation, and you would be careful to keep the vehicle lubricated and free of dents.

How much more should you be concerned about your own human body? The body with its sixty trillion cells and cellular memory equal to the content of two hundred New York phone books needs more committed attention than a car … It's the only one you have![9]

Our body is ours to take care of. We need to take more responsibility for ourselves than we would expect our doctor to take. As the primary care physician of our own health, we need to recognize the liabilities as well as the benefits of our health practice. If we were a licensed doctor, we could be subject to being charged with malpractice. Many of us can acknowledge that we have been guilty of some form of malpractice in our personal health habits. It is never too late to correct the way we have cared for ourselves.

Many of us can acknowledge that we have been guilty of some form of malpractice in our personal health habits.

As our mind, will, and spirit interact, the brain becomes a communications center for the entire clinic. So let's allow Dr. Swenson to resume our tour of this remarkable personal clinic:

The brain—pride and joy of the nervous system—is staggering in its abilities and complexity. Despite all of our modern scientific research, we are only beginning to penetrate the brain's secrets.

The basic cell of the brain is called the neuron, of which there are ten billion (some estimate as high as 100 billion). In addition to long extensions called axions, each neuron has ten thousand tiny branching fibers and filamentous projections called dendrites, a name derived from the Greek word for tree. Each neuron is thus in contact with ten thousand other neurons, for a total of 100 trillion neurological connections.

If you were to snatch out all the neurons and dendritic connections in the brain and lay them end to end, they would reach for one-hundred-thousand miles and circle the earth at the equator four times.... The capacity of the brain is such that it can hold information equivalent to that contained in twenty-five million books, enough to fill a bookshelf 500 miles long. In contrast, the Library of Congress has seventeen million volumes. (Members of Congress may do well to use more of their brain's capacity than they use their library.)

Assuming that 10 percent of the brain's cells are firing at any given time, this implies a rate of a thousand trillion computations per second.... Unlike the parts of a computer, nerve cells are highly individual. No two cells are exactly the same, nor do they respond to the same incoming information in the same way. Each neuron is unique to the entire universe. God, it seems to me, really outdid Himself.[10]

When God designed the brain, He became the original computer scientist. He built a unity of remarkable sophistication, complexity, and beauty. Despite the fact that the entire brain creates only about twenty watts of power, its performance is astounding. The brain's curriculum vitae, according to brain expert Todd Siler, reveals it to function in more than 200 ways: alignment equipment, altitude and heading reference systems, data processing equipment, direction finders, closed circuit television displays, distance measuring equipment, optical guidance systems, information retrieval systems, night vision equipment, noise measurement equipment, recording equipment, strategic and direction-finding systems, frequency synthesizers, velocity-measuring equipment, and so forth.

It would appear to me that with an entry like the brain, God would be in the finalist competition for the Westinghouse Science Award.[11]

While the brain contains more high-tech capacities than any instrument created by mankind, another source of information is needed for the brain to function at its best. That capacity comes from another mind—the mind of God. His mind is interactive with ours through the Holy Spirit.

We are offered this interface as part of our learning experience. Here is a promise from the apostle John's letters: " ... as His anointing teaches you about all things, and is true and is not a lie, and just as it has taught you, you abide in Him" (1 John 2:27).

Dr. Swenson has valuable insight into God's part in our understanding of spiritual reality:

The brain is the realm of data, information, and knowledge. The spirit, however, is the realm of understanding, wisdom, and truth. The brain and the spirit need to register for classes together in the halls of education, and their togetherness needs to be fixed. Harvard University, for example, had in its original charter this statement: "Let every student well consider … that the main end of his life and studies is to know God and Jesus Christ." Somewhere in the process of gaining prestige, they lost Eternity. And such a loss can never be compensated.

God has ordained from the beginning that worldly learning will never be sufficient to reveal Christ. This does not, of course, mean that the message of Christ is irrational, but only that it is extra-rational. Its meaning is not accessible through neurons and synapse, no matter how exceptional. To see Christ requires that a light be turned on in our understanding, and the light switch is controlled by God and not by the brain.[12]

It is clear Dr. Swenson is inviting God's presence to be part of our tour through the clinic. I, too, am inviting His presence to guide us. Join us as well, and the three of us will acknowledge God's presence to guide in gaining the wisdom we need. Now the four of us—God, Dr. Swenson, you the reader, and myself—can continue.

Quite honestly, if we wish to be straight about it, the brain is having trouble even understanding itself, let alone God. When someone challenged Woody Allen to explain God, he quipped, "I can't explain God to you. I don't even know how my toaster works."

The brain is quite spectacular in its own right, and it does not need inflated claims about its potential. Let's challenge it diligently to learn, but then let's accept the borders it cannot cross. Even given its limitations, the brain's amazing capacity speaks to the genius of the God who endowed it.[13]

Memory and learning are essential parts in gaining the knowledge God wants us to experience. He pointed out that we perish for lack of knowledge (Hosea 4:6). The opposite of memory is forgetfulness. God's mind both re-members and forgets. Our minds must also engage in this same balance. We cannot maintain a healthy emotional mind-set while storing and maintaining every event in life.

Forgiving is an important part of forgetting. God forgives and forgets our sins. We draw forgiveness from our account with God and forgive those who wrong us. Love does not remember the wrongs done.

When the ancient Greek Simonides offered to teach Themistocles the art of memory he refused. "Teach me not the art of remembering," he said, "but the art of forgetting, for I remember things I do not wish to remember, but I cannot forget things I wish to forget."

"In the practical use of our intellect, forgetting is as important a function as remembering," said William James. "If we remembered everything, we should on most occasions be as ill-off as if we remembered nothing."[14]

Learning how God forgets is an important aspect of thinking like God thinks. It is His love shared in the cross of Christ that enables Him to forgive, and never remember again, our sins as we turn to Christ. Love, which is the nature of God, does not take into account wrongs we experience (1 Corinthians 13:5).

In this quick look at the brain and its functions that affect every part of our physical clinic, we need to pursue further the aspect of memory and how it relates to our health. Memory not only makes up an important part of our brain, it is found in every part of our body. This clinical tour will help us get to the core issue of our health and to the core of who we are.

If you were to read two hundred books with a thousand pages each the size of a New York telephone book, and you read at the rate of ten characters per second, and it would take you nine and a half years to finish, you would be reading the codes of your body. And you might ask, "What am I reading?" You are reading about you! You are reading the human genome or DNA sequence contained in your body (a paraphrase of Dr. Swenson, p, 66).15

A Mammoth Project Found Language from God

The Human Genome Project was a mammoth undertaking extending over a ten-year period. Dr. Francis Collins led this project involving more than two thousand scientists. His book, *The Language of God*, reviews both his life and his experience in the vast research of the hereditary code of life. In part of his book, he describes his own journey from atheism to faith in God and knowing Jesus Christ. He believes that within all the trillions of cells making up our body, the "language of God" is found as encoded by God in creation.

Dr. Collins consulted with the speechwriter for President Bill Clinton to shape a statement made at the White House on June 26, 2000: "'Today', he said, 'we are learning the language in which God created life. We are gaining ever more awe for the complexity, the beauty, and the wonder of God's most divine and sacred gift.'"

Dr. Collins asks this question: "Why would a president and a scientist, charged with announcing a milestone in biology and medicine, feel compelled to invoke a connection with God?"

He then answers his own part of the question: "For me the experience of sequencing the human genome and uncovering this remarkable of all tests, was both a stunning scientific achievement and an occasion to worship."[16]

Every student of Scripture should take notice that the wording Francis Collins uses to describe our cellular encoding is *the language of God*. Words are the building blocks of language. A word is a thought that has found a voice. God's thoughts became a word and were heard in a voice.

Why would a president and a scientist, charged with announcing a milestone in biology and medicine, feel compelled to invoke a connection with God?

Creation is described in John's gospel as originating in the Word. John 1:1-4 declares that in the beginning there was *the Word*. Then John identifies that Word became flesh in the person of Jesus Christ (v. 14). This Word, God's presence—including His language—created all things. God's creative communication can be found even in the cells of our body. Stated another way, our cells contain a part of the dictionary of God's language that He chose in creation.

Cells are the foundation of life. So this tour of the medical clinic will include the most basic part of any structure: the foundation. Without a good foundation, no structure can withstand the stress coming against it.

Good news awaits us. We get a completely new foundation every seven years and we get foundation repair continuously.

The Sound of Music in Our Body

The cell, composed predominantly of carbon-based ingredients, is the basic structure of living matter. An adult human body contains tens of trillions of cells. Because trillions of these cells die every day, the body always has a repair kit on hand to make duplicate copies as rapidly as the old cells disappear.

Each individual cell floats in a swimming pool called the interstitial fluid. This fluid is rich in molecules that have just come from the bloodstream and are now dog-paddling their way over to the cell. Once they arrive at the cell door, they knock at the tiny pore openings in the cell membrane and request permission to enter. If the cell has need of their services, molecules such as oxygen, glucose, and small proteins are invited in.

Once inside, these newly arriving molecules probably gasp in astonishment. The cell's interior must feel like a combination of a video arcade and Radio City Music Hall. Things are popping everywhere, for they have entered a protoplasmic pyrotechnic factory in hyper drive. In fact, it is a shrine to God's efficiency and precision. He probably visits it now and then, lingering in the lobby just to enjoy that which He has made.

… The membrane is a microscopic miracle all its own, functioning crucially in the exchange of important materials. Electrical forces (each cell has an electrical potential difference across the cell membrane) play an important role in cellular functioning, with perhaps a lightning strike from time to keep the mitochondria entertained. Speaking of the mitochondria, they are the tiny engines of each cell busily making the fuel ATP. Food is oxidized in the cells … But you don't have to worry about these structures other than to realize that the cell is a very active, crowded place.

… Buried deep in each cell is the nucleus. This is the center of the cell's functioning. If the mitochondria is the heart of the cell and membrane is the skin of the cell, then the nucleus is the brain of the cell. The nucleus contains twenty-three pairs of chromosomes and here the story becomes interesting.

All of these tens of trillions of cells began very inauspiciously as one single, tiny, minuscule, microscopic, almost invisible speck—the fertilized egg … Within this tiny first cell, measuring mere microns, is the blueprint for an entire human body with a complexity that is incomprehensible…. Sometime within the first couple of weeks, in addition to dividing, the cells also begin to differentiate.

The secret of this differentiation—which will eventually result in over 200 different kinds of tissue and organ cells—is somehow mysteriously locked up in the DNA. Within each cell are chromosomes consisting of tightly coiled DNA, and encoded with this DNA are instructions on how to recreate the entire human body.

[May I pause for awe!]

This initial single-cell DNA, which determines everything from your handedness to eye color to foot size to whether you are at risk for premature heart disease, weighs 0.2 millionths of a millionth of an ounce. The combined initial single cell DNA of every person alive today (all six million) would weigh one thousandth of an ounce.[17]

These studies have impacted me with information I never had before. No wonder the Lord said, "My people perish for lack of knowledge." He built knowledge into our entire being, starting with the cells which reach a crescendo in the brain leading to the development of a mind.

These studies have impacted me with information I never had before. No wonder the Lord said, "My people perish for lack of knowledge."

Now take a deep breath and let this intricacy of communication throughout the body sink in—or better yet link up!

The chain of DNA is built by linking these base pairs, rather like God playing with Legos. For example, at one level you might have an A linked to T; then at the next level you might find a C linked to G; and you just keep linking and building, up and up, for a very long way.

There are three billion such base pairings that make up the human genome, leading to a staggering level of mathematical and biochemical complexity....

The purpose of the chromosomes and DNA is to carry the genes. And the purpose of the genes is to make proteins. And the purpose of the proteins is to ... well do everything. "A typical cell," explains Michael Behe, " ... contains thousands and thousands of different types of proteins to perform the many tasks necessary for life, much like a carpenter's workshop might contain many different kinds of tools for various carpentry tasks." Each gene knows how to make one specific protein. Thus if there are 100 thousand genes, there are also about 100 thousand different proteins. "The best way to look at it is like a gene is like a sentence in an encyclopedia," explains geneticist Maxine Singer. "The gene instructs the cell how to do some one thing." ... It is like a computer, copy machine, and *Encyclopedia Britannica* combined.[18]

Now hang on a little longer. If God took the time to build all of this into our being, let's allow the time for Dr. Swenson to finish this initial part of his presentation.

In addition, a portion of this extra DNA guards against faulty copies. Obviously with a job this big—three billion base pairs, at a time, trillions of time a day—there are bound to be mistakes. The DNA has its own spell-checker of sorts, an enzyme that examines the newly copied DNA for errors. When an error is found, the segment is replaced. If the error if not found and corrected, the resulting flawed DNA then carries a "mutation." This is thought to be the mechanism (at least in part) behind many birth defects, cancer, and aging.[19]

It is important to note that God built a "spell-checker of sorts" into cells to prevent wrong mutations. Our spell-checker for misspelled words or the wrong usage of words in thought has been damaged. Sin has created a flawed thought process. God wants to repair our "spell-checker" so we can think with ease.

Usually the DNA replication occurs with remarkable accuracy, making only one error in a billion copy steps. Nevertheless each of us carries about half a dozen defective genes.... Because we carry two copies of every gene—one from the mother and one for the father—in the majority of cases one normal gene is sufficient to avoid all the symptoms of genetic disease.[20]

The Language of God Can Become Our Language

Thoughts from God and His creative genius abound in our cellular network of memory. The need for our conscious thoughts to align with God's thoughts should be easily understood in light of this cellular language identified as the language of God.

Countless people have found the benefits of aligning their thoughts with God's thoughts. Without the knowledge filed in our brain being in agreement with the memory recorded in our cells, our body does not enjoy the peace God intends.

We are meant to be at ease. God's thoughts offer that right. It is His eternal plan that we know His peace.

One of the noteworthy points Richard Swenson makes in an earlier quote, as noted, is the fact the cells know which replacement cells to welcome and which to refuse: "Once they arrive at the cell door, they knock at the tiny pore openings in the cell membrane and request permission to enter. If the cell has need of their services, molecules such as oxygen, glucose, and small proteins are invited in."

If we are wise, we will recognize that thoughts entering our consciousness must be reviewed, just as cells review the possibility of welcoming their replacement cells. Not every thought should be made welcome. Just as we are the most important physicians attending our bodies, we are also the most important counselors guiding our thinking. We will become what we think, because what we think will determine what we do and eventually what we are.

We cannot change the language of God in our cells. They are encoded. We cannot change God's Word. His Word is fixed forever. But we can change the thoughts in our mind. God gave us that right of willful response. We set our mind by choice. We set our mind on God, on ourselves, or on countless other alternatives. We set our mind on time and eternity with God, or we set our mind without God in both time and eternity.

We cannot change the language of God in our cells. They are encoded. We cannot change God's word. His word is fixed forever. But we can change our thoughts.

A Father's Love Leads to a Medical Breakthrough

When a father learned his two-year-old daughter had been diagnosed with Type 1 diabetes, he chose to seek alternative methods of treatment. That required him to think in new ways. His thinking included research, prayer, and even further schooling. With well-developed skills in research as a successful attorney, he realized he knew little about physiology. Love never counts the cost, but always seeks the best. His love sent him back to school. Studies in biomedicine alerted him to possible innovative ways to address the needed insulin supply from the pancreas. With a new way of thinking about the functions of the body, he began drawing from all of his previous experience.

Dr. Ford Gilbert was devastated when his daughter, Trina, received the diagnosis of having diabetes. He knew this condition could lead to a lifetime of potential debilitating issues. Understanding of the human body, some skills in mechanics, a mind highly trained in legal research now sought God's mind for guidance. At the time of his daughter's diagnosis, he was an attorney in a highly prestigious law firm.

Having built a pump before, he wondered how hard could it be to develop a pump that gave exactly the insulin his daughter needed. But that was when he realized that diabetes is about carbohydrate metabolism. As he worked with several medical doctors, he changed his design criteria to making a pump that injects insulin intravenously and gives a strong signal to the liver that is missing in people with diabetes.

Realizing that the original ideas were flawed, it was only his dedication to pressing forward—against all normal convention—that resulted in success. "I am not overly skilled, but I am skilled at not quitting," he tells everyone. This persistent pioneer refused to believe in failure.

Instead of the pump releasing the insulin under the skin, as do other insulin pumps, it released the insulin in intervals of six-minute bursts intravenously. After he was already working with patients and had his FDA clearance, it turned out that he was perfectly mimicking God's design of a normal pancreas, and that this was not known to medicine until 13 years after he finished his pump development. Ford Gilbert is quick to point out that he feels he is only a willing vessel, not the inventor, as "it is all God's design."

When people with diabetes were tested with the infusion they began experiencing remarkable benefits. Diabetes is not cured, but the complications from diabetes are reduced, sometimes dramatically, and many complications are reversed. Ford Gilbert believes that he sought to invent a certain pump model only to discover that God would assist the process by making an adjustment that he did not know to make.

It took years and many successful treatments for the Bionica Pump to be FDA-cleared for usage. Part of the validity of the therapy is the fact that Ford's daughter is now the mother of five children and had no problems in her pregnancies. That is most significant for a person with diabetes.

Trina Health Clinics are now available in many cities in the U.S. I was one of four men who founded a Trina Health Clinic in Fort Worth, Texas. Two in our group are very respected medical doctors. One is a gifted administrator with years of experience in hospital administration. My role is that of a counselor and encourager.

Part of the emphasis in this book came from my experience in the clinic. The clinic came out of my concern for a health crisis in America, as stated in my last book. I began engaging in prayer and discussions with people in the medical community. In our culture, the disconnect between people of faith and people on the front lines of medical services is conspicuous.

Doctor friends, nurses, technicians, administrators, and people of prayer all contributed invaluable insights. When I learned the therapy used in the Trina methodology activated cells that were not being regenerated, I began asking questions. My questions led to an answer from Ford Gilbert, that our cells have memory because they are encoded. From there I began to read, research, and draw from the insights of medicine, physics, and correlations with Scripture—God's thoughts.

Included in the list of complications from diabetes are sight, feeling, muscle weakness, kidney failure, heart and blood vessel complications, wound healing, mental alertness, sexual dysfunction, and more. The North Texas Trina Health Clinic has been been open for nearly two years. All of the usual complications from diabetes have been addressed with most satisfying results.

This journey became very personal. I first became concerned about the complications from diabetes as I watched a pastor friend gradually lose feeling in his feet and legs. We attended a conference together. He needed assistance walking to and from events. In his own church services it was no longer possible for him to walk up the steps to speak without assistance. Later I learned his vision was also slowly diminishing.

Bob Phillips, however, is no ordinary pastor. He trained at Southern Baptist Theological Seminary in Louisville, Kentucky. From that foundation, he became a student of God's presence as manifested in supernatural ways. After cofounding Times Square Church in New York, he became a pastor in Houston. There, he often led people in healing services. I have seen him pray for people to be healed when he was in greater need of healing than the people for whom he prayed! Part of the mystery of God is the mystery of healing.

When I learned he had gone to Newport Beach, California and received a new medical therapy with accompanying benefits, I was extremely thankful. He was soon able to walk up the steps to the pulpit without the assistance of two thoughtful men. He found he had improved eyesight as well.

Part of my gratitude for God's guidance and goodness to Bob Phillips was the possibility of Him meeting a need for my older brother Joe. Joe's neuropathy had progressed to a point in which he could barely feel his feet. Walking was very limited, and driving his car was no longer safe. With an engaging mind, he now faced limited activity, possibly being confined to a bed and a wheelchair. Having been mayor of his town for years, a leader in his church, and a leader in business endeavors, he faced limitations he never expected.

This led me to drive to Southern Missouri and convince him to get the therapy offered at Trina Health in Newport Beach. After three treatments, feeling returned to his feet and legs, enabling him to walk much better as well as drive safely again.

The most significant personal aspect of this experience was to realize God's ways manifested in expressions that were unknown before. It was clear that medicine had benefited from faith, the faith of Ford Gilbert to persist to find benefits for his daughter. Just as clear was the fact that faith had been rewarded in Bob Phillips. His faith took him to a medical therapy that will extend both his quality of life as well as his length of life given in service to others because of God's love.

The most significant personal aspect of this experience was to realize God's ways manifested in expressions that were unknown before.

Cells awaken from this therapy. Thousands of cases affirm this fact. Once the pump imitating the pancreas releases the insulin, the liver responds. In turn, the liver releases enzymes for the body's proper carbohydrate metabolism. A more normalized energy production occurs in every cell in the body—potentially all 60 trillion! Several people whom I know well have said, "It is like a cloud was pulled out of my brain!" Or they say, "I can think more clearly and more quickly."

I am inviting you to join me in pursuing this possibility—if a pump can stimulate such positive cellular response, what will happen if, instead of an imitation, we get the genuine original? These are God's thoughts. They were intended, from creation, to agree with all of the encoded cells in our bodies, starting with our mind!

Let's pause in this brief tour of our medical clinic to give Dr. Swenson a break, and let's use our time now to review some of the case histories of other lives and how their personal clinics functioned.

We will turn now to the amazing story of a blind man given sight again.

CHAPTER TWO

We See with Our Brain, Not Our Eyes

After forty-three years of blindness, a man began to see again. Though he could see, he could not fully comprehend what he saw. This true story has remarkable insight for every person. We all see things that we do not comprehend. Ideas of great importance enter our consciousness, yet we do not know how to recognize their worth.

Learning to see what exists begins in our childhood. A child can be told, "There is a deer standing in the edge of that field," and they cannot see it. Or we might point out a bird in the tree, but the child cannot see anything but the tree. Their eyesight is perfect, but their comprehension of shapes, textures, and colors are not yet developed in the brain. Until they know with their brain how to see a deer or a bird, they have no comprehension of that reality. They cannot see without the needed development of the brain to utilize the billions of neurons found there.

We See with Our Brain—with Eyes of Understanding

Eyes do not furnish us with understanding. They only project to the brain imagery which thought will interpret. "The retina is comprised of photoreceptor cells that are light-sensitive, converting the image into electrical signals that can in turn be interpreted by the brain. In contrast to a camera, the eye 'takes pictures' continuously and develops them instantaneously—a process we couldn't stop even if we wanted to."[20]

It is in the brain that sight occurs. Our understanding is the source of our sightedness. That makes this communications center of our medical clinic all the more significant because nothing we experience can be properly assessed without correct thinking.

The smartest person to ever teach on this earth said we can have eyes and yet not see, or have ears and yet not hear. The issue is looking to the right source for the disclosure of what vision or sound has recorded. Our eyes are more than cameras, but they are less than our vision. Our ears are more than microphones, but they are less than clarification of the sound that was transmitted.

We see with our mind and we hear with our mind. Improved and transformed minds are obtainable. Jesus came offering us a renewed mind. This mind can be taught to properly comprehend what the lenses and microphones furnish. Transformation of life occurs in the transformation of the mind.

Improved and transformed minds are obtainable. Jesus came offering us a renewed mind.

One of the most compelling stories I have ever read is the story of a blind man who was offered the gift to see. It was not, however, a quick or easy choice for him to make. His life as a blind person was full of events, enjoyment, and fulfillment.

Robert Kurson tells the amazing account of Mike May in the book *Crashing Through*. These are the opening lines from a book you will enjoy reading:

> The forty-six-year-old businessman had been invited to present the prestigious Kay Gallagher Award for mentoring the blind, an award he'd won himself the previous year. Dozens in the audience knew his history: blinded at age three by a freak accident; three-time Paralympics gold medalist and current world record-holder in downhill speed skiing; entrepreneur on the verge of bringing a portable global positioning system (GPS) to the blind; co-inventor of the world's first laser turntable; mud hut dweller in Ghana; husband to a beautiful wife … loving father; former CIA man.[21]

When he began to see, he did not know *what* he was seeing. His world of sightlessness was well organized because of the careful cataloging of his experiences with comprehension. Sight added complications to his life that he could never have imagined. It was exhilarating to see the color of his wife's hair, to see the faces of his two boys, and the colors of familiar objects. Yet, what he saw brought a complexity to his life he could not have imagined.

"Crashing Through" Helps in Seeing Through

This story has insights into everyone's story. None of us knows how to correctly assess and respond to what we experience. I want to walk you into the world of a sightless man who achieved remarkable things. After breaking world records in downhill skiing, inventing devices for others in a sightless world, developing successful business practices, and leading a family of four in normal family engagements—all while sightless—this man had vision again. With sight he found himself struggling in a world that he could not easily comprehend.

This rare case is a one-in-one-hundred-million example, illustrating that sight does not occur in the eye. A remarkable individual became an invaluable resource to prove research that was being done by scientists.

Crashing Through is not written from a spiritual perspective using spiritual language or illustrations. Yet it is a spiritual book without the language or the suggested applications. For the spiritual is, like beauty, "in the eye of the beholder." Or in reality, "in the mind of the knower."

Robert Kurson reflected his best seller's status through his ability to make a powerful, gripping story an even more moving, arresting account. It is written with a quality of excellence anyone would enjoy, and I was totally absorbed in a world of thought I had never pursued.

Now, I am committed to take from this book realities that I firmly believe are God-given—kingdom-of-God operatives. These insights were invaluable to me in being able to see more of God's ways.

Entering into this insight-expander, I had to consider how to relate the story while honoring the writing and storytelling skills of Robert Kurson, yet not simply quote him verbatim on page after page. With profound appreciation for the original, not-to-be-improved account, I will give my own reflections of the story along with some direct quotes.

Crashing Through

Even the book title itself has spiritual implications. Crashing through barriers was the common thread for most of Mike May's life experiences. Whatever barrier was in his way he dared to take on.

Breakthroughs always mean that a barrier has been challenged. The greatest barrier is always within us. The barrier, however, was kept at the lowest possible level for Mike May because of the influence of a mother's love and wisdom as well as a family's flare for adventure.

Breakthroughs always mean that a barrier has been challenged. The greatest barrier is always within us.

Mike was born with normal vision. His mother, Ori Jean May, who remained his hero all of his life, had good vision. Her vision included seeing God in the most traumatic emergency of a three-year-old boy's life.

Needing supplies for making mud pies, an energetic, imaginative three-year-old Mike climbed to the rafters of the family garage. There he found a jar filled with powder.

Inside the house, Ori Jean dried the last of her dishes. A moment later she heard an explosion. She ran to the backyard and found Mike lying on the ground, drenched in blood and sharded in glass. He was in shock and whimpering…. Ori Jean picked up her son and ran inside where she wrapped him in a blanket and dialed frantically for help. Mike's injuries did not hurt. He just wanted to crawl away and put his head down.

Ori Jean … followed the ambulance fifteen miles to the nearest hospital, drawing a curtain over her fears in order to stay on the road. Emergency room doctors swarmed around Mike. He had lost massive amounts of blood from his face, neck, arms, and stomach—everywhere. Critical veins in his wrists had been slashed…. A doctor found Ori Jean in the waiting room. He told her that Mike was going to die.

Ori Jean pleaded with God. "Please let him live, please let him live. Do it to me. Do anything to me. Anything is okay if you just let my baby live."

The doctors kept working. Staff scrambled to find a helicopter to rush him to specialists in El Paso, Texas. "We don't think he's going to make it," they told Ori Jean, and she could not believe the words…. [She prayed again.] *That boy does not die, that boy moves and laughs and tells jokes, he does not die.* The helicopter came …

Mike was still in surgery when Ori Jean reached El Paso. She waited for hours. Doctors told her to prepare to say good-bye to her son. More hours passed. Finally, a surgeon delivered different news. It had required five hundred stitches to quilt Mike together. His eyes had been badly damaged. But he was going to survive …

Mike remained in the hospital for three months, Ori Jean by his side. His face and head and skinny body were bandaged, and his system so stunned that he did not realize he couldn't see …

Doctors told Ori Jean it could take a year for Mike to recover. And they told her that he was blind.[22]

In keeping with her Catholic heritage, Mike's mother had cried out in prayer for her son to live. Her prayer was more than answered. In addition to his life being extended here on earth, his life can teach many of us principles long overlooked.

His mother was the daughter an American family that had moved to Chile for adventure and an opportunity to gain wealth. They experienced both. Her father knew no fear even after being kidnapped by bandits. When freed, he returned with a show of courage and fearlessness by riding the same horse on the same trail where he was captured.

This mother who set a standard for Mike's life of adventure joined her father in adventures through the long chain of mountains in Chile. Her father and mother practiced a lifestyle that displayed a desire to find a way to do whatever they considered important.

When Ori Jean and Mike arrived home after nearly a year in the hospital, his mother told a social worker she wanted Mike to attend public kindergarten and experience the activities of any boy. She was quickly reminded that Mike was blind. When asked what activities she thought Mike was to enjoy, her reply was: "All of them."

At home, Mike climbed out of his bed and into his new world. It did not look black to him—he remembered black. Rather it looked like nothing, like the space directly behind one's head. He climbed kitchen counters, squirmed out windows, ran down toy-littered hallways—a constant ballet of tripping and colliding he hardly noticed for his excitement to get to the next place. Mike felt no surprise at being unable to see. To his four-year-old brain, he just was who he was.[23]

When Mike reached school age, this mother who always lived with a quest for adventure insisted that Mike attend a neighborhood school rather than going away to a school for the blind. Several weeks of persistence and persuasion finally convinced school officials that she would take all responsibility for his safety.

With dark glasses and a sack lunch, he joined his sister in walking to the bus stop. When he climbed onto his seat on the bus and fell to the floor because he faced the wrong way, he only then thought of being blind. Fifteen months had passed since the accident, and this was the first time he remembered thinking about being blind.

The desire to have him experience school as other children spurred the May family's move to Walnut Creek, California; Ori Jean's research had uncovered that blind and sighted students were integrated in this community. Out of six hundred students, fifteen were blind. Mike thrived in school. It was his first experience with other blind people.

With a freedom from fear and accompanying cautions that most parents would teach their sighted children, Mike's mother stood by her little man. When he wanted to be a safety patrol officer helping children safely across the street, it was this believing mother who took his case to a principal who couldn't imagine a sightless person in such a role. Mike insisted he could hear traffic as well for others as he could for himself. His mother and one of his teachers were united in the argument for it. Wearing a vest symbolizing his authority and carrying a stop sign, Mike started escorting children across the street to and from school.

Mike thrived in school. It was his first experience with other blind people.

When he was near the end of grade school, his mother faced a new test when she recognized there was a place in which he should be afraid.

He wanted to ride his bicycle three miles into downtown Walnut Creek. With a stomach knotted with anxiety and images of emergency vehicles attending her son again, she kept her concern to herself.

Don't Be Afraid—Even of Being Afraid

"'It's important to stay on the right-hand side of the road,' she found herself saying as tears rolled down her face. 'If you hear a car or truck, just stop and pull over. If it gets to be too hard, don't be afraid to turn around and come back. And don't be afraid to be afraid—it's important to know when you're afraid.'"[24]

She may have borrowed from the famous quote: "We have nothing to fear except fear itself." Franklin D. Roosevelt in his inaugural address as President of the United States, in 1933, said, "The only thing we have to fear is … fear itself—nameless, unreasoning, unjustified terror which paralyzes needed efforts." That is believed to be a paraphrase of Sir Francis Bacon, who said, "Nothing is terrible except fear itself." Ori Jean was telling Mike, "Don't be afraid—even of being afraid."

There Was Little Place for Fear

Reading the account of Mike May's life, so wonderfully described by Kurson, impacted me most when I saw what little place fear was allowed to hold in his life. It started me thinking how fear stalks so many children, how fears and phobias that have no justification stalk our inner lives. I will address this in detail later.

Kurson's account records times when fear was a part of Mike's boyhood. But it was a controlled fear that permitted him to finish what he started. In climbing a 150-foot radio tower swaying in the wind, he describes "terror" as being part of the experience. He nevertheless finished his job by rotating the receiver he was there to fix to its desired angle.

From that experience, Mike made the decision to build his own radio antenna in his backyard. First, he laid a concrete foundation. Using ten-foot sections, he climbed and placed the components together to reach a height of 80 feet. His mother had to drive away when he reached the 40-foot level. But again she did not utter the words *shouldn't* or *couldn't*. When she returned, she heard him on a short-wave radio asking where he was being heard.

From riding a motorcycle to driving his sister's car (though not very far), to learning to ski the most challenging ski runs, Mike defied his supposed limitations. Skiing was mastered with the aid of a fellow skier giving him verbal directional instructions to avoid objects or other skiers. His skiing skills resulted in special recognition from President Ronald Reagan as part of the 1984 U.S. Winter Olympics Team.

An Unexpected Examination–an Unexpected Offer

Later in life, Mike was accompanying his wife to a routine examination at her optometrist. The doctor finished quickly and surprised them both by asking if Mike would mind him checking his eye. Mike was puzzled, but also OK with the idea. After a quick look at the one eye that remained from the accident so many years before, another request followed that his partner, an ophthalmologist, do an exam as well. With the explanation that the partner, Dr. Dan Goodman, was one of the best in the country, Mike granted the request.

Dr. Goodman learned the nature of Mike's injury and did the exam. It turned out that Dr. Max Fine, a legend in corneal transplants, had been Dr. Goodman's teacher. Dr. Fine had been the doctor who had sought every means known to restore sight in Mike's eye so many years earlier. After many attempts, he had told little Mike and his mother that he would never see again.

So an unexplainable connection between the legendary physician, his student, and his patient was now coming full circle. From the mouth of the expert with the latest methods of treatment, Mike was hearing something he had never expected to hear: "'Mike,' Goodman said, 'I think we can make you see.'

'Despite your horrible corneal disease, it looks like there is a good potential for vision in your eye, and that it can benefit from a stem cell transplant,' Goodman said. 'I have done maybe six of these procedures. Most ophthalmologists in the world haven't done any. It is not something anyone specialized in. And I don't know of anyone who has done one on a patient who has been blind for as long as you have.'"[25]

Mike began to process this possibility and listened to the answers offered to his questions. But months would pass before he made the final decision.

There were risks and no guarantees. There was a fifty-fifty chance of success. Chances of rejection at any time could occur. He did have some perception of light, and that was potentially at risk. Side effects that Mike might face from the necessary drug, cyclosporine, included cancer as well as the failure of healthy organs such as the liver and kidneys.

There were risks and no guarantees.
There was a fifty-fifty chance of success.
Rejection could occur at any time.

He took all the time allotted before deciding to pursue the possibility of seeing. Both pluses and minuses were weighed carefully and, like other decisions that contained risks, he was confident he should undergo the medical procedure. He would later apply that decision when he said to Jennifer, his wife, "I never back out."[26]

After four months it was confirmed the stem cell implant had resulted in the needed reproduction of other cells called daughter cells. That meant a cornea transplant could follow. That too was done with excellence and without incident.

The next morning Dr. Goodman suggested that Mike come by his office for a quick checkup. "'Good morning,' he said, washing his hands. 'How did things go last night? Any bad reactions to the painkillers?'

"'No, this time it went really well,' May said. 'I ate a good dinner and slept all night.'"[27]

Then, with the well-practiced skills of an exceptional surgeon, Dr. Goodman began opening the prized eye to inspect his work from the day before. Instead of the routine cleaning followed by more bandages for protection, Mike could instantly tell the doctor was taking unusual steps.

Goodman wasn't talking about dressings, he was doing something strange and asking something strange, too … he was pulling open the eyelid with his thumb and forefinger and he was asking, "Can you see a little bit?"

A cataclysm of white light exploded into May's eye and his skin and his blood and his nerves and his cells. It was everywhere. It was around him and inside him, inside his hair, on top of his breath, in the next room, on his hands. It was fantastically bright —such intensity had to be bright … but not painful, not even uncomfortable … it rushed toward him and around him, yet it didn't move. It was always moving and it was always still, it came from nowhere—how could something come from nowhere? … It was all white, and now Goodman asked again, "Can you see anything?"

May's face erupted into a smile and someone inside him made him laugh and then talk, and he said, "Holy smoke! I sure can!"

May could feel his adrenaline asking to be allowed in, begging to do its job and tell him that something overwhelming was occurring, something sublime and colossal, but his instincts wouldn't turn him over to such emotion, to allow him to say what was in his throat—"Oh, my gosh, it's happening"—because he sensed that he could not pay attention to feelings and to this new world at the same time; that if he were to think, the images would disappear; that the images required more than just his eye for their existence. They required all of him, and he knew that he didn't want those images to go away, even if it meant postponing the explosions of joy he could feel bubbling underneath.[28]

Mike May had sight. Yet into this near miraculous offer of light and sight came the realization that he did not know what he was seeing. Shapes and colors were clearly in view and could be identified from the sound of voices. He was seeing his wife Jennifer for the first time. Seeing a blue patch, he concluded she had worn a blue sweater that day.

He looked for her face above the blue and there it was, just where it was supposed to be, pink and different from the blue, and a perfect shape, his wife's face, his wife's shape, her face, and he needed to see more. He wanted to cry for fear of losing the image, so he concentrated on the fact that hair came above the face, and he tilted his head back and there was another new color, a soft white, not like the fluorescent lights above it, a white with some yellow in it … he looked at that soft white above Jennifer's face and thought, "So that's blond."

From seeing his wife for the first time, he moved to seeing himself in a mirror across the room. He had not seen himself since he was three. "Is that really me?" he wondered to himself, and he knew he would need to spend more time looking in a mirror when he got home in order to know more.[29]

The Small World of Home—a Big World Beyond

A new world awaited a man now able to see. Details of the trip home required explanations as to the meaning of certain shapes. Road signs had shapes and colors that required explanation. "What's that?" became the most frequent question from the inquiring mind of one with new sight.

Home meant seeing his small world in a way he had never seen it and with the same required explanations of what he was seeing. Then came a hallowed time—the first time he saw his sons. His newly gained sight allowed him to see their hair color and the freckles on seven-year-old Carson's nose. Love was now joined with images of these so valued in his life.

It was as if a new world entered the old world of Mike May. This world had details he could not have imagined. Yet this world also required more explanations and identifications than he could have imagined.

He was seeing, but he didn't know *what* he was seeing much of the time. Explanations helped. Yet, as time went on, the most unimaginable accompaniment to sight occurred: sight brought a dimension to his life so pleasurable that he was enthralled by it, yet the same sight brought a burden of confused images he could not identify.

Simple things he had mastered in his one-dimensional world of sightlessness now were there in the three-dimensional world—but without identification. Going to the grocery store was totally frustrating, because what once was a simple method of feeling the shape of a ketchup bottle or a mustard jar now called for the perplexing problem of seeing something with a shape and colored markings he could not identify. His was suddenly loaded with issues that required so much mental and emotional energy he found himself exhausted from carrying the weight of it.

He assumed there was lack of clarity in his vision that would in time be corrected. But as time went by without resolve, his exasperation continued in several areas of vision.

His was suddenly loaded with issues that required so much mental and emotional energy that he found himself exhausted from carrying the weight of it.

Something Wrong in the Brain

Frequent visits to Dr. Goodman's office with the usual testing methods offered the same results. Mike could not see the giant E atop the familiar Snellen eye chart from twenty feet away. From five feet away he could read it as well as the next two lines.

"So what is wrong with my eye?" May asked.

"There is nothing wrong with your eye," Goodman said. "In fact it's an almost perfect eye. Optically, I'd say you're 20/40."

"I am not sure I understand," May said.

"I'm not an expert on this," Goodman said, "but I'm pretty certain the problem is your visual cortex."

"My brain?"

"I think so. I mean, I can see your entire optical system, and it's excellent. Eyes seeing as beautifully as yours should be able to read all the way down the chart. That leaves the brain."[30]

With that information Mike assumed time would allow the brain to begin to see normally. One of his strengths was brain skill. Forty-three years of being blind would necessitate the brain taking some time to catch up.

Now, a whole new paradigm would have to be processed by what seemed like an already overworked brain. Time and further tests offered the same conclusion. The problem was not in his eye, but in his brain.

> ## One of his strengths was brain skill. Forty-three years of being blind would necessitate the brain taking some time to catch up.

Following a television interview with Mike, a call came from Dr. Ione Fine, a research scientist at the University of California-San Diego. She wanted to do tests on his newfound sight and accompanying comprehension. She later explained that, from her research, Mike was believed to be one of fewer than twenty people in known history to have gained sight after being almost totally blind.

Lengthy tests followed. Many trips to San Diego led to a bond of friend-ship with Dr. Fine and her colleague, Dr. Donald MacLeod. Fine's fiancé, Dr. Geoff Boynton, also engaged in vision research at Salk Institute.

Mike May was now poised to enter a new realm of understanding, one that had been first explored in Germany in 1850 by a scientist named Her-man von Helmholtz. Sight required knowledge to interpret the visual data being transmitted through the eyes.

Let the excellent research and writing of author Kurson give the needed information of this important realm of brain activity:

> Today it is virtually impossible to find a vision scientist, a researcher and psychologist, who does not agree that knowledge and vision are highly related, and that without our knowledge about the visual world our ability to understand visual scenes would fall apart.
>
> The human brain contains approximately 100 billion neurons. Neurons are a particular type of nerve cell designed to process and transmit electrical impulses. Some of these neurons transmit signals from the world outside, bringing signals to the brain from the eyes, ears, fingers, and even the stomach wall.
>
> To learn something as staggeringly complex as vision—with all its subtleties, shadows, cues, clues, priors, exceptions, contexts, and conclusions—a person needs massive amounts of neurons available and ready for that purpose.
>
> "But who owns a supply of neurons like that?" Mike asked.
>
> "Young children do"[31].

Mike learned that he had forgotten how to see certain things. Now, with-out the needed neurons, he would not be able to gain those skills he could have acquired at three years of age and following.

Dr. Fine compared his attempt at learning to see with that of an adult learning a second language. Mike affirmed that experience—being just like learning a second language—as exactly how it felt. "Imagine doing that every working moment of every day," he said.[32]

People who have been deaf and receive cochlear implants experience this same heavy cognitive lifting. They are often confused and annoyed. In fact, there are some in the deaf community who are totally against cochlear im-plantation to restore hearing. Spiritually we face similar adjustments as we learn to see what God sees and hear what God says.

During a lengthy time with Fine and her team, Mike heard the essence of her conclusion. "May didn't seem to possess the neural structure necessary for normal vision—it just wasn't there anymore…. Fine's best guess was May's vision would remain a process of heavy cognitive lifting, assembling clues, figuring things out, and managing the constant overflow of information and its resultant fatigue."[33]

With this honest and yet virtually hopeless conclusion about potential improvement, Mike was not deterred. He would resort to building a plan in the same way he had made plans all his life. His plan called for using both his sightless skills and his skills with sight.

> Over the next few weeks, May continued to practice cooling his vision while moving his other senses to the forefront of information delivery. He started to see faster and more accurately. Some days he stumbled in these efforts. Some days he stumbled to the pavement. He kept practicing. Seeing the world kept getting easier. He wasn't automatic, and he wasn't close to normally sighted. But he was better. He was thrillingly better.[33]

This journey with a man I will probably never know has been a most important and meaningful journey in my life. I have called on all the neurons in my brain to properly record what I am to see and hear out of this incredible story. I have also asked the wonderful Teacher assigned by Jesus to continue His teaching role to aid me as well, and to supply the needed neurons for better brain insight.

Mike May faced more challenges, yet with each new one he had the courage and determination to continue to "crash through." Thank you, Mike, for living such a life, and thank you, Robert Kurson, for writing in such an arresting way.

People of Sight Need Insight from God

Now let me get to the point: Spiritually, we are people of sight. Being born again brings sight we never had. Without a new beginning—a birth coming from the Holy Spirit—there is no comprehensive vision of God or of His kingdom.

As a newborn child of God, the Holy Spirit furnishes us with the needed neurons for spiritual recognition. In the new world of spiritual sightedness, being like a child is required in our learning engagements. The reality of this new world of consciousness requires childlikeness. Jesus said, "Whoever humbles himself like this child is the greatest in the kingdom of heaven" (Matthew 18:4).

The reality of this new world of consciousness requires childlikeness.

We have much to learn about thinking—about knowing—and about knowledge and how to process what we experience with every one of our God-given senses. Our bodies are wonderfully made and connected in such a way that every function is interdependent.

Until we see what God sees and think like God thinks, we cannot experience what Jesus promised—a life that is abundant, full and running over.

America has a thinking crisis. When we learn we have an illness, the way we process that fact can, at the least, influence the outcome and, at most, determine the outcome.

We can't document how many people could be well instead of sick if not for their faulty thinking. But many doctors know they are treating patients whose illness is a symptom. The cause is wrong thinking. The illness is real. Yet the illness may not have occurred had the patient not carried the toxin in his or her thought processes to incubate it.

I want to remind you of what the man known as the father of medicine said: "It is more important to know what sort of person has a disease than to know what sort of disease a person has." The "sort of person" we are determines the sort of life we live as well as the sort of conditions our body contains.

Sight for Mike May was a cataclysm of white light—light so penetrating, so invasive that everything was attended by this gift to him. Kurson described light inside and outside, upon and through, present and yet beyond. We will take a look at the fact that God is light and His first utterance was, "Let there be light" (Genesis 1:3).

We will look at that light shining on us to make us an extension of that illumination. Returning to the ease of life is part of the light God gives us. Let's take the journey together.

Chapter THREE

God's Visit to a Doctor's Brain

The brain of a respected doctor in Fort Worth was laboring with incessant noise created by a rare disease. A tangled mass of blood vessels on the surface of the brain resulted in a constant noise in his left ear.

To Dr. Russell Lambert, it resembled the sound of a rushing wave crashing against the seashore. Though he used his stethoscope to listen to the heartbeat of patients in his family practice, while doing so he had to tune out hearing his own heartbeat along with the attending noise created by the rush of blood pushing against the mass of blood vessels.

He had coped with the problem for four years. But the condition worsened and he was unable to sleep lying down because of the exaggerated noise level as well as the elevated pain. His abbreviated sleep times occurred in a chair.

He knew the diagnosis was a dural arteriovenous malformation. He also knew that this tangled mass of blood vessels could rupture at any time, causing brain damage, stroke, and even death.

And with a progressive increase in the noise level, he realized he must find a solution soon.

The Need for Superglue

Research led him to a new method of treatment. It called for a specially developed glue to be squirted through a tube inserted in a main artery in the groin and threaded up into the brain. The glue would harden instantly and block the blood supply to the arterial venous malformation, thus diverting the blood to normal channels and blocking off the abnormal vessels. A derivative of that glue today is a common household commodity: Superglue.

But all of the blood vessels needing to be blocked could not be reached. So the medical team believed that though a complete cure was not possible, the condition would be greatly improved. While risk accompanied the procedure, the process appeared to be Doctor Lambert's only hope.

A teaching doctor, Dr. Charles Kerber, in the University of California Medical School in San Diego, was chosen to do the surgery. Dr. Lambert reached that decision after carefully drawing from his own medical training, research, and prayer that extended for several weeks.

As one who believed Jesus Christ is God and could be trusted with his spiritual needs, Lambert was challenged to trust Him also for His physical needs. His faith was challenged, yet he chose to release his life and condition to the care of the Lord—somewhat in the way that he chose to trust the surgeon with renowned medical skills.

The skills of Christ in caring for him physically—these were not as well known to Doctor Lambert. He knew Christ could take his sins from him and grant forgiveness. He knew Christ could care for him eternally when he died, as evidenced in the resurrection of Christ. But thinking of Christ as an attending physician, along with the doctor he was trusting for surgery, was a new dimension of faith.

Time in prayer and time reading the Bible began to strengthen his faith, just as time spent in physical exercise can strengthen muscles. He wife and daughter shared in this exercise of faith building. Friends also played an important role in prayer and encouragement.

Arrangements to Give Russ Lambert New Vision

Just before he was to leave for San Diego for the surgery, God arranged a series of events that served as preparation for the miraculous experience that awaited him in California. Prayer times became meaningful. He became more conscious of God's part in his life and in his thoughts than he had in the past.

The Bible was coming alive with meaning. Personal messages from God that he could claim for his own assurance were frequent. One Scripture became a promise of hope and assured him God was at work on his behalf.

"For momentary, light affliction is producing for us an eternal weight of glory far beyond all comparison, while we look not at the things which are seen, but at the things which are not seen; for the things which are seen are temporal, but the things which are not seen are eternal" (2 Corinthians 4:17, 18, NASU).

Like Mike May, whose story we learned in chapter two, Russ Lambert was seeing things not seen before. He was also receiving God's explanation for what he was seeing.

I had several conversations with Russ before writing this story. As we talked, his face would radiate the awe for what God *said* to him from Scripture as much as what God *did* for his medical needs. God gave him a passage of Scripture that, he said, became like an intravenous feeding. This passage flowed into his thought life and became the sustaining infusion for him through the trauma we will visit in a few paragraphs.

God gave him a passage of Scripture that, he said, became like an intravenous feeding.

It is important that we get as familiar with the passage as he did. His familiarity came from memorizing it and making it his watchword.

The LORD is my strength and my song;
He has become my salvation.
Shouts of joy and victory
resound in the tents of the righteous:
The LORD's right hand has done mighty things!
The LORD's right hand is lifted high;
the LORD's right hand has done mighty things!"
I will not die but live
and will proclaim what the LORD has done
(Psalm 118:14-17, NIV).

He could not have imagined that that these words, memorized, would be like a life-support system for his body in the operating room of the hospital. As a doctor, he not only received them as a life infusion in that moment, he also shared them with the attending doctors and medical students who filled the room to observe the surgery. But more on that is coming shortly.

Before his surgery in San Diego, another surgery was needed in Fort Worth. That surgery was one that would help his thinking. Doctor Lambert will acknowledge that he carried an offense toward a well-known spiritual leader in the area, Kenneth Copeland. Though he did not know Kenneth Copeland, nor had Kenneth done anything to Russ personally, he nevertheless carried this offense.

In one of my conversations with him, Russ said it was an offense that led to him making a judgment that further developed over time. Occasionally, as he drove in his routines in the city, he would listen to a radio broadcast by Copeland.

"I just didn't like the way he said, 'Well, bless God,'" Russ related to me. Though the offense was unwarranted and had no good rationale, it was nonetheless extremely strong in Doctor's Lambert thoughts.

To avoid being irritated by his thoughts about Kenneth, he never listened to radio stations that might broadcast Copeland's programs. So, to his complete surprise, as he was on his way one day to visit patients at the hospital, he heard the voice of … Kenneth Copeland. In his inimitable style, Kenneth was saying to his wife, "Gloria, there are only two kinds of people we ought to pray for—those who deserve it and those who don't."

Amazed that his radio was tuned to a station carrying the Copeland broadcast, Russ was nonetheless stunned at the logic and wisdom of the statement he had just heard. His mind reviewed the truth that we *ought to pray for those who deserve it as well as those who don't.*

He realized what he was hearing was good insight and advice from a man he had judged—and sentenced—in his own thinking. Russ made clear to me that, at the beginning of his physical problems, he was not a spiritual man. But by this time he was processing issues by asking for God's perspective. He recognized that he must get God's perspective on Kenneth Copeland rather than form a characterization from his own rationale.

So while driving toward the hospital, he said, "Father, I have judged Kenneth Copeland, and I want your forgiveness. I also want to know how to ask him to forgive me, either in a letter, a phone call, or face to face."

As he arrived at the hospital, he was aware of the Lord's presence in the car. More importantly, he was aware of a newfound peace in his heart. The root of unforgiveness and judgment toward a man he didn't even know was gone. God's peace was now filling his consciousness and guiding his thoughts.

But Russ and his family were carrying another burden in their lives. It was a burden for the wife of one of his colleagues, Dr. Jim Marr. She had become part of their prayer focus. Her diagnosis was as serious as his, if not more so. A tumor had been diagnosed in her brain and surgery was scheduled that very day.

As he entered the hospital, a nurse approached him with excitement. "Have you heard the report on Dr. Marr's wife?" she asked.

"No, haven't heard anything. What's the report?" Russ replied.

"They did the surgery and when they opened to the location of the tumor, it was gone!"

"Wow—I must congratulate them! Where are they?" Russ asked.

"They have already taken her back to her room," the nurse answered.

With that news, Russ called his longtime friend, colleague, and fellow Christian. Dr. Marr explained that he and his wife had asked Kenneth Copeland to pray for his wife. Kenneth had not only prayed, but he had come to the hospital and was with them in the room at that very moment.

Jim Marr suddenly said to Russ, "Here, talk to Kenneth Copeland. I am putting him on the phone so he can tell you about the miracle."

Not much time had passed since Russ had cleared his own heart of wrongful thoughts about the man whose voice was on the other end of the call. Having asked God for the right to ask Kenneth to forgive him, he waited as Kenneth shared the remarkable report of a tumor being removed by God's power. Kenneth gave all the credit to the Lord's presence and power supplied by His grace and love for this dear couple.

Then Russ told Kenneth he wanted to ask his forgiveness for having carried an offense toward him, with its attending judgments and false conclusions.

Kenneth Copeland granted that request for forgiveness as if the offense had never existed.

Two Brain Surgeries in One Day

Two surgeries occurred that day in Fort Worth. One was performed in the car of Dr. Russ Lambert as he humbly accepted a better way to think, which is called *repentance*, and as he asked God's forgiveness, which is called *grace*. That ready supply of forgiveness was implanted in his heart. New thoughts and attitudes were implanted in his mind. God successfully completed that surgery as a prelude to another one that would happen in San Diego.

The second surgery occurred in the sterile, germ-free, well-lighted operating room of St. Joseph's hospital. With help from the light that streamed from the fixtures above, a woman's skull was opened and layers of tissues were parted to disclose that, where a tumor had existed, there was now nothing but normal brain matter. God had been there before the scalpels of the surgeon. No one knew when God took the tumor. What the doctor's surgery did was verify God's earlier surgery, an operation that could be done only with the skills only He possesses.

God had been there before the scalpels of the surgeon. No one knew when God took the tumor.

The impaired thinking in Russ Lambert's brain was as serious as the entangled blood vessels in his brain yet to be treated. Entangled thoughts, which he had nurtured, were impairing his life also. Those thoughts didn't send a constant noise to his eardrum, but they did send debilitating signals, prohibiting healthy thinking.

His tumor of wrongful thoughts that were without justification was just as damaging as the brain tumor that God removed from his friend. He too had a surgery! The sequence of events occurred in such an unexplainable way that it became obvious God was preparing him for the highly specialized procedure in his own brain. God was offering Himself, and Russell Lambert was willing to accept His offer.

The Right Hand of the Lord on the Right Arm of Russ

Accompanied by his wife and daughter, he made the trip to San Diego. In a document he wrote before leaving from California to return home, he gives this account.

We arrived in San Diego on Sunday, May 16, and I was admitted to the hospital. I was thoroughly examined by several doctors and medical students. On Monday afternoon the neuroradiologist who was to do the procedure examined me. After he left, I was discussing the 118th Psalm with my wife, Ireta, and daughter, Lizabeth. Present also was my friend Ernie Horn, who had flown from Fort Worth as a surprise to be with us.

Lizabeth suddenly asked me, "Dad, what are you going to do if the doctors do not find anything wrong when they get inside your head?" I was deeply touched by her expression of faith. Later than evening, alone in the hospital room, I told the Lord that if my daughter could express that kind of faith, I could also. I thanked him for His presence. During the night I was restless. There was no fear, but it was as if something was taking place inside my head.

I went to the special procedure room the next morning. I mentally shut out all the activity in the room and totally concentrated on the presence of Jesus at my side. The procedure began. The catheter as put into my femoral artery, threaded up into my aorta and up into my head. The first series of pictures were taken. As soon as they finished, Dr. Kerber, with much excitement, told me that the branches of my internal carotid artery, which were feeding my arterial venous malformation, were nowhere to be found! These were the most worrisome branches, as they could not be eliminated by the planned gluing procedure. Brain surgery would be necessary to eliminate them. Their unexplainable absence meant God was at work.

My faith soared. I asked the doctor if he knew where the branches could have gone, and he said he didn't. I told him that the Lord had removed them and I also told him of the many people who were praying for me. His reply was for me to keep praying.

What happened next is impossible to understand. I know the Scripture says, "His ways are not our ways," and we know His timing differs from ours. In any event, I suddenly had intense pain in the left side of my head, [which] I reported to the doctor. After a quick look into the fluoroscope, the doctor came up to me and said that a complication had occurred and that there was a tear in the lining of my left internal carotid artery, which was the main blood supply to the left side of my brain. He said that the procedure would have to be stopped immediately and the gluing that was planned could not be done.

Suddenly I lost the feeling and the use of my right arm. Intuitively, I wanted it to move, so I reached over and picked it up with my left hand. My right arm was completely paralyzed. In addition, my right side had gone numb also. Then I remembered the truth in Psalm 118:16: "The LORD's right hand has done mighty things!" (NIV)

I prayed and asked the Lord to share the power of His right hand. Then I suddenly knew that I would be able to use my right arm. So, I told the doctors and the attending students who were observing all that was happening. "I am going to use my right arm," and I lifted it up to a normal position. Instantaneous strength was returned to my arm and the right side of my body.

Because of the unusual physiological reactions of my body, the doctors were implementing every medical procedure they knew to protect me from further damage and even death. So, they ordered me sent to intensive care for observation and for preparation for possible brain surgery. That surgery would have been an attempt to prevent a stroke.

Two neurosurgeons began examining me and questioning me. They were amazed to find no weakness whatsoever. Their extensive exam included asking if they could listen for the noise in my head that I had experienced for some four years. Of course, I invited them to listen as needed. The surgeon put his stethoscope up to my head and listened. That sound [should have been] easily heard because of its volume, but he reported, "I can't hear any noise."

I had been so preoccupied with all the events and the movement in the ICU, I had not thought about the noise. Normally my lying down would have created such intense noise and discomfort I would have been aware of it without the aid of a stethoscope. I reached for the amplifier that I so frequently used in practice to listen for myself. The noise with which I had become so familiar was not to be heard.

I called for a resident who had listened with great interest and attentiveness during my admission procedures. She came to the ICU along with a neurologist, a medical student, and my primary doctor. No one could find any sign of the malfunction, yet nothing had been done to eliminate it because of the emergency.

I suddenly knew that I had been completely healed! I began to praise God and give Him thanks for so gracious a gift. The doctors said they did not understand what had happened, but they wanted me to lie quiet and rest. So I began lying flat on my back without any of the unusual pressure or noise I had experienced for over a year. Previously, I could not lie flat for more than 10 minutes at a time. It was so gratifying to realize that I was completely at rest and free from any discomfort or noise in my ear.[35]

A Friend Drops By

Let me break into this account of the sequence of events to share more evidence of the remarkable ways of God. Ernie Horn, the friend who accompanied Dr. Lambert and his family, has also been a friend of mine for years. He has distinguished himself as one who honors the heroes of education in the Greater Fort Worth area, both students and teachers.

Russ told me personally how much it meant to him that Ernie showed up at the hospital unannounced and casually said, that epic day, "Well, I was just in the neighborhood and thought I would drop by."

Ernie's account of this in my interview with him was equally helpful. "The Lord did everything just short of mailing me an airline ticket to go to see Russ," Ernie said. "He was speaking to me about being there to encourage Russ as well as witness something He was going to do."

Ernie arrived and gave his "I was in the neighborhood" explanation and he and Russ prayed together. He remembers Russ being somewhat anxious, but his wife showed an amazing calmness. In the prayer, Ernie remembers Russ saying to the Lord several times, "You are my strong right arm."

When Russ was taken to the operating room, Ernie asked to be excused to get some personal supplies he had forgotten to pack for the trip. He walked across the parking lot and back into the hospital at the time one of attending the doctors came out in his scrubs, now drenched with perspiration. "His hair was even wet with sweat," Ernie recalled.

With a smile of approval for God's ways as well as His timing, Ernie recalls the doctor saying: "I am having trouble breathing. I just came out here to get some air." In the inimitable style that Ernie has about him, he responded, "How may I help you?"

"No, no," the doctor said. "I just saw a miracle, and I need some air— some time to collect my thoughts."

"Well, I just came out here early this morning from Fort Worth to be with a friend having surgery."

"What is your friend's name?"

"Dr. Russell Lambert."

The doctor showed his amazement at the connection between his patient and the stranger engaging him in conversation. The doctor said, "We just barely got started on our procedure, and someone in Heaven healed him."

Now back to Dr. Lambert's report, which includes his conversation with this highly skilled doctor:

The next day Dr. Kerber came into my room and sat down to review the amazing events. He said he could not understand how I could be perfectly well considering the magnitude of this untoward event. First he cited that the branches of veins that were so concerning because they could not be reached had disappeared. He had no explanation.

Further, he said they had even less explanation how the tear in the carotid artery, with the resulting paralysis to my right side, was instantly repaired. He pointed out that the paralysis would have likely spread resulting in a complete paralysis to my right side, loss of speech, and even impairing my intellect. That was all reversed, and there was no aftermath of it ever happening.

As I tried to take all of this in, I asked the doctor, "Where did the noise go? How [did] the vessel that was going to be injected with glue get closure and get blocked without the procedure being completed? What caused the tear in the artery to repair itself, and how did the paralysis suddenly leave?"

My doctor had no medical explanation. As far as he was concerned, it was unexplainable. He was so pleased with all the current tests and my apparent condition that he told me he was dismissing me from the hospital the next day. He concluded that nothing further needed to be done for me.

I was totally healed and symptom-free. Again the words of Psalm 118 played from the recording of my memorizing these verses:

The LORD has done this, and it is marvelous in our eyes. This is the day the LORD has made; let us rejoice and be glad in it (vv. 23, 24).

It was clearly the Lord's doing, and it meant not only a day the Lord had made for me, but it also meant a new day was dawning in my life for knowing His love, His favor, and His faithfulness.[36]

Russ wrote this short addendum to his report after he arrived home:

I had been home about two weeks when I received a call from Dr. Kerber in San Diego. I gave him my report that I was still completely well.

Then I asked him what I should tell those who asked about what happened. He told me to tell anyone who asked that the Master Physician had healed [me], not him. I told him, "You are the world-famous physician, and if that is good enough for you, it is good enough for me."

I am in awe God's mercy and goodness to me, and I will praise His name forevermore.[37]

Untangled Thoughts, Untangled Blood Vessels

Instead of a tangled mass of blood vessels being glued to alleviate pain and noise, a work only God could do had occurred. And yet, the untangling of thoughts Russ had toward an honorable man was just as significant. A significant part of the healing of Russ Lambert was granting forgiveness leading to freedom from the malignancy of judgments he had carried.

Equally important was his willingness to allow God's thoughts to become His thoughts as he memorized Scripture and then, in a time of intense trauma, use this life-carrying power of God's own Word. As if he was hooked up to an intravenous flow of life, he claimed, "God's right hand has done mighty things." Not only was his right arm restored, his right side was restored, which meant his left brain was being freed from any damage.

This account has great relevance for anyone. God wants us to know the way He thinks so we can draw from His mind—just as we would draw from the skill and training of a renowned physician—as He attends to our medical needs. God is for us. God loves us.

Our thinking is the issue. We cannot think our way to health without learning how to think by using the organic computer God supplied in creation. If our thinking does not lead us to God, we are not thinking correctly. The master programmer of this amazing capacity to think must be consulted if we are to enjoy a life of being at ease.

Russ Lambert experienced the unexplainable ability of God's power to repair the damaged veins in his brain. More importantly, he learned how to experience God's guidance in rerouting the errant thought patterns in his mind. His contribution to us has limitless implications. We can learn how to access the same power he accessed.

> **If our thinking does not lead us to God, we are not thinking correctly. The master programmer of this amazing capacity to think must be consulted if we are to enjoy a life of being at ease.**

More importantly, we can learn how God thinks, with the attending result of His thoughts can become our thoughts.

CHAPTER FOUR

Thank You:
The Fitting Response of a Thinker

Few in my generation have been equipped to *think* as was Dallas Willard. Gifted of God with a brilliant mind, he carefully developed his mind to align with God's thoughts. The same skill he used to pursue the thoughts of God, he used to review the thoughts of men.

While he knew mental brilliance, he also knew gentle humility before God and everyone. Though he set out to be a pastor, he found himself accepting a role in academia as a well-respected professor of philosophy. Instead of feeling conflict in studying the thoughts of men as well as the thoughts of God, he knew a calling to gain from *God-thoughts* answers for the *men-thoughts* as well as learning God-thoughts *from* men who know God.

Such a monumental life and manner of life would lead many to conclude there is little reason for average people (like me) to find encouragement from his life. But the opposite is true. John Ortberg writes of his humble beginning in *Christianity Today*.

> Because Dallas wrote extensively on spiritual formation and taught philosophy, one might think he came from abundant education and culture and resources. In fact, he grew up in rural Missouri in poverty. Electricity did not come until he was mostly grown up. His mother died when he was two years old; her last words to her husband were, "Keep eternity before the children."
>
> He once read a book by Jack London that described the world from an atheistic point of view. Dallas said that he'd never known books could

contain such ideas and afterward [found] that his mind was never the same. He was 9 years old. He became an insatiable reader: "When I left home after graduating high school, I left as a migrant agricultural worker with a Modern Library edition of Plato in my duffel bag. It sounds kind of crazy, but I loved it. I loved the stuff. Before I knew there was a subject called philosophy, I loved it."

He attended Tennessee Temple and did graduate work at Baylor University before receiving his PhD from the University of Wisconsin-Madison. He then taught for 47 years at USC [University of Southern California], where for a time he chaired the philosophy department.[38]

Dallas joined the faculty of the School of Philosophy at the University of Southern California in 1965, and was eventually asked to serve as chairman of the department for two years. He valued the administrative work, but it caused him to cut back on his teaching time, which he treasured most. As a professor, he discussed the thoughts of God as freely as the thoughts of renowned men. His plumb line for truth was always the Word of God.

At home in stacks of books with philosophical positions in libraries across the world, his measurement of their value was always what God thought and what God said. One of the most important books he authored is simply titled, *Hearing God*.

With unmistakable clarity, he affirms his confidence in our ability to hear God, because God enjoys conversing with us:

> Today I continue to believe that people are meant to live in an ongoing conversation with God, speaking and being spoken to. Rightly understood, I believe that this can be abundantly verified in experience. God's visits to Adam and Eve in the Garden, Enoch's walks with God, and the face-to-face conversations with Moses and Jehovah are all commonly regarded as highly exceptional moments in the religious history of humankind. Aside from their obviously unique historical role, however, they are not meant to be exceptional at all. Rather they are examples of the human life God intended for us. God is indwelling His people through personal presence and fellowship. Given who we are by basic nature, we live—really live—only through God's regular speaking to our souls and thus "by every word that comes from the mouth of God."[39]

Dallas took the road less traveled as a follower of Jesus Christ teaching philosophy in a very respected school of secular academic excellence—simply because he knew God. This road was as appealing to him as a conventional school of theology because he had a comprehension of the kingdom of God in operation.

God's kingdom includes theology, or a study of God, but includes all centers of influence or domains. God is at home on a university campus as He is at a church campus or a divinity school campus. So Dallas Willard, a man of much learning, was at home there as well.

Few in our generation have known the reality of the kingdom of God as he did. His most well-known book is the classic, *The Divine Conspiracy*. Conspiracy theories exist for almost all issues, from government to finance. Those who espouse a conspiracy theory usually believe a few members of the world's most powerful families successfully rule the world by making decisions in secretive chambers. These are, of course, families of great wealth as well as power.

God is at home on a university campus as He is at a church campus or a divinity school campus. So Dallas Willard, a man of much learning, was at home there as well.

Dallas Willard dispelled the conventional conspiracy theory by declaring there *is* a conspiracy. Someone runs the world. A family does indeed influence all of life on this planet.

However, this family does not meet in clandestine secrecy. It is God who has conspired to rule. He opens the windows of His meeting place so He can been seen and heard. It is His desire to make His will known for us to follow on earth. This rule, by love, invites all who will accept His offer to rule with Him. God further intends that His family join Him in His rule over all things.

God even invites all to join actively in planning and in strategy meetings with him. He wants His conspiracy known and the reason for such a plan understood.

Intuitively, every person on this earth knows there ought to be a way for every realm of life to result in our fulfillment. We were meant to *be at ease*. The search for that quality of life is unending for those who have not found it. Those who have found it, as did Dallas Willard, know life as God intends it for everyone. They are at ease as he was at ease.

During my writing of this book, Dallas Willard stepped even further into the dimension in which he already lived. It is a dimension of knowing God's presence, with His attending peace and without limitation.

His mother's insight was to forever mark his life. "Keep eternity before the children,"—her last request before her death—was honored by Dallas's father. Eternity was not only kept before him as a child growing up, eternity became as much a part of his thought life as was his time zone.

One of the most remarkable things he ever shared came toward the end his journey: "I think that when I die, it may be some time before I know it."[40]

Like many of his insights, much thought is required to fathom the depth of his meaning. He so lived in the presence of God's affirming love that he believed he might be out of his body for some time without knowing that his earthen body had been vacated. He lived in the presence of God here, which meant it was *not* a long-distance move to get to Heaven. It was more like a move to the next room—another dimension.

Stepping into that dimension of the invisible realm of God's presence can happen in many ways. One way is to hear the report from one whose life experience makes the invisible visible. Just as we saw that principle in an earlier chapter, we find that we do not know what we are seeing without the needed disclosure from someone who does know. Spiritually, we know only what or whom we are seeing when God—who knows all things—tells us.

His Report of God Visiting Him

An unexpected report of seeing God's invisible presence occurred during one of the treasured times I was in the presence of Dallas Willard. It was a meeting before he was to be interviewed by James and Betty Robison on the *Life Today* television program. James and Betty always have dinner with their guests at the studio, during which they get to know their guests and simply enjoy being real people discussing real issues of life. James had been impacted by the book *The Divine Conspiracy* and wanted his viewers to enjoy the remarkable insights Dallas offered.

He called Dallas in Los Angeles and talked with him extensively. They spoke of the weighty issues Dallas believed and taught. When someone blesses James, he wants others to be blessed by their insights through his TV program. So he arranged for Dallas to come to the Dallas/Fort Worth area with Jane, Dallas's wife. Dallas and Jane already knew James and Betty because they watched and enjoyed the *Life Today* program.

It was my privilege to be part of the dinner meeting before taping the programs that would air later. It was an engaging time in which I got to know

Dallas and Jane better while they, likewise, came to know James and Betty and the staff.

At the end of the visit, which included a review of the topics to be discussed on the program, James asked if anyone else had a question for Dallas. Dallas answered several questions with his usual gracious manner and keen perceptions.

I felt compelled to ask a question about which I had long wondered: How was he led to take a role in teaching at a university?

Dallas's eyes, filled with love and acceptance for me, looked into my own soul as I looked into his. With his clear, resonant voice and the cadence of words coming from a seasoned teacher, he opened a hallowed moment in his life.

An Epiphany as a Student–A Life as a Teacher

What followed was an account of his early days as a student at Tennessee Temple College in Chattanooga, Tennessee. He described God's presence visiting him in his dorm room. Because he had chosen not to share this experience in his writing or his interviews, I am not going to share the details here. This encounter with God's presence as a student ushered Dallas deeper into the realities of the kingdom of God.

When he finished the story of that experience, a hush fell on the room. No one knew what to say, and no one wanted the awesome presence attending the account to be interrupted. We sat in silence for some time until the production director reminded James that the studio was full of people waiting for him to appear with his guest.

When he finished the story of that experience, a hush fell on the room.

Jane slipped to my side and said: "I am so glad you asked him that question. I have so wanted him to tell it through the years, but he did not want people to think that he saw himself as more special than others. I once mentioned it in general terms in an interview with *Christianity Today*. Thank you for asking him."

During that epiphany, a man experienced the living Christ, whose manifest presence was there with him. Because this epic experience occurred while he was a student, it may have guided him to share his life with other students. Dallas then took the role of a teacher and impacted countless students through their studies with him. An even wider circle of people have been touched through the study of his writings. That circle includes me and thousands of others.

Hearing God Is Important—But Not to Make Us Important

I believe an explanation for Dallas's reluctance to share that encounter with the eternal Christ can be found in his book *Hearing God*. I have already said that he knew from Scripture and experience that God desires—even enjoys—speaking to us. But he also went on to explain that people have difficulty believing that God is interested in them.

> We might find it hard to believe if we were told that a high government official or some other important, though merely human, dignitary had called to talk to us. We might think, on the one hand, that we are not important and, on the other hand, that such a communication might seem to make us important.
>
> Similar thoughts may be stirred up at the suggestion of God's talking to us. But these thoughts are irrelevant to his purposes in dealing with us. Moreover they contain tragic misconceptions that have the power to shut us off from the individualized word of God.
>
> In the first place, we are that important. We were important enough for God to give his Son's life for us and to choose to inhabit us as a living temple. Obviously then we are important enough for him to guide us and speak to us whenever that is appropriate.
>
> In the second place, *his speaking to us does not in itself make us important.* Just as when he spoke to the ancient people of Israel, his speaking to us only gives us greater opportunity to be and to do good, and greater responsibility, too, for the care and guidance of others. But if we allow God's conversational walk with us (or anything else, for that matter) to make us think we are people of great importance, His guidance will pretty certainly be withdrawn. For we cannot be trusted with it. Under the kingdom of the heavens, those who exalt themselves will be abased, as Jesus taught, and pride is the condition that comes right before the fall.[41]

Dallas never wanted people to see him as one whom God had endowed in ways others were lacking. Like Paul, he knew he was what he was by the grace of God. "But by the grace of God I am what I am, and his grace toward me was not in vain" (1 Corinthians 15:10).

On the other hand, Dallas Willard was quite willing to recognize that others could experience God's presence and hear His voice. He never lost appreciation for those who were used by God to shape and influence his own life.

His early years were spent among the most conservative and fundamental students of God's Word. Affirmation and appreciation for their influence was acknowledged often in his life. Such a tribute is found in his classic *Divine Conspiracy*. There, in the dedication page, he listed the names of those he honored: R. R. Brown, Joe Henry Hankins, John R. Rice, Lee Roberson, and J.I. Willard. Then, with a Scripture, he gave this appraisal of their stature: "In those days there were giants in the land" (Genesis 6:2).

His Brother's Encounter with God

It was part of his family heritage—as it is part of God's family heritage—to recognize family members who shaped his life. (God was always quick to make clear He was the God of Abraham, Isaac, and Jacob.) So in this list of high-profile men who write, found churches, build universities, and lead thousands of people to embrace Christ as their own treasure of life, Dallas included his older brother, J.I. Willard.

My acquaintance with J.I. came long before I knew Dallas. J.I., like Dallas, was gifted with an excellent mind and a character to equal it. He served in a modest church in Nevada, Missouri, one made up of wholesome, God-loving people.

J.I. often spoke with me of his younger brother and the unusual journey he had taken to the halls of academia. His primary reason for speaking of him included a prayer request that he would be guarded and guided in his pursuit of knowledge outside the conventional realm of studies. I would pray *with* a very dear man *for* a man very dear to him, his younger brother, Dallas.

During my first meeting with Dallas, he told me of the step J.I. had taken from this world of sometimes-blurred vision into the full presence of God's glory. Sorrow was reflected on my face as I voiced my regret that J.I.'s council and fellowship were no longer possible. With beaming face, Dallas replied, "Oh, but think of all the great understanding and enjoyment he is having in the fullness of life and with those dear to him already there."

I will never forget that moment. It was as if the Lord Himself had come to say to me: "Jim, don't you really believe what you teach and tell others to believe?"

No wonder, then, in his very helpful book that encourages and instructs us in how to hear God, he tells a story very similar to his own. It was a holy moment to have him share his own account of the presence of God being made known to him.

God Wants to Make His Presence Known

It is clear enough that one person's conscious concentration upon another frequently evokes a reciprocal awareness. Since that is known to be true among human beings, we should not be surprised that God's attention to us should result in our reciprocal awareness of *His* presence.

Sometimes, of course, the sense of God with us becomes much more distinct. My oldest brother, J. I. Willard, served for over thirty years as a minister under the blessing of God. But his entry into ministry came through long and intense struggles with personal and financial issues.

One evening he faced a major decision that had to be made the next day, a decision that would commit him for years into the future. He prayed long into the night, falling asleep at around 1:30 a.m. But, he relates, at 2 a.m. "that room lit up with the glory of God. I saw a figure. I did not see a face, but I recognized it to be the person of Christ. I felt a hand on my shoulder, and I heard a voice that said, 'feed my sheep.'"

As had been the case of many others who have been given such experiences, the presence of God almost overwhelmed his consciousness, and it also transformed various aspects of his personality. He was suddenly living in the study of the Bible, memorizing much of it without trying to do so, even though his days were spent in hard physical labor.

He had been painfully addicted to tobacco all of his adult life; desire for it was removed without his asking. According to him, the "aroma" of that room full of the presence of God has stayed with him ever since. Many others would testify that it is so.[42]

In my trips to Calvary Baptist Church to be with J.I. and Bertha Willard, I had been honored by J.I. sharing with me his encounter with the manifest presence of Jesus. When Dallas shared that astounding account about the same presence visiting *his* life, I was in awe that God would entrust this manifestation to both brothers.

In my own reflections, I wondered why Dallas did not include his own account of the visitation of the manifest presence to him, as he had shared the similar, though unique, account of his brother, J.I. It would have fit so well along with the story of his brother.

I believe he was being careful to not suggest that such a manifestation is a normal part of God showing us reality. So I am using the illustration with the desire to take the care Dallas would have taken. Do not assume that unless you have this kind of experience you are *inferior*, nor that if you have had this experience you are somehow *superior* to others.

With his usual insight, which comes from thinking through issues many never take time to address, Dallas comments further on why some may have visions while others do not: "Notice that Jesus never had a vision, but Paul had visions. Why would that be true? God does not have to get certain people's attention, because they are already paying attention in that interchange that characterizes the conversational relationship. Because they are not as in tune with what God wants done … if we do have a vision that turns out to be of God, we should not feel inferior however. We simply give God thanks."[43]

The visual presence of Jesus is not a greater presence than His presence *without* the accompanying sight. As we have already reviewed, in chapter two, sight without understanding is not sight at all. Children can see, yet not know what they have seen. We have His presence because He promised He would be with us always. Sight aids us to know He is there. But when the visual manifestation does not occur, His presence is no less a reality.

The old adage that "seeing is believing" is not true. In fact, just the opposite is true. *Believing* is seeing, because by believing what God is saying, we are made to see. Sight occurs in our mind through the choice to believe God. That is why Brother Lawrence could advocate practicing the presence of God by consciously being aware of His presence.

Sight aids us to know He is there. But when the visual manifestation does not occur, His presence is no less a reality.

Dallas often referred to Brother Lawrence in his writings. With a humility that made everyone important to him and a desire to experience God from the insights of others, Dallas found that a cook in a monastery was one he could learn from! Brother Lawrence was not formally accepted in the religious order of his monastery, so he became a cook to serve the monastic order. Despite not being part of that religious order, Brother Lawrence knew and enjoyed the presence of God in his kitchen, and Dallas loved his insights.

This same humility was extended to me. After some treasured time with Dallas, I gave him a copy of my book, *The Supernatural Skyline—Where Heaven Touches Earth.* I never expected to get a letter from him, one on USC School of Philosophy letterhead!

Having no advanced degrees and no notable material published, I never imagined reading these words from him:

> Dear Jim,
>
> I have kept *The Supernatural Skyline* within eyesight and arm's length so I could return to it over and over and savor the truth and the writing. Thank you, thank you for holding still long enough before God and writing the incisive truths you have been given in your trip to the better land…. God exalt you, Jim, and let the blessings of truth flow from you with power.
>
> Love, Dallas.

I had hoped to visit with him about thoughts and conclusions presented in this book. But Dallas's going home meant I would not be able to directly gain insights from his vast knowledge of God and his attending excellence in wording the understanding of complex issues. So I have drawn from his words of blessing: "Let the blessings of truth flow from you with power."

A Significant Life That Lives On

Years flowed by in the significant life of Dallas Willard. That disclosure of God's presence was not the only confirmation that He was part of what Dallas was doing. Dallas knew His presence through faith. Believing Him was part of his life, because he knew that the knowledge of God is the foundation of faith. Thus, he was devoted to knowing God and sharing the knowledge of God with others.

His journey here concluded in the presence of God. His experience of God's presence when he was a student was not repeated—that we know of. But he was so aware of being in the presence of God that, toward his last days, he made that astounding statement: "I think that when I die, it might be some time until I know it."

That statement was like many of Dallas's thought-stoppers—it requires some time to process. Knowing the agility of his mind to compute difficult issues, you know it was not an indication that his mind was slowing down. He was stating that the presence of God was so real to him that stepping beyond the veil between earth and Heaven—time and eternity—would possibly go unnoticed for a time.

John Ortberg titled his tribute to Dallas, in *Christianity Today*, "A Man from Another 'Time Zone.'" Dallas lived in eternity and in time simultaneously, and with an equal interest in both. Jesus Christ did that as well, and He was the model for Dallas Willard.

His last words on this earth are of great significance. As Dallas approached the last stages of this journey he reported he was going down a hallway lined with a "cloud of witnesses." (This referred to those who had gone before him, both Bible heros and those with whom Dallas had walked.) He was seeing here *and* there simultaneously, just as he had expected.

Then from out of all the words that flowed with such precision from his mouth or from his pen, he spoke two last words and was gone. Those two words impacted me as few others have, even though they are as familiar as any words I know. They are not unusual words for anyone, and certainly were not unusual for him. But their significance must not be lost merely because we are so familiar with them. For they express the only true response we can make to the reality of all that God is and all that God has for us. Are you ready for Dallas Willard's final two words?

"Thank you!"

Dallas spent his last conscious minutes sharing insights just as carefully as those that characterized all of his life. He was given clarity of thought to the end. So this final step from his body to God's engulfing presence of glory occurred with enabling grace, allowing him to know and to share what he knew.

At that junction of earth and Heaven, time and eternity, a man is saying what faith, reality, and a proper response embodies when all is complete.

"Thank you" is the only fitting response to the One giving all of Himself from one who welcomed and treasured everything he had found in Him.

At that junction of earth and Heaven, time and eternity, a man is saying what faith, reality, and a proper response embodies when all is complete.

It is the fitting response to the "with-God life" as he defined it.

It is the fitting response to God's grace that enables and empowers.

It is the fitting response to those who shared the journey with him as contemporaries and now are part of the "witnesses" that he saw.

It is the fitting response to those who took the journey before him as patriarchs of the faith, in exploits so well documented by Dallas.

It is the fitting response to those who were at his side as family and friends.

It is our fitting response if we really believe the report the knowledge of God affords us.

Knowing God and communicating the knowledge of God was the primary focus of Dallas Willard's life and teaching in the last phase of his life. In the knowledge of God, Dallas knew there was life now—and life eternally.

I want to offer his final words to the Father of our spiritual family, to the Willard family, and to Dallas, who possibly can read as well as observe them, now, as part of that cloud of witnesses …

Thank you!

CHAPTER FIVE

A Gifted Mind
Guides Gifted Hands

Gifted Hands is the title of a bestselling book. It is also the remarkable story of the man whose hands saved countless lives, and it became a movie with the same title.

Before his hands could extend hope to people, his mind had to embrace the gift of thinking correctly. Had it not been for a mother's wisdom and a science teacher's encouragement, God's thoughts for Ben Carson might never have been realized.

Dr. Ben Carson, a renowned neurosurgeon, attained legendary levels of success as a physician. Early in life, his potentially brilliant mind languished in doubt, anger, and despair. Good thoughts replaced wrong thoughts because he learned to think selectively. He went from being known as the dumbest kid in his class to being the smartest.

When feelings of inferiority changed to feelings of superiority, he learned to add humility and love for others to his thoughts. The way his own brain processed things led to his becoming a brain surgeon with few peers.

Early fame came when he led a team of 70 specialists in performing a surgery never done before. Twenty-two hours of intense procedures led to the successful separation of Siamese twins. The Binder twins of Germany were conjoined at the back of their heads. Dr. Carson led the team in the intricate procedures necessary for two boys to attain individual freedom of movement.

He was catapulted into the media spotlight when he spoke at the Presidential Prayer Breakfast in Washington. The President and many governmental leaders listened as he shared his faith in God, as well as his belief that God is America's hope and source of true wisdom. Words spoken in love captured people's awareness of a thinker and leader who had answers for issues facing our government.

I was honored recently to meet Dr. Ben Carson. I shared with him the many times I have spoken to audiences about his life stories. He is a living example of a man at ease with himself, with others, and with God.

Reports for One Who Could Not Read

Ben Carson was not born with a silver spoon. If any of us are indeed born with spoons, his was perhaps bent plastic. The bend included a father who deserted his mother, leaving her with two small boys. With little formal training, she worked at two jobs to meet the needs of her boys and herself.

> **Ben Carson was not born with a silver spoon. If any of us are indeed born with spoons, his was perhaps bent plastic.**

While formal training was lacking, training about thinking was abundant. She knew God as her source of wisdom. She relied on God's wisdom and required that her two boys read and write book reports, for which she would give approval—or disapproval.

Dr. Carson writes:

> She didn't know what to do to help change our path, so she asked God to give her wisdom on how to inspire her sons to work hard and make something out of themselves. That's when she came up with the idea of turning off the television and making us read two books apiece from the Detroit public libraries each week.[44]

Ben and his brother submitted the reports punctually. They did not know their mother was illiterate and could not read their reports. But the reports were not for her mind; they were for theirs. Her wisdom from God was cultivating a garden of thought in young Ben that developed into a splendor later to be admired in medical practice around the world.

Long admired for his skills in bringing medical healing to many patients, Dr. Carson more recently became known for attempting to bring healing to a troubled nation by helping us think clearly. His speech at the national prayer breakfast was a classic time of reasoning about God's ways, ways that could properly guide our nation.

His wonderful book, *America the Beautiful,* also gives great insight into our nation's beauty and what we need to do to maintain and improve this gorgeous landscape of human engagement and governmental structure.

As he gave a keynote address at a conference that I was honored to part of, he shared how reading took him from being the kid who was laughed at and called dumb to being the best in his class. The pages of books gave him entry to a world he had never seen.

It is probably more than coincidental that both Ben Carson and Dallas Willard found the books of Jack London, opening a world of reality they never knew existed.

> In the beginning I sure hated reading those books. After a while, however, I actually began to look forward to them because they afforded me a fantastic escape from our everyday poverty and sense of helplessness. There in the city, books about nature captivated me … I began to imagine myself as a great explorer or scientist or doctor. I learned things no one else around me knew. Every single day my knowledge of our world expanded.[45]

Sight that comes from many sources has the ability to shape the lives of those willing to know God's ways. When I read these lines from Ben Carson, I was reminded that Jesus described how the kingdom of the heavens can enable us to see a world that we would otherwise never know.

With the skill of reading came the increased skill to reason and retain knowledge, and that led to a scholarship to Yale University. From those early literary trips, even at age eight Carson knew he wanted to become a medical doctor.

That required enrolling in courses necessary to qualify for medical school, chemistry being one of the basics. High school had become so easy; he assumed he could achieve the same good grades with the same amount of study at the university level.

A Dream Came True at Yale University

> By the time final exams rolled around, however, my grade in chemistry was so low I would have failed the course even if I had gotten an A on the final exam. In an act of great compassion (or sadism, I'm not

sure which), the chemistry professor offered to give anyone who was failing the course double credit for the final exam—which gave me one last glimmer of hope. I suspect he believed that people like me had no chance of passing the final exam if they had done so poorly throughout the course of the semester; therefore, there was little or no risk in making such an offer.

The night before the final exam I sat in my room with my thick chemistry textbook, a barrier to all my hopes and dreams. I poured out my heart to God, asking forgiveness for squandering such a wonderful educational opportunity. I asked him to show me what he really wanted me to do with my life, since I obviously wasn't going to get to go to medical school. Preferably, I asked him to work a miracle. As I tried futilely to memorize my entire chemistry textbook, I fell asleep and entered a dream.

During the dream I was the only student in a large auditorium and a nebulous figure was writing our chemistry problems on the chalkboard. I awakened early that morning with the dream so vivid in my mind that I quickly consulted my chemistry textbook to corroborate what I had seen in the dream.

When I opened the test booklet the next day during the chemistry final exam, I was flabbergasted when I recognized each of the problems in the booklet as one of the problems that the nebulous figure was working out on the chalkboard in my dream. It felt like I was in the twilight zone as I hurriedly scribbled down the answers, afraid that I would forget them if I waited too long.

I knew the minute I finished the exam that God had granted me my miracle. I promised God that he would never have to do such a thing for me again and that I would be a diligent student and make Him proud of me. It was a scary lesson to learn, but it profoundly changed my attitude about my purpose in college.[46]

Lessons on Thinking from God

Lessons Ben learned in medical school illustrate for us that we absolutely *can* consult God about what to think. A brilliant mind was being prepared for further service to countless people, including you and me right now.

God's testimony included him. He made provision for him. Now his testimony includes God. Just think: a great gift to medicine, countless lives helped, and now help for our nation that was once all but lost. All *would* have been lost, except Ben Carson knew how to think by asking God for His input.

> The rest of my time at Yale was relatively smooth sailing, but medical school was another matter. The amount of new material that must be mastered in medical school is equivalent to learning several foreign languages simultaneously, and many students flunked out before their first year was over. I had learned my lessons in college and was very diligent about studying and attending all my lectures, but I still did horribly on the first set of comprehensive examinations.
>
> As a result, I was required to see my counselor who had been assigned by the university to help me get through medical school. He told me that I should simply drop out of medical school since I obviously wasn't cut out for medicine. Of course I was crushed, because the only career I had aspired to since I was eight years old was that of a physician.
>
> Following the meeting, I returned to my apartment and again poured out my heart to God, begging for wisdom. As I prayed, a thought occurred to me. *What kind of courses have you always struggled with,* I asked myself, and, *what kind of courses have given you no difficulty?* It dawned on me that I did very well in courses that required a lot of reading, and I struggled in courses in which the material was communicated through boring lectures.
>
> Unfortunately I was being subjected to six to eight hours of boring lectures every day in medical school. Right there and then, I made an executive decision to skip the boring lectures and spend that time reading. It was a risky move, but if it didn't yield results, I would have been in no worse shape than I was in already. It turned out to be a fabulously successful strategy, and the rest of medical school was a snap.
>
> That traumatic episode taught me how important it was to learn your own strengths and weaknesses from your mistakes … I'm convinced that much of the success I have experienced in life is a result of learning from my failures.[47]

We are reviewing the testimony of a humble man of great acclaim. His story perfectly reflects the role he allowed God to play in shaping his life. The book and movie of his life, titled *Gifted Hands*, could have so appropriately been titled *A Gifted Mind*.

A Gifted Mind and Gifted Thinking

Without a gifted mind, his hands could never have provided the skills used in miraculous surgery. Without a gifted God offering Himself to a young and very troubled Ben Carson, this story would never have been told.

Gifted thinking resulted in gifted hands extended in medicine, education, and now in leadership for our nation's future. Had these gifts from God not been received, we could not have spent this time reviewing a significant life.

I have never met a man more at ease with himself and with others than Ben Carson.

But it was not always so.

Angry Thoughts Removed By God

He readily admits in his writing and speaking engagements that anger once ravaged his young mind. Like Russ Lambert, a tangled mass of thoughts that did not come from God at times ruled his life.

In the recent conference, he openly shared the anger issues that led to his struggle. One of his accounts details a time when, in anger, he drew back a hammer to strike his mother. But for Curtis, his brother, grabbing his arm, he could have severely, even fatally, injured the mother who gave him life and continuous love.

> Because of the racial and socioeconomic injustice I experienced as a boy, in my anger I began to retaliate by going after people with baseball bats, rocks, and knives. One day a boy pushed me too far. I told him to back off, but he wouldn't quit pestering me. Finally, I pulled out my knife and lunged at him striking him in the abdomen. He fell back, and for a moment I thought I had killed him, but just then my knife blade fell to the ground. It had hit his belt buckle and it snapped in two.

> I ran to the bathroom and locked myself in, terrified that I had just tried to kill someone—and over something so trivial. If his belt buckle had not been there, I would have seriously injured or killed him and I would have been on my way to reform school or jail, following the path of so many around me.

All my life I had attended church services, and I knew—at least in theory—that God could radically change a person's life for the better. I also knew that I had tried to gain control of my temper time after time with repeated failure.

Although I was only fourteen years old, I was familiar with behavioral modification therapy from reading *Psychology Today*—but I was also acutely aware that we had no money for behavioral modification therapy. By that time I was a straight-A student, yet I realized that I would never achieve my dream of becoming a physician as long as I harbored an uncontrollable temper.

So, I fell on the bathroom floor, pleading with God to remove my temper. There was a Bible in the bathroom, and I opened it to the book of Proverbs. Verses about anger and the folly of a fool's actions all seemed written to me and about me.

Other verses encouraged me, such as Proverbs 16:32, which says that mightier is the man who can control his temper than a man who can control his city. I stayed in the bathroom for three hours reading, contemplating, and praying.

My selfishness had made me so angry inside, and it dawned on me that if I could just step outside myself and look at things from someone else's point of view, I might see the world differently and not feel so persecuted.

My new, God-given perspective worked like a charm. He became very real to me that day, and I have never had another angry outburst of uncontrollable temper since then. There would be other tests, of course, and I would make my share of mistakes. But that, after all, is how we learn and grow.[48]

With simple yet profound language, a renowned brain surgeon is describing how he moved outside himself and got a perspective from God. By gaining a new perspective, he allowed God to tell him what he was seeing.

This principle of getting outside ourselves to see what God has for us started early in Ben Carson's life. He stepped outside himself when he began reading—and he found a new world. A dream filled with answers to complex chemistry equations supplied answers from outside himself. Three hours with an open Bible, an open heart, and an open mind resulted in a life-altering removal of anger that never again dominated his thought life.

Not a single convoluted thinking pattern—nor any combination of patterns—is beyond the realm of God's provision to repair and renew. Every person has access to God's skilled ways of renewing and restoring the mind when we step outside ourselves and into God's presence.

Flawed thinking can be repaired by God's thoughts. So our proper response rightly should be …

THANK YOU!

CHAPTER SIX

God's Testimony Includes ... You

We have looked at four testimonies—Mike May, Dr. Russ Lambert, Dallas Willard, and Dr. Ben Carson. Each relates to the purpose of this book: leading us to a fuller understanding of how to think better and discover how to be fully at ease.

All of the testimonies are about people who learned to *think* accurately. The last three highlighted how they chose to make God part of their lives. This next testimony is God's own. It highlights how He made us part of His thoughts and ways.

The idea of His having a testimony is probably a bit surprising to consider. In God's testimony, you will discover that He is interested in every aspect of your life. Usually, we don't think of God as having a testimony, yet Scripture refers to "the testimony of God."

If we receive the testimony of men, the testimony of God is greater, for this is the testimony of God that he has borne concerning his Son.

Whoever believes in the Son of God has the testimony in himself. Whoever does not believe God has made him a liar, because he has not believed in the testimony that God has borne concerning his Son.

And this is the testimony, that God gave us eternal life, and this life is in his Son.

Whoever has the Son has life; whoever does not have the Son of God does not have life (1 John 5:9-12, ESV).

We Are Part of God's Testimony

Most testimonies from people highlight how God has become part of their lives. We see that in the testimonies we just reviewed. God's testimony is about His Son—and includes us. He describes His Son and His desire to make all of us part of His family. This gift of life is God's greatest desire for us. You are meant to be part of God's testimony.

Paul knew this reality, that God's testimony actually gives us a testimony of knowing life and being at ease with God and with ourselves: *"And when I came to you, brethren, I did not come with superiority of speech or of wisdom, proclaiming to you the testimony of God"* (1 Corinthians 2:1, NASU).

Paul explains God's testimony in the simplest and clearest way possible. Understanding God's testimony leads to our understanding of how we can better think. This testimony is sometimes referred to in Scripture as the "mystery of God." Yet this testimony has led Paul to a new, more precise way of thinking.

Out of all that Paul knew as a highly educated man, he had narrowed his focus to this testimony of God. Paul was one of the better scholars of his day. He was privileged to study with Gamaliel, who was renowned for his scholarship and wisdom.

Initially, Paul could not have been more wrong in his thinking about God. He thought Christ was an impersonator of God. Then He met Him in a dramatic encounter. With that encounter he knew Christ was the embodiment of God to the degree that He was even willing to live in a body like his.

Christ called to him, "Saul, Saul why are you persecuting me?" The love and compassion of Jesus flowed out to a man who was the enemy of men that Christ loved. Calling his name twice was the same way Jesus addressed a city He had sought to transform: "Jerusalem, Jerusalem, how often I would have gathered you as a hen gathers her chicks under her wings."

His dual call to Saul did not reveal anger. Nor was it a threat. It was a question: "Why?" An honest answer to "why" would make Paul rethink his assault on others. Jesus asked, "Why are you assaulting me?" His assaults on others had been blows landing on Jesus as much as on those he killed. What we do to the least, whether it is good or bad, we do to Jesus, because of His love for all people (see Acts 9:4; Matt 25:40).

From that encounter with Christ came the understanding that God must guide our thinking. God became Paul's teacher. The next three years Paul spent alone with Christ learning God's thoughts.

> But, as it is written, "What no eye has seen, nor ear heard,
>
> nor the heart of man imagined, what God has prepared for those who love him"—
>
> These things God has revealed to us through the Spirit. For the Spirit searches everything, even the depths of God.
>
> For who knows a person's thoughts except the spirit of that person, which is in him? So also no one comprehends the thoughts of God except the Spirit of God.
>
> Now we have received not the spirit of the world, but the Spirit who is from God, that we might understand the things freely given us by God.
>
> And we impart this in words not taught by human wisdom but taught by the Spirit, interpreting spiritual truths to those who are spiritual (1 Corinthians 2:9-13).

Thinking with God–Not Just About God

Instead of thinking independently *about* God, without God's guidance, Paul began thinking *with* God. He moved from being antagonistic toward Christ to being fully appreciative of Christ. In summary, he said: *"For me to live is Christ and to die is gain"* (Philippians 1:21).

Instead of thinking independently *about* God, without God's guidance, Paul began thinking *with* God.

Paul's focus on the testimony of God was related to the cross and all that God was saying in the event that changed history. He had narrowed his focus to the cross. In the cross, God proved—or demonstrated—His love for us (Romans 5:8).

In the cross God made payment or atonement for the sins against Him and against all mankind. That work of Christ was the means of God reconciling or making right all that was wrong from the past.

Reconciling is like the balancing of books by an accountant. To reconcile, God took from His account what was needed and added it to our account. The negative balance of our record received the assets of God's account. That balance sheet covers our past, present, and future.

God's Account, When Received, Gives Us "All Things"

Here is that new balance in your account found in the report from God's testimony: *"For all things are yours, whether Paul or Apollos or Cephas or the world or life or death or the present or the future—all are yours, and you are Christ's, and Christ is God's"* (1 Corinthians 3:21-23).

Notice the phrase, "For all things are yours." Again, the thought is repeated: "all things are yours." Also repeated is the reason for it: "you are Christ's and Christ is God's." A giving occurred in the giving of Christ's life that enabled God to credit to your account what previously did not exist.

For now, I want to focus on why Paul would choose an awareness of such a limited body of information. Our thinking cannot accommodate God offering us everything as a gift unless we learn to think *with* God.

Years ago, a professor training young men in ministry asked them this question: "Young men, is the gospel you preach a demand or an offer?"

With one accord they replied, "A demand."

"Think again," the professor said.

And then these young men came to the conclusion that if it was the Gospel, it was an offer.[49]

How to Access the Offer

The offer is ours to accept or refuse. To use this account we must understand the fact that the account is set up jointly. It is a trust account. Christ's name is on the account, and our name is on the account. Without a relationship with Him that enables us go to Him in faith to accept this offer, we cannot draw from what is already on deposit.

To agree to the relationship, one signs under his or her name on the line marked with an X. Christ has already signed under His name. He signed with His life found in blood given on the cross.

If you have not already signed, you can do it now by agreeing in your heart. It is a trust agreement. He has trusted you with the right to choose.

Agree with Him and acknowledge you trust Him. He has trusted you. You can now trust Him!

If you want to think about it, He gives you the right to make that choice as well. You see, He has more faith in us than we do in Him! He also has more patience toward us than we do toward Him.

Though you may not want to sign now, I invite you to walk on with me through this book. The book will be more understandable to those who have already signed, but the lack of signing now won't keep you from understanding if you really want to know.

He has more faith in us than we do in Him! He also has more patience toward us than we do toward Him.

God Means for You to Have Everything He Has

Let's return to the report found in God's testimony. You have everything others who know God have, and that includes Paul, Peter, and Apollos. Paul, who wrote the report, is saying you have everything he has.

The list of what you have can boggle the mind, so let me encourage you to brace for the boggle. After you have braced for the amazing offer, you need to embrace what God is saying and what He is offering you.

What God Has You Have—When Received

Through knowing God … you have the world … you have life … you have death … you have the present … you have the future.

Here is how the Living Bible says it: *"He has given you the whole world to use, and life and even death are your servants. He has given you all of the present and all of the future. All are yours"* (1 Corinthians 3:22).

The list is amazingly encompassing, isn't it? You move through time zones, through life, and through a vast world. All that you move through God says belongs to *you*. Yet there is one thing missing in this list—one thing here is not yours.

Everything that is yours belongs to you because it is God's, and He has chosen to give it to you. Have you determined what is missing yet? It is the past!

The Past Is Past in God's Presence

The past is *not* yours if you have signed the trust agreement with Christ. The past is *not there*. In Christ our past is wiped from the record, because His record becomes ours. God does not remember our sins or our past again, because His past becomes ours.

> *"This is the covenant that I will make with them after those days,"*
> *declares the Lord: "I will put my laws on their hearts, and write*
> *them on their minds, I will remember their sins and their lawless*
> *deeds no more" (Hebrews 10:16, 17).*

The extensiveness of this arrangement of God on our behalf is the most assuring reality we can consider. It is all part of God's plan for us from before the clock of time was wound.

God wants us to be part of His family so that, as our Father, He can share all that belongs to Him and all that jointly belongs to His Son, Jesus. His will has been executed and reads that we are heirs of God and joint, or equal, heirs with Christ. *"If children, then heirs—heirs of God and fellow heirs with Christ"* (Romans 8:17).

This clear statement that we are heirs with God verifies the reality that all things are ours. Not to be overlooked or taken lightly is the fact that not only are we heirs of God, we also share in all that is God's as joint heirs with Christ.

A thoughtful reading of God's will and testament, or "testimony," makes it clear that you are included. He has given you everything He has, along with His Son Jesus Christ. It was His Son who first received it and is conferring it on us—if we are willing to receive it.

Now let's look at this testimony of God. Paul had adjusted his thinking so that he could think well. His focus was on Christ's life and victory being shared with us through His death.

The people to whom he wrote at Corinth also needed to change their thinking. Their behavior reveals how confused and off track their thinking had become. Behavior is always the outcome of thinking.

Not Good Christians–Good Children Like Jesus

Jesus did not come to make people "good Christians." He came to share the full rights of family membership that He enjoyed. It was His purpose to make everyone who is willing to accept the offer a child of God every bit as much as He is.

Paul knew this. He knew this life exchange took place in the cross. The people in Corinth had become members of God's family, but they weren't acting like it because their thinking was so muddled.

Our permissive expression of life today in America comes out of wrong thinking as well. Culturally we have become what we think, and what we think has been divorced from the brilliance of the greatest mind that ever thought—the mind of Christ.

God's thinking was downloaded into the mind of Christ. In just a few more pages we will spend time with Jesus as He tells us what He knew God was thinking.

Paul's thinking had been changed and he knew the distorted, sometimes grotesque thoughts of these people could be changed. God loved them, and love does not write people off. Love writes us back into the storyline of God's eternal purpose.

God loved them, and love does not write people off. Love writes us back into the storyline of God's eternal purpose.

Here are some of the realities that Paul knew:

- God's testimony is that His wisdom is available to everyone—to you and me. God's wisdom can't be accessed except by being in relationship with Him as a family member (see 1 Corinthians 2:7).

- Our minds, without God's disclosure, could never fathom all that God has for us. Things that are already prepared are ready for delivery for those willing to receive them (1 Corinthians 2:9).

- Their delivery comes through the delivery system of the Holy Spirit. We know what they are because we let God tell us. And as we saw earlier in the quote from Dallas Willard, God likes to talk to us (1 Corinthians 2:10).

- Knowing is a problem when we don't allow God's thoughts to be our thoughts. With God's thinking *we know*—we know God and we know what He has given to us.

- It is His sharing that enables our knowing. *"Now we have received, not the spirit of the world, but the spirit which is of God; that we might know the things that are freely given to us of God"* (1 Corinthians 2:12, KJV).

Natural minds are limited without the Spirit. They may even think so foolishly that there is no understanding of God at all. Only the Holy Spirit, who is God with us, can bring clarity and reality to us.

• Spiritual wisdom frees us from the judgments of others, and then lets us make judgments and decisions correctly.

> *The natural person does not accept the things of the Spirit of God, for they are folly to him, and he is not able to understand them because they are spiritually discerned. The spiritual person judges all things, but is himself to be judged by no one.*
>
> *For who has understood the mind of the Lord so as to instruct him? But we have the mind of Christ* (1 Corinthians 2:14-16).

Being enamored with others can be part of our wrong thinking. We can be so enthralled with the skills or gifts of others we do not recognize what belongs to us. Honor is to be given to others, but we must not see them with an adulation divorced from God's grace, a grace that enables Him to use them.

These Corinthian followers of Jesus were enamored with Paul, with Simon Peter, with Apollos. But Paul told them all three men were but instruments of God's grace. He told them that they were no more special to God than anyone else.

Honor is to be given to others, but we must not see them with an adulation divorced from God's grace, a grace that enables Him to use them.

God's love offering of grace makes everyone special!

More insights from Paul follow that use the analogy of a building to illustrate life as God arranged it. You are the building. God is the builder. Christ is the foundation. As a building, you house the presence of God as a temple. God was not only *with* the apostles—He was *in* them.

> *"Do you not know that you are God's temple and that God's Spirit dwells in you? If anyone destroys God's temple, God will destroy him. For God's temple is holy—you are that temple"* (1 Corinthians 3:16, 17).

Wisdom from God Is Our Gift to Receive

The Corinthians are then reminded that wisdom from a source other than God is not wisdom at all. God sees it as foolishness. Paul tells them to look past the men whom they see as having a relationship with God that is unavailable to them. We too must look past those in our culture who would be marquee names—names like Billy Graham, Pope Francis, Rick Warren, or many others, depending on our heritage. Honor is due them. But honor without knowing them as God's instruments is not the honor God intended.

God gives His testimony through Paul. He said to them—and to you and me—that these men have no more of His love, His favor, His acceptance, or His provisions than we have.

Let's look again since it seems almost too good to be true:

> *So let no one boast in men. For all things are yours, whether Paul or Apollos or Cephas or the world or life or death or the present or the future—all are yours, and you are Christ's, and Christ is God's (1 Corinthians 3:21-23).*

We Have What God Has–That Is All Anyone Has

We have as much as those who seem to have everything. They have what they have because they are Christ's, and Christ is God's. In the trust agreement with Christ, you have the same.

Perhaps you are already asking, "Why then does there seem to be so much discrepancy among followers of Jesus? Some have so much; yet many seem to have so little."

This is because God is not keeping what is ours in Christ *from* us—He is keeping it *for* us until we are ready for it. We are not ready for it until we begin to think with the humility needed to allow our thoughts to be in agreement with His.

Jesus gave Simon Peter the keys to the kingdom. They were his from that time on, but Peter didn't know how to use them for some time afterward. Peter did not fully appreciate and receive God's thoughts until he had a personal meltdown, in which he denied that he even knew Christ.

Following this, Jesus came to Him offering His unconditional love. Then He asked him three times, "Do you love me?" This was Peter's training in correct thinking. He did love Jesus and needed to have it drawn out of him. Jesus was there to meet him where he was and lead him to where he could be.

Every person has access to God's skilled ways of renewing and restoring the mind. Since all things are yours, let's move further ahead and access what belongs to us.

All things are ours, and our proper response is …

THANK YOU!

CHAPTER SEVEN

A Garden with God's Presence

God's first press conference was delayed for more than two thousand years. He prepared a man named Moses and called him up into a mountain. That mountain came alive with God's presence. A selected replay occurred. Moses accompanied God through a selected account of beginnings—God's activity in creation.

The Bible begins with God and the account of a garden. The Bible ends with God and the disclosure of a garden. There is reason to conclude that what occurs between the opening and the closing of the Bible is about a garden either enjoyed or forfeited. This may account for that instinct within us that wishes to enjoy a garden teeming with life and beauty.

I sat one day in a lovely home in one of the most affluent sections of Fort Worth. Through the window, I saw a carefully groomed landscape surrounding the house. I had entered this garden upon arrival. Only the driveway and parking area interrupted this display of nature's art.

The house itself contained many famous displays of fine art depicting nature and the beauty of creation. The family living in the house plays a major part in developing a world-famous art museum in our city. Suddenly, my mind was filled with the memory of many gardens attached to houses I had visited in countries around the world. Some were houses in the poorest countries on earth, including India.

God's DNA: A Garden Is His Desire

I concluded that, if people can afford to build a garden, there is likely a natural instinct within us to do the same. We have the innate desire in our DNA, given us in God's creative act, to live in or near a garden. This DNA still reaches toward the beauty of life's beginning.

From my studies since then, I have learned that some students of history have concluded that we are restless, or ill at ease, because we long for home—a garden home. Our longing is for a place called Eden. Scholars have found evidence that this desire can be traced throughout history. Professor Jean Delumeau offers extensive research to support the inner quest for Eden in *History of Paradise: The Garden of Eden in Myth and Tradition.*

> Many civilizations believed in a primordial paradise that was characterized by perfection, freedom, peace, happiness, abundance, and the absence of duress, tensions, and conflicts. In that paradise human beings got on well together and lived in harmony with animals. They also communicated effortlessly with the divine world. This belief gave rise in the collective unconsciousness to a profound nostalgia for the lost but not forgotten paradise and to a strong desire to recover it.[50]

From these studies, I was further impacted at the thought that all people want a garden if they can afford it. Mapmakers in ancient history carefully laid out the world and marked the believed point of Eden as the reference point to their known world. Those maps are copied in Professor Delumeau's book just referenced. Writers both secular and sacred wrote of their awareness of a place like paradise.
Delumeau gives vivid descriptions of these views:

> In the mentalities of earlier times, a quasi-structural link existed between happiness and garden…. Inside a favored area, the generosity of nature was joined to water, pleasant fragrances, and unvarying springtime climate, of absence of suffering, and peace between human beings and animals. Three major themes kept alive this memory of a happy portion of earth: the golden age, the Elysian Fields, and the Happy Isles, the three being sometimes combined, sometimes kept separate.[51]

Their description of a garden remained consistent, though their names for such a place varied. Plato, Homer, Virgil, Horace, and others were among those who referred to a utopia of beauty. Many Christian writers, such as Justin Martyr, Clement of Alexandria, and Tertullian believed that the Hebrew records of Eden influenced Greek and Roman myths.

In fact, Justin Martyr wrote that Homer had read Moses' account of creation and then changed the language to mythology. "Tertullian, like Justin, was convinced that the teaching of the Bible is older than pagan culture and therefore has a superior claim to acceptance. In fact (he says) the pagans honored the God of Moses without realizing that they were doing so. What their poets had to say about the Elysian Fields was in reality derived from the description of the earthly paradise in Genesis."[52]

This nostalgia for a return to a garden paradise carried into the 16th and 17th centuries, even though the Renaissance was focused more on science and education. Walled gardens flourished in well-kept estates and in some monasteries. These gardens of enjoyable beauty often included a fountain as a source of water for the garden.

I believe that the longing for home—the longing for Eden—resonates in everyone. It is likely part of the unidentified restlessness found in our culture as well as the culture of the world.

In short, we desire a return to the garden. And this desire is found and fulfilled in the kingdom of God! Jesus came offering us the right to return. What Adam and Even were removed from, for their protection, is now offered to us again.

Jesus Taught Us Not to Fear

A truth that Jesus spoke captured my attention as a teenager, just about the time I had come to know Him. Though I understood little of the verse, it was highlighted in my mind. In recent years it has become a favorite of mine. A doctor named Luke quotes Jesus. It was probably a favorite of Luke as well.

> *"Fear not, little flock, for it is your Father's good pleasure to give you the kingdom"* (Luke 12:32, ESV).

We have no reason to fear, though we feel small and insignificant. Our Father gets pleasure in giving us His kingdom. That kingdom is a return to the original purpose He had for every person.

Understanding the garden which God created for His children becomes a foundational understanding of life as God intended it. Though our desires may be confused and twisted with corrupted thinking, what God originally intended for mankind remains a yearning is us … a desire for something that *works*. Innately, we long for order and symmetry, for something that has beauty and inspiration and comes to us with our most basic need—love.

Scripture abounds with these disclosures of God's love on display in creation.

> *He has made everything beautiful in its time. Also, he has put eternity into man's heart, yet so that he cannot find out what God has done from the beginning to the end. I perceived that there is nothing better for them than to be joyful and to do good as long as they live; also that everyone should eat and drink and take pleasure in all his toil—this is God's gift to man. I perceived that whatever God does endures forever; nothing can be added to it, nor anything taken from it (Ecclesiastes 3:11-14).*

This summary of the eternal nature of our being deserves to be carefully considered:

- Everything was intended to be beautiful.
- Eternity is a reality of God's existence and is also placed in our heart.
- Only God can show us life from the beginning to the end. He gets pleasure in giving us this understanding.
- Life is about being joyful and doing good.
- To toil or work is a gift from God, in which we are to find pleasure.
- God's creation cannot be added to or destroyed.

God the Eternal One has made everything beautiful, and eternity has been put in our hearts. Intuitively, we want life and life that lasts. Yet our quest of this life, and the beauty that God created, cannot be found apart from Him.

Eternity is there as part of God's creation masterpiece, yet we "cannot find out what God has done from the beginning to the end." Only God can show us. Like Mike May, we can see but not know what we are seeing. Or, like him, we labor trying to comprehend the parts we do see or know only partially.

God Speaks Up–In, Out, Around, Beyond–Forever

A better understanding occurs if we consider two things that God did in the beginning. When He created He said, "Let there be … " Both in His creation and in His speaking, He disclosed Himself as well as His continuing participation in His workmanship.

In the beginning, God created the heavens and the earth. The earth was without form and void, and darkness was over the face of the deep. And the Spirit of God was hovering over the face of the waters.

And God said, "Let there be light," and there was light. And God saw that the light was good. And God separated the light from the darkness. God called the light Day, and the darkness he called Night. And there was evening and there was morning, the first day (Genesis 1:1-5).

Light was the first thing He called into existence with: "Let there be!"

God's speaking not only brings into being whatever He declares, but also defines and clarifies what He has done. He had already created the heavens and the earth.

His presence, or Spirit, was hovering over or engaged with His artistry. Without His speaking there would have been no way to see the excellence of His workmanship. It is still true for us today that without His speaking there would be no understanding of Him or what He has made.

Light was given a place of significance that no other part of creation experienced, because God spoke and light was active. When we think through this reality, we can better understand by knowing that God is light! God reflected Himself in all of creation, but He also gave everything its definition. Without light there would be no ability to see what He had made. Science has found that light is the most basic factor in all of God's creation.

Again, Richard Swenson gives clarity to this important reality:

Nothing in the created order is equal to the remarkable essence God assigns to light.

It establishes the speed limit for the entire universe.

Its speed is the only constant in the universe.

It is outside of time.

It never ages.

It anchors the laws of relativity.

It is both a wave and particle.

It allows us to see.

It comforts us with its presence and depresses us by its absence.

It conveys the energy and warmth that allow us to live.

It consumes darkness but itself is never consumed by darkness.

It is mentioned as the first thing God created after the heavens and the earth.

It, apparently, has a divine aspect to its nature.[53]

God spoke and still speaks. File a marker to the fact that God speaking to us is part of our understanding, just as light gives definition to what God has made. Without light, we could not see physical reality. Without God, we cannot see spiritual reality.

While we are marking spots in beginnings, let's mark the fact that God continued to create by speaking. The refrain in chapter one of Genesis was "and God said." Whatever God said became what the Word of His power declared.

A Change of the Order–God Did Not Speak

Suddenly the order changed. He did not speak. Instead, He took from His already existing creation a substance to fashion a new likeness. This was as much a defining moment in creation as when He began speaking. He spoke to make light, which was an evidence of Himself. Then without speaking, He sculpted a likeness of Himself.

> *The Lord God formed the man from the dust of the ground and breathed into his nostrils the breath of life, and the man became a living being (Genesis 2:6, NIV).*

Instead of speaking His pinnacle of creation into existence, He scooped from the earth what he had already made and began to craft a likeness. What He crafted was not a likeness of Himself but a likeness taken from His creation.

Instead of speaking His pinnacle of creation into existence, He scooped from the earth what he had already made and began to craft a likeness.

Then he breathed the breath of His Spirit into that likeness of the earth. Now the image of Himself was embodied in the likeness sculpted from the earth. Heaven and earth were one with Adam and with each other.

Remember that God is a spirit without a body. So the body of man was not a likeness of Himself but the masterful linkage of heaven and earth. Within the crowning complex of His creative genius, God arranged a body to contain both a soul and a spirit. In that spirit was a perfect likeness of Himself.

God's breath in man contained eternal life with the accompaniment of eternal love. Adam's first look at a face was the face of His Father. The first voice Adam heard was his Father's voice. Skin never before touched felt his Father's touch. Love resonated in his thoughts and emotions with His Father's love for him.

Apparently, a home for Adam, however, did not yet exist. The account in Genesis suggests the creation of the garden was yet to occur. My imagination contains enough creativity to stretch to the likelihood God that wanted Adam, at the least, to observe the next phase of creation. At the most, he may have participated as an apprentice being trained for management.

> *Now the Lord God had planted a garden in the east, in Eden; and there he put the man he had formed. And the Lord God made all kinds of trees grow out of the ground—trees that were pleasing to the eye and good for food. In the middle of the garden were the tree of life and the tree of the knowledge of good and evil* (Genesis 2:8, 9, NIV*).*

If you have an issue with my license to imagine, we can talk about it when we both know as we are known. By then neither of us will have a need to be right, and we may find that neither of us is right! Our error will be due to the fact that God created in a way exceeding all that we could think or ask.

More Excitement Awaited Adam

God does not follow a pattern—He creates a pattern. He enjoyed his creation. His goodness was affirmed in all that was made by Him. "It is good!" … was the familiar sound of His voice following, "Let there be" … whatever He said was to be.

Then the pattern was broken.

> *The Lord God said, "It is not good for the man to be alone. I will make a helper suitable for him"* (Genesis 2:18, NIV*).*

"It is not good" had never been said before. Therefore a *helper* was needed. The word *helper*, used 80 times in the Old Testament, means "to save" or "to rescue." Adam needed to be rescued or saved from having no one to share all the love God was lavishing on him.

Rescue would include wanting to share the grandeur of the garden with another like him. Another important part of the chronicle of events in creation occurred next.

Notice how *involved* Adam has become. That suggests to me part of the reason I believe he may have been involving in planning and creating the garden. (I give the other reason in the final chapter of this book.)

> *Now the Lord God had formed out of the ground all the beasts of the field and all the birds of the air. He brought them to the man to see what he would name them; and whatever the man called each living creature, that was its name. So the man gave names to all the livestock, the birds of the air and all the beasts of the field. But for Adam no suitable helper was found* (Genesis 2:19, 20, NIV).

Adam was promised another like himself. Then he was told to review and name all the animals and birds that passed before him in pairs. With brilliance beyond our comprehension, he named each pair. The dictionary of zoology was dictated by the sound of Adam's voice that day.

He identified and named each species. Our ability to give proper identification to every issue of life is one of the basics for *being at ease*.

The dictionary of zoology was dictated by the sound of Adam's voice that day.

In short, God gave Adam naming rights. His mind, given in creation, was capable of knowing names that never existed. We too have naming rights, but now we need to consult God so we name things by agreeing with God. Calling something by a different name than God calls it may be a likely source of being ill at ease.

A highlight of this account is in the words: "But for Adam no suitable helper was found." This suggests that each pair coming before him was potentially the helper God had promised. Yet Adam never broke ranks. He never waffled in his naming assignment in hopes of gaining what God was giving to him.

Then the promise came while he slept. This place of rest for Adam is a lesson we must not miss. The rest God induced in Adam is a picture of the rest God is about to enter. Adam rested. God worked. When we learn to rest in God's ability, we give God working room.

> *So the Lord God caused the man to fall into a deep sleep; and while he was sleeping, he took one of the man's ribs and closed up*

the place with flesh. Then the Lord God made a woman from the
rib he had taken out of the man, and he brought her to the man
(Genesis 2:21, 22, NIV).

Now one had become two so that the two could become one. Without God, the idea of two becoming one is impossible. Two cannot be one until each of the two know and enjoy the One who is love.

Our being at ease is as basic as two becoming one. We become one with God. We become one with our companion for life. We become one with all of God's family.

Then God said, "Let us make man in our image, in our likeness,
and let them rule over the fish of the sea and the birds of the air,
over the livestock, over all the earth, and over all the creatures
that move along the ground."

So God created man in his own image, in the image of God he
created him; male and female he created them.

God blessed them and said to them, "Be fruitful and increase in
number; fill the earth and subdue it. Rule over the fish of the sea
and the birds of the air and over every living creature that moves
on the ground."

Then God said, "I give you every seed-bearing plant on the face
of the whole earth and every tree that has fruit with seed in it.
They will be yours for food. And to all the beasts of the earth
and all the birds of the air and all the creatures that move on
the ground— everything that has the breath of life in it … I give
every green plant for food." And it was so (Genesis 1:26-30,
NIV).

The questions "who am I?" and "why am I here?" now begin to receive their answers. These two children of God are like all the children of God. All are born with encoded cells. We are born to be His children, but the choice is still ours to make—just as was true for these children.

We are also born for the management of His creation. There is never unemployment in God's creative order, His operative kingdom. All are created for co-management with the Father, Son, and Holy Spirit. Recently, a very successful man asked me: "Why am I here?"

The answer is found in Moses' report: We are here as co-managers with God of all He has created. That was His purpose for us. We get to do what He is doing. We labor together with God. Nature cries or groans for the sons or children of God to take up management (see Romans 8:19).

I grew up on a farm where I did whatever my dad was doing. We didn't even know it was work. It was the family dairy business, and we were all managers because we were co-owners. It was ours to enjoy together.

God was at home in the garden that was placed in the very being of man. Man was at home in the garden of God both around him and within him. Adam and Eve knew a garden within and without.

Now note this important process concerning why eternity takes so long: Two people, lots of pairs of animals, and birds living in a garden with God. Their role was to be fruitful, multiply—fill the earth and subdue it. This was a development plan.

The garden did not cover the earth. It was part of the earth, awaiting expansion as God's family grew in size as well as skills. All the earth was intended to be a garden. That will be realized as a new Heaven joins a new earth, one still on schedule to come.

Back to an earlier point: Adam and Eve were now developers with God to extend garden boundaries across the mass of their good earth.

That is the reason I believe God took Adam with Him to create the garden. That continued engagement was meant to take eternity for him as well as Eve, children, grandchildren, and children who would follow for all the days of their eternal lives.

With 100 billion galaxies undeveloped, you can see why I think eternity will take so long. We have a family business that operates as no business anywhere on this planet—as long as God's thoughts are known.

The eternal kind of life starts now. We are co-laborers with God.

And our proper response to being co-laborers with God is …

THANK YOU!

CHAPTER EIGHT

The Temporary Closing of the Garden

Shock waves must have slammed Moses as he relived the awful decision made by two people who had possessed everything. They had everything just as we have everything, as we saw in God's testimony in chapter six. And like us, they had a choice to make.

As in all of Moses' reporting of the earliest events, brevity prevails. Let us review:

> *The Lord God took the man and put him in the Garden of Eden to work it and take care of it. And the Lord God commanded the man, "You are free to eat from any tree in the garden; but you must not eat from the tree of the knowledge of good and evil, for when you eat of it you will surely die"* (Genesis 2:15-17, NIV).

The likeness of God's sovereign nature was shared with Adam. God gave him the sovereignty of choice. No one could take it from him. God's sovereignty was not lessened with his choice.

God had faith in Adam, just as Adam had faith in God. Eve was not created yet. She likely learned God's instructions from Adam.

For there to be a choice, two alternatives were—and are—necessary. Every tree was good for food except one. That one, the tree of the knowledge of good and evil, was forbidden. The penalty was clear—death!

Two trees were named—life and knowledge. Knowledge of good and evil would lead to death. They had life. No death existed.

Now the serpent was more crafty than any of the wild animals the Lord God had made. He said to the woman, "Did God really say, 'You must not eat from any tree in the garden?'" The woman said to the serpent, "We may eat fruit from the trees in the garden, but God did say, 'You must not eat fruit from the tree that is in the middle of the garden, and you must not touch it, or you will die.'" "You will not surely die," the serpent said to the woman. "For God knows that when you eat of it your eyes will be opened, and you will be like God, knowing good and evil." When the woman saw that the fruit of the tree was good for food and pleasing to the eye, and also desirable for gaining wisdom, she took some and ate it. She also gave some to her husband, who was with her, and he ate it. Then the eyes of both of them were opened, and they realized they were naked; so they sewed fig leaves together and made coverings for themselves (Genesis 3:1-7, NIV).

Suddenly, the focus in the garden changed. God was no longer the center. Adam and Eve became the center. A serpent identified elsewhere in Scripture as the devil, or Satan, appears (Revelation 12:9).

Satan never comes with a name tag for easy identification. He comes with subtle, cunning deception. Nothing had changed in the garden except the focus. Our focus determines what we seek. What we seek guides our lives.

Instead of expressing truth, a question was asked: "Has God said … ?" It was followed by an offer. The existence of God was not questioned, but the issue was raised: "What has God said?" That issue contains the inference: "What does God think?"

Is God Trustworthy?

That leads to the question, "What is God like?" Is He trustworthy? Does He speak the truth in love? Is He one who loves or one who lies?

That is our issue today as well. Knowing what God has said because of how He thinks comes from who He is. That still defines our life. The suggestion was to eat what God said not to eat. The "offer" given to the young couple sounded even more amazing: "You can be like God."

No more noble idea, seemingly, could have been presented. Eve was not challenged to rebel against God but to *be like* God. All religions offer the same subtle way of suggesting what we can do to be like God, or draw closer to a version of God through our own ingenuity. Instead of knowing and enjoying God through His own disclosure, the offer was to be *like* Him ... *without* Him.

No more noble idea, seemingly, could have been presented. Eve was not challenged to rebel against God but to *be like* God.

God, who is love, had not changed. But from a question leading to a suggestion, He was under review in the mind of Eve. Eve could remember what God said: "You must not eat fruit from the tree that is in the middle of the garden, and you must not touch it, or you will die."

Though she could remember what God said, she added her own thoughts to God's. She added, "You must not touch it."

She gave the right answer in part, though she added to God's statement. She could not make the right response, though, because God's council no longer guided her.

What was she thinking? This offer of a choice could only be made because they were already like God. Nothing they could do would make them more like God. They were God's masterpiece of creation.

What We Do Never Makes Us Like God

Becoming like God never begins with what we do. It always begins with accepting God's workmanship in making us like Himself. We become God's workmanship by accepting Him for who He is.

Adam and Eve not only lived in a garden, a garden lived in them. Everything within them was adorned with God's perfect harmony. That arrangement of beauty in them is described in what our inner life looks like when our thinking is guided by God: *"Finally, brothers, whatever is true, whatever is honorable, whatever is just, whatever is pure, whatever is lovely, whatever is commendable, if there is any excellence, if there is anything worthy of praise, think about these things"* (Philippians 4:8).

Beauty was enjoyed *within* them as much as around them. Their entire beings were harmonious with God, reflecting His created likeness. They were at ease! At ease with God, at ease with themselves, at ease with each other, and at ease with where they were.

Their yoke was easy; their burden was light. It was easy being at ease.

The Step Away from God: Not Believing God

A step away from God led to what we know as the fall of man. Rebellion did not occur. The step away was not from not knowing. The step away was from *not believing* God.

Eve knew what God said. But she did not believe the answer she gave. God is either love speaking truth because of His love, or He is a liar not worthy of believing.

The devil told Eve God was lying: "You will not surely die…. For God knows that when you eat of it your eyes will be opened, and you will be like God, knowing good and evil." The suggestion that God knew something He would not disclose was a defamation of God's character.

Author Peter Kreeft has helpful insight into this moment of cataclysmic change based on a lie. We will either get it and understand the consequences of false conclusions, or we will repeat the same practice of thinking without God. This was "one small step for man," but it was also a leap into the dark for mankind.

> Whom do we choose to believe? Whom do we trust? To whom do we entrust our heart? That is, whom do we love? Love determines faith. Faith is not an intellectual opinion arrived at by abstract reasoning. It is a lived relationship of trust with a person arrived at by love and will, choice and freedom. That is why we are personally responsible, even eternally responsible, for our faith or our faithlessness.

> When we believe God is something other than a lover, it is inevitable that we will sin. The devil tempted Eve to believe that God was selfish, arbitrary, and jealous in forbidding the forbidden fruit. Perhaps God was evil, the devil implied, for he described God as "knowing good and evil." This "knowing" probably means experiencing good and evil …

> Once Eve began to believe that God might not be pure love, an opening for sin was created. If all of me believes that God loves me, then nothing in me would want to disobey Him.[54]

Adam and Eve had not committed adultery. They had not murdered anyone. Nothing had been stolen from the forbidden tree. The tree was theirs to manage along with all of creation; their ownership included the responsibility of not eating from it.

They sinned because their spirits, in perfect likeness of God, chose to sever their relationship with Him and attach to the evil of unbelief. Sin starts inside in what we believe before it moves outside to exhibit disobedience to God's ways.

Dallas Willard often collected the test papers of his students with a question: "Do you believe the answers you gave to the questions on the test?" He understood that believing what we know is as important as knowing correct answers. To not believe comes from questioning the character of the source of our information.

Repeating religious clichés or Bible verses without believing them can be a way of deceiving ourselves. Memorization leading to quoting Bible verses can assist us, but God is not impressed with our good memory. He asks for our believing confidence. Our church culture is saturated with this practice of saying the right words without believing them.

Craig Groeschel, pastor of the 50,000 members of Life Church, acknowledged what all of us have experienced at times. He characterized himself as a practical atheist in his book, *The Christian Atheist*. With his usual candor, I have heard him say he was doing what he is gifted to do without God. Like Eve, we quote God yet do not believe Him.55

Our church culture is saturated with this practice of saying the right words without believing them.

Many of us can quote God while not believing God. We practice the atheism of unbelief while quoting Bible verses, religious clichés, and keeping to religious habits.

Jesus defined sin as, "not believing in me" (John 16:9). Every step away from God is a step taken by unbelief. Scripture calls it "an evil heart of unbelief in departing from the living God" (Hebrews 3:12, NKJV).

It may be only one step, but it is evil because God's character is questioned while another alternative is believed. Sin starts with the right to make a wrongful choice, which God allows us make because of His love.

Believing an Alternative to God Is Believing an Idol

"Everything that does not come from faith is sin" (Romans 14:23, NIV). Faith, or the action of belief, either rests in God's proven character of love or in an alternative to God. That alternative becomes our idol. Our idols are often ourselves.

"An evil heart of unbelief" always leads to departing from the living God. We would not be shocked if the evil heart was defined as the heart of murder, slander, rape, or robbery. But to hear that evil exists in the heart of unbelief is to understand that this one step led to a monumental leap—a decision made by Adam and Eve— which led to the Fall.

They were God's children, but in their hearts they had left home. Their spirits were now severed from God in death. We will see later how God arranged in His Son, Jesus, to return us to Himself.

The "evil heart of unbelief" turns from the living God. The replacement god is an idol embraced and believed in our minds. But replacement gods are lifeless.

The living God has proven His life-giving power by choosing death on the cross to destroy death. Resurrection power is the power of life in the living God.

Thinking Without God

Two people who had known only the excellence of completeness as God's son and daughter were now plunged into thinking in a way they had never experienced. They wanted to think like God, but do it *without* God.

Their thoughts were not better, but very different, and the difference was a distorted, ill-conceived way of processing what they saw. They thought differently about Him, and they thought differently about themselves.

Everything Changed Except God–His Love, His Plan

Everything had changed, or would change, except two things: God's love for them and God's eternal plan. God did not come announcing that He had decided to create a replacement couple. He still loved these two, not for what they did, but for who they were. What they *did* changed. Who they were in His eternal purpose had not changed.

God always acts like Himself. He is the same yesterday, today – forever. God's nature of love resulted in an action not a reaction. Replacement was not God's solution. The solution was found in a covenant God had already made as Father, Son, and Holy Spirit. Instead of replacement, God's Son would live in a body through natural birth after the Holy Spirit's fertilization of an egg in the body of a young woman, Mary. The living God's own life already in His Son was placed in the body of Mary, developing the likeness of God in man again.

Jesus Christ, God's Son, would live and die as He and the Father agreed in the covenant before creation. The same Holy Spirit who placed God's own cell of life in a human body raised that body in resurrected power. Death was conquered!

All who had believed God and chosen life from the time of Adam forward—from now through forever—can return to the garden and carry eternal life to full term.

Adam is forever listed in the family tree. He was not disowned, disinherited, nor disgraced by God. Again Luke, the doctor/author, details the genealogy of Jesus. From Jesus, Luke heads upstream.

Adam is forever listed in the family tree. He was not disowned, disinherited, nor disgraced by God.

The purity of the stream found in Jesus is not consistent in some of the ancestors. But purity in Jesus purges the stream for those who believe in both time and eternity.

Luke's account starts in 3:23 with this statement: "Jesus son of Joseph, who was the son of Heli." Then sixteen verses follow that we usually never take time to trace. The long stream of generational names contains very familiar biblical personalities. Just a few of the better known as you work you way back are: Joshua, Joseph, Jesse, Jacob, Isaac, and Abraham.

Then we come to verse 38 and read: *Who was the son of Enos, who was the son of Seth, who was the son of Adam, who was the Son of God."*

Let that sink in! Adam was not disinherited. He is forever memorialized as the one through whom the entire lineage to Jesus is connected. More than that, he is identified as the Son of God in time, just as Jesus was the Son of God eternally.

Adam was birthed in creation from the dust of the earth. Jesus was birthed supernaturally from the womb of Mary. God loved his first Son, Jesus, who was before Adam. He loved His second son, Adam, just as much. Jesus took all of sin right back up through the family tree. Adam was made whole by the exchange of Christ's life for him, just as we are made whole. The stream of history was backwashed with the cleansing, forgiving power of Christ for those who believe.

God Comes Where We Are

*Then the man and his wife heard the sound of the Lord God as
he was walking in the garden in the cool of the day, and they hid
from the Lord God among the trees of the garden. But the Lord
God called to the man, "Where are you?"*

*He answered, "I heard you in the garden, and I was afraid
because I was naked; so I hid."*

*And he said, "Who told you that you were naked? Have you
eaten from the tree that I commanded you not to eat from?"*

*The man said, "The woman you put here with me — she gave me
some fruit from the tree, and I ate it."*

*Then the Lord God said to the woman, "What is this you have
done?"*

The woman said, "The serpent deceived me, and I ate" (Genesis
8:13, NIV).

God came to them for who they were. He had made them who they were.
Neither their decision, nor their disobedience, nor their current blaming
game changed how God saw them. They didn't need to tell God who was at
fault. He was not there for faultfinding, but for truth-finding. Truth would
come from love, and truth would lead them to faith.

"Where are you?" was not a question God asked to determine Adam's
location. It was a question for Adam to locate himself. Adam started back
from where he was.

Thinking that is skewed beyond recognition of reality must start there.
When we are willing to admit where we are, regardless of where it may be,
God is always there to start us on the journey to where we need to be.

Jesus told a story about a son who got as far from home as a son in that
culture could possibly get. He had gone from riches to rags and then to deg-
radation. To avoid starvation, he took food from the pigs he was hired to
feed. That was the greatest disgrace possible in Jewish culture.

Jesus said that the young man then "came to himself." He located himself.
In that moment of rationality, he decided to go home.

That is the moment we see in the experience of Adam. He came to himself by locating where he was. The journey home starts wherever we are at the
time God asks, "Where are you?"

God asks each of us to get real. "Where are you?" is not a condemning question—it is a loving question. In the identification of *where we are* comes the realization of *who we are.*

Three Essential Things to Know

The account in the garden gives us the three most basic things we must know:

We must know who we are.
We must know where we are.
We must know whom to believe.

The son in Jesus' story went home from his distant location, and he took with him a well-rehearsed speech. But before he got home, home came to meet him.

It was not a house he wanted. It was a father he wanted. The father saw him when he was still far away and ran to meet him. He hugged him, kissed him, and gave him love's total acceptance.

Moses saw a burning bush and turned aside to see it. God was in the bush. This is a burning bush story showing us God's way of accepting us. God arrived with love's embrace and the kiss of affection. No speech was offered, only His heart.

The son had a speech. He delivered it: "I have sinned against heaven and in your sight and no more worthy to be your son; make me a hired servant in your house."

This is a burning bush story showing us God's way of accepting us. God arrived with love's embrace and the kiss of affection.

Carefully, even slowly, read this well-prepared speech of the son. Sin was acknowledged, sin that had not only violated earth but had reached Heaven. The violation included what he had done to the father.

Love does not hear what grace does not provide.

Grace did not provide a house, but a home. Grace did not provide a servant's job, but a son's management. Grace did not provide a job description, but a relationship of love's lavished affection. (See Luke 15:11-24 for the entire story.)

Our Speech to God or God's Speech to Us

Jesus is telling you and me how the Father comes to meet us. Our speech will not set the agenda. God's thoughts, not ours, will create the arrangements that await us.

Jesus said the Father did not even discuss the son's thoughts. The Father's speech was rehearsed long before the son's was even planned. "Bring the best robe, mine, and put on him. Put the family signet ring of authority on his finger. Put shoes for walking with me on His feet. Serve the finest foods in the hall of joy as we celebrate that he is alive again." (This, by the way, is my paraphrase, with a level of imagination that is probably too low, not too high.)

Where We Are Is Not Where God Leaves Us

Adam knew where he was. He was hiding, and any tree would do! He didn't know how he looked because he did not know who he was. For none of us know how we look to God! We must hear from God who we are and how we look, then decide who to believe.

The man Moses, who has done us such a favor with his written account, his "press release" of creation, also once couldn't see himself as God saw him. He kept telling God he could not make speeches. God did not want a speech maker, but a speech reporter. God would make the speech, and Moses would break the story of creation, as well as God's speech to Pharaoh, the one in which he said, "Let my people go!"

Adam's Speech to God, God's Speech to Adam

Without knowing who he was, Adam began describing himself to God: "I am a man full of fear. I am naked and ashamed." What an amazing transformation had occurred. He had gone from a man full of love to being one full of fear. He had gone from being clothed in God's glory to believing he was naked. He felt shameful wearing some leaves he had patched together. His self-image had been shattered as if the mirror where he saw himself was splintered, with pieces missing.

God's response is most revealing. "Who told you that you are naked?" God did not agree with him. He had not consulted God about whether to eat from the tree of knowledge. Once again, he had not asked God for the truth about his appearance.

Adam had clothed himself with the leaves he thought would conceal his shame. God said, "I still see you as before. I see you wearing the clothes I gave you."

Now the issue of who to believe was just as before. It was a choice Adam had to make. It is our choice as well. Either we are in Christ and covered with the clothing of His righteousness, or we must piece together the leaves of our own efforts with an attempt to make what only God can correctly tailor for us.

Much of our being ill at ease is in the clothes we have made that don't fit. They bind us; sleeve lengths are not matched, and worst of all, the crotch cuts into sensitive parts of our body. But we made them and can't seem to give them up.

When we stop to listen to what God thinks, we can think properly. *Who are we? Where are we? Who are we going to believe?*

It is always God who tells us who we are, where we are, and who we can believe.

God Gave Them Identity, Location, and a Choice of Belief

Their next step was to learn from God. God's creative love gave them their identity as His son and daughter. God's creative love gave them their location. God's creative love would guide them to a safe place, a place to learn to think and choose again.

First, I want to discuss why they were no longer safe in the garden. Then I want to discuss how the same choices in the garden continued outside of Eden. We too have the same choices.

They now knew good and evil, but they did not know truth from a lie. Love was no longer their assurance of security. Fear dominated their thoughts and actions. Their thoughts were unsafe. They wore their leaves instead of God's clothing for them: Himself. Because the garden inside them had been ravished by death, the garden around them was no longer safe.

Love was no longer their assurance of security. Fear dominated their thoughts and actions. Their thoughts were unsafe.

And the Lord God said, "The man has now become like one of us, knowing good and evil. He must not be allowed to reach out his hand and take also from the tree of life and eat, and live forever." So the Lord God banished him from the Garden of Eden to work the ground from which he had been taken. After he drove the man out, he placed on the east side of the Garden of Eden cherubim and a flaming sword flashing back and forth to guard the way to the tree of life (Genesis 3:22-24, NIV).

The garden was temporarily closed. God had not deserted them—He was outside the garden as much as inside. Another garden would be opened one day that would never close, but the original was closed for repairs, repairs that would allow them to know God properly.

Most of my life was spent believing in tradition. Tradition said, "God's punishment expelled them from the garden." Truth comes with what God said, and truth says, "God took them out to protect them, not to punish them."

"He must not be allowed to reach out his hand and take from the tree of life and eat, and live forever." Punishment would have *left them there* to live in a state of wrong thinking, shame, being incomplete and disease.

This is why: God's truth was spoken in love that death would come if their choice was to choose against Him. That choice was in favor of knowledge instead of God. The first idol ever embraced was in the *mind* of Eve and then the mind of Adam. That choice was made and love was truth; death did come.

Adam and Eve would now die. They now lived in bodies containing disease. Science still does not fully know why cells finally stop being replaced by new healthy ones, but that state is called death. Death that was cultured in their cells was destroyed by Christ when He destroyed death.

Access to the tree of life would have left them trapped forever in bodies not fully functioning as God intended. They forfeited life as God intended. But he would not leave them in that condition for eternity. God's love reached out to them by honoring their choice. Love would not leave them marooned with less than His fullness of life. Death would be necessary for them. The tree of life was no longer safe for their consumption. They needed to die so that, following the death of God's son Jesus, resurrection life would be theirs with all who know God.

God's love reached out to them by honoring their choice. Love would not leave them marooned with less than His fullness of life.

The resurrected body is a body that needs no cellular replacement. No more pain, disease, or death is experienced.

God Took Them to School to Think Like Him Again

We do not know where God took them except that He removed them from the garden. Historically, it became known as East of Eden. It is my studied opinion—meaning I have thought of this enough to be satisfied—that there is a connection to the rest of Moses' writings.

Moses covered the creation, and then he began exhaustive writings of history. Contained in his next book, Exodus, was his experience in the presence of God. He reported Adam and Eve's exit from the garden in Genesis, but in Exodus he records his own visit with God. God was still available to talk, and Moses talked to Him face to face. The theme of Exodus is about freedom.

Pictures of God and principles of access to God were found in Leviticus. Next, the book of Numbers was not about a training school for CPAs. It is an account of God's regard for every person. Every person counts. What counts most is that every person is to return to belief in God.

Deuteronomy is the farewell address of Moses, the epic figure God equipped to reopen access to His truth. Moses is seen one more time in the Bible after Deuteronomy. The next time he appears, Moses is with Jesus on a mountain of transformation in which Heaven and earth were interfaced as in garden reality (Matthew 17: 3). Peter, James, and John accompanied Jesus up the mountain.

> *There he was transfigured before them. His face shone like the sun, and his clothes became as white as the light. Just then there appeared before them Moses and Elijah, talking with Jesus* (Matthew 17:2, 3, NIV).

These monumental disclosures must not be taken as extraneous, unimportant issues. Moses continues a theme he first saw when he regressed into God's presence with His children in the garden. He saw the trees. He heard the alternatives.

Two trees were named. *Life* was the name of one tree. *Knowledge of good and evil* was the name of the other. Having been trained in the highly developed sciences of Egypt, Moses did not need a scientific mind to understand one tree contained life and the other tree contained death.

"Remembering" is the theme most scholars agree marks the book of Deuteronomy. "Remembering what?" is a good question. I believe Moses is seeking to encourage the people to remember the choices the two trees offered. So his summary is beyond significant—it is essential.

> *See, I have set before you today life and prosperity, and death and adversity; in that I command you today to love the Lord your God, to walk in His ways and to keep His commandments and His statutes and His judgments, that you may live and multiply, and that the Lord your God may bless you in the land where you are entering to possess it.... I call heaven and earth to witness against you today, that I have set before you life and death, the blessing and the curse. So choose life in order that you may live, you and your descendants, by loving the Lord your God, by obeying His voice, and by holding fast to Him; for this is your life and the length of your days, that you may live in the land which the Lord swore to your fathers, to Abraham, Isaac, and Jacob, to give them* (Deuteronomy 30:15-20, NASU*).*

God's call to remembrance is a call for both Heaven and earth to witness. It was time for everyone to remember. This is a loud crescendo in the song of Moses. And it is part of the clarification of why Adam and Eve left the garden.

They left to attend school again with God, to know the difference between life and death, truth and lies, love and fear. Twice he gives the alternatives found in the two trees—life and prosperity, death and adversity. God had set before them life and death, the blessing and the curse.

A Change of Mind, A Change of Clothes

Now I am going to present a bit of scientific evidence to make a case for the importance of understanding the two trees. Adam and Eve would need to revisit the two trees and change their minds. They had changed their minds once, and their change of clothes followed. Now the changing of their minds again would bring back the clothing of God's presence … to make them, once again, at ease.

"Trees" Grow in You

In the 1940s, Betty Smith wrote *A Tree Grows in Brooklyn*. Its popularity warranted a movie. The title itself suggests that an unlikely tree was enjoyed in the congested inner city of New York. But the most amazing location we will find trees growing is in our brain, right in the most congested area of our cerebral center.

Within the communications network in our mind are dendrites. The Greek word, *dendron,* meaning "tree," is the source of the word *dendrite*. We have "trees" in our brain essential to our thinking capacity. More trees than you can imagine. Gerald Schroeder writes:

> In an adult brain, the axon of each neuron connects with as many as a hundred thousand dendrites of other neurons. The branching is stupendous, a million billion connections. That's 1,000,000,000,000,00 points within our heads at which neurotransmitters are racing, sending information from nerve to target nerve.[56]

These dendrites, or transmitting trees, look like trees with trunks and branches. There are no leaves. The leaves could have been lost in the fall. (Just a needed chuckle from the intensity of writing!)

Not Seeing the Forest of Reality Because of the Trees

Most of life is regulated within this forest of trees carrying messages that create our mind. Schroeder: "We've seen how the brain develops, but that still does not tell how our thoughts arise…. What happens when the brain does its work is to understand the beginning of the mind."[57]

Caroline Leaf, with her trained trees in research, has greatly advanced this understanding of the importance of the dendrite.

> Your brain is made of nerve cells a hundred billion more or less, and each cell looks like a tree with a central cell's body and branches. Every thought makes up one of these nerve cells, with memories and other information growing off of it—the branches of the tree.

For every "thought tree" you have in the left side of your brain, you have a duplicate, a mirror image, in the right side…. On the left side of your brain you draw on details to form the big picture, while on the right you draw from the big picture to find the details…. That means, in order to understand something and build a stable memory that augments intelligence, the mirror images of the same "thought tree" have to communicate with each other.[58]

Revealing these smallest parts of our composition becomes a key to our knowing how to function. God sees each detail, having chosen each part, whether it is microscopic or beyond being observable.

We get input from the environment, our body, and our thoughts. This information is then transmitted via a structure called the thalamus to the outer cortex of your brain where memories (thoughts) are stored. This area of the brain looks like a big forest, because these thoughts look like trees.

The information flies through these "trees"—your memories/thoughts—alerting them to the new incoming information, much like the preview of a movie does…. It is literally "switched on" as the information sweeps through the memory trees like a breeze—"the breeze through the trees."[59]

The time I have spent on this point must be carefully considered. The health of our "trees" will depend on it. All of us need tree service. Spending just a little more time in the garden, and to the east of Eden, can help.

Trees in Adam and Eve Twisted in a Storm

Can you imagine the intensity of the storm that swept through the trees in Eve's mind and then Adam's mind as they stood face to face with thoughts never before entertained? *God* was being questioned. Did He love them with truth?

You will not die as He said. This was the thought that raced through their trees with high-wind velocity. It was followed with: *You will be like God and know what God knows.* With that thought came a soft breeze; it was from a direction never experienced. It was the breeze of fear. The fear of being left out. A fearful breeze of missing something others possessed swayed their trees and even fanned their faces.

With that thought came a soft breeze; it was from a direction never experienced. It was the breeze of fear.

They turned their faces from God. (I pause to weep as I write this, because I too have turned my face from Him when fear came. Yet fear could only come because I gave permission through unbelief.)

Then their trees of thought came to a consensus. They would choose a lie's fear instead of love's truth. Now the "trees" began bending under tornado-force winds greater than an F-5. Trees that once stood strong were ripped from the soil and hurled into space.

The memory of love was gone. The wind of fear blew their once beautiful minds that resembled the garden into the twisted, mangled, splintered debris of confusion. Fear and shame was inside them, so they wore it under their leaves. They no longer wanted God with them, even though His name is "with us."

When their trees of mental computation were changed, everything they saw was changed. Do I need to emphasize again that we see with our *mind*, not our eyes? Where our eyes focus is not what we see. Where our mind is focused is what we see. Everything they now saw looked different.

Once, the tree of life was their joy of life. Now, leaves from any tree were their most important possession. How many times do we walk past the tree of life to shop for more leaves that others think are so valuable?

Fear was born that day in a garden where only love had lived. Now two trees vie for our attention—from which all our thoughts and behavior will be derived. Either the tree of God's love as our source of life, or the tree of fear, offering a substitute existence.

Our dendrites/trees need to go back for replanting, or regrafting, so the needed changes will allow us to think with God. Now it becomes very apparent, at least to my satisfaction, why God took the parents of the human race outside the garden. A school was opened for them to learn, once again, from which tree they could take love's truth.

One day on a hillside that school was enlarged, and Jesus taught how the garden was open again—this time as the kingdom of God.

East of Eden was not east of God. Where you are, with thoughts of *God can't be found*, or, *He can't find me*, exists only in your trees—and those can be replanted. God is with you. He is truly "God with us."

Our proper response to Emmanuel, God with us, is …

THANK YOU!

CHAPTER NINE

Back to School: God's Kindergarten

God did not stand at the gate of the garden as the guard. He stationed an angel with a flaming sword to guard against further wrong thinking. Now death was embedded in the thoughts of Adam and Eve, because fear always presents the most fearsome thought—fear of death.

Death is never the end of thinking. As it was not for Adam and Eve after their spiritual death, neither is it for anyone.

Where was God? He was in attendance everywhere in His creation. He was with Adam and Eve in their East-of-Eden home. In light of the summary of Moses, He was teaching Adam and Eve once again that life and death were their choices. Moses' summary to his contemporaries was a continuation of the teaching God gave east of Eden.

It is our choice today as well. We have life and death set before us.

Since we have been in the heavy traffic of thought for a few pages, let's take a route that's less intense. I have already offered the probability that God was going to retrain the thinking process of the two He loved. So may I suggest He sent them from postgraduate experience back to … another kindergarten?

The basics of life needed to be replanted again in their neurons and dendrites. "Trees of truth" were needed to replace the "trees of lies" they had chosen.

The German word *kindergarten* literally means "children's garden." The term was created by Friedrich Fröbel for the institute that he created in 1837 in Bad Blankenburg. His goal was that children should be taken care of and nourished in children's gardens, just as plants are taken care of in a garden.

With a tongue-in-cheek title, Robert Fulghum stated: *All I Really Need to Know I Learned in Kindergarten.* His acclaimed book became a number one *New York Times* bestseller. It is a fun book to read.

But he had not learned everything he needed to know. Fifteen years later he did a rewrite and acknowledged a needed truth he didn't get in kindergarten.

Fulghum's first list reads like this:

All I really need to know about how to live and what to do and how to be, I learned in kindergarten. Wisdom was not at the top of the graduate-school mountain, but there in the sand pile at Sunday school. These are the things I learned:

Share everything. Play fair. Don't hit people. Put things back where you found them. Clean up your own mess. Don't take things that aren't yours. Say you're sorry when you hurt somebody. Wash your hands before your eat. Flush. Warm cookies and cold milk are good for you.

Live a balanced life—learn some and think some and draw and paint and sing and dance and play and work every day some.

Take a nap in the afternoon.

When you go out into the world, watch out for traffic, hold hands, and stick together.

Wonder. Remember the little seed in the Styrofoam cup: The roots go down and the plant goes up and nobody really knows why, but we are all like that.

Goldfish and hamsters and white mice and even the little seed in the Styrofoam cup—they all die. So do we.

And then remember the Dick-and-Jane books and the first word you learned—the biggest word of all—LOOK.

Everything you need to know is there somewhere. The Golden Rule, love, and basic sanitation. Ecology, politics, equality, and sane living …

And it is still true, no matter how old you are—when you go out into the world, it is best to hold hands and stick together.[60]

Fulghum reminds us that the biggest word in the basic primers of books he read as a child was: LOOK. And this is clearly one of the most important desires of God for us: LOOK.

There is "more than meets the eye," as the title of Dr. Richard Swenson's book accurately declares. It is true: we have already seen things not seen, and there is much more to come.

If there were nothing to see, there would be no reason to LOOK. There is much to see, and there is someone to teach us what we are seeing.

There was more to see for Robert Fulghum. A 15th-anniversary edition followed. The subtitle reads, in part: "Reconsidered, Revised … "

A new addition came because Fulghum revised his thinking. While looking, he learned a greater truth than he found in kindergarten. He was looking at a bumper sticker that read: DON'T BELIEVE EVERYTHING YOU THINK.

His classroom was his car while driving in a snowstorm at night. The lights of his car and the red taillights on the old blue Ford pickup in front of him created a kind of marquee. The bumper sticker offers sound advice for us as well:

DON'T BELIEVE EVERYTHING YOU THINK

These words left a permanent afterimage in my mind. They provoked me to recall the dumb and useless or naive ideas I've held in a lifetime. Ideas I once thought were indelibly tattooed on my brain cells. Ideas I have since discarded when new evidence and further experience forced me to change my mind.[61]

No doubt Adam and Eve could have given the same advice in their exit interview from the garden: "Don't believe everything you think." Making God's thoughts our thoughts, and God's ways our ways, are the only ways we can believe everything we think.

From our time in the Garden, here are some thoughts worth believing:

- Everything began with God.
- God is good and everything He made He declared to be good.
- God wanted others like Himself, so from the earth He took dust and made a likeness where His breath, or life, would live.
- Life is good, and life that is shared is very good. So God took from the side of the one another who would share God's likeness.

- Be aware that you can flunk kindergarten—and even asked to leave school.

- The right to choose comes from God, but needs to be done with God's guidance.

- Eat what God furnishes and refuse what God says is harmful.

- God's thoughts come with His life for you.

- What you think will lead to what you eat. What you eat will also lead to what you think. So think before you think and ask God what He thinks. What God thinks is what you are to eat: "Taste and see that God is good."

- Beware of an idea from a source not introduced to you by God.

- When you are misled, don't blame others. Just get real. Let God guide you out of the mess you have made.

- Let mistakes teach you how to make the right choices.

- Don't try to cover for yourself. God will cover you *and* cover for you.

- God and fear don't go together because God is love, and fear can't co-exist with love.

- If you are afraid to let God come to you or you are afraid to go to God, don't believe what you just thought.

- Going to God with fear will lead to leaving with love.

- Believing God is choosing and acting in faith, which pleases God. God is pleased because His faith in us is joined by our faith in Him.

We are to be one with Him in thought, will, and actions. We think, and then choose to believe or not believe. Not believing God is to believe an alternative. There is never a belief vacuum. Choice occurs at the crossroads of what we believe.

God's gift of choice says He has faith in us. Our choice of faith in Him is a choice made by believing.

Our proper response to God's faith in us that leads to our faith in Him is …

THANK YOU!

CHAPTER TEN

Replacing Thoughts and Replacing Cells

Our bodies are replaced, except for our skeletal structure, every five years through the replacement of our cells. About every seven years new bone structure completes the body's replacement. Thought replacement is even more important than cell replacement. Life and death are the alternatives to our choosing thoughts.

Adam and Eve started with life surging through them as well as around them. They chose death. Death occurred when they took the essence of themselves, their spirits, from God.

One of the attributes of death is separation. Spiritual separation occurred immediately. Death would follow eventually in their bodies.

In a later chapter, I will discuss how the choice to take their spirits from God was reversed in the choice of Jesus. On the cross He commended, or entrusted, His spirit to the Father (Luke 23:46). Through His choice, our spirit is joined to God again—if we join ourselves to Christ in faith.

The immediacy of death in their spirits resulted in the loss of their consciousness of God's presence. God's omnipresence was at first fully enjoyed. There is no indication there was ever a sense of God's absence until they chose to disobey. They practiced the presence of God without a cognitive awareness they were doing it—it was part of their spiritual likeness.

Oneness with God contained no awareness of anything other than being who they were. Their lost consciousness of God became a crescendo when they "heard the voice of God in the garden." Instead of rushing to embrace the one they had loved as part of His nature in their spirit, they ran from Him in fear and shame. Their death spiritually was now evident. They had distanced themselves from God, and that is spiritual death.

> *When we know who God is, we can learn who we are.*
> *When we know where God is, we can learn where we are.*
> *When we know God is love's truth, we can learn to believe God.*

Their souls experienced death's advance as well. They dreaded God instead of delighting in God. Love no longer resonated in their thoughts. Instead, fear gripped their soul's engagement of thought. Death in the soul was destroying the healthy experience of enjoying God's unchanging nature: love.

Death to their bodies was also activated, and now necessary. Without death physically, though they lived for years, they would never have returned from death's shadow to the full power of light. All of life would have been seen through a cloudy glass that obscured much of the exquisite beauty of God and all of life.

We will take a good look at life that has moved from behind the smoked glass later. That is an experience of knowing—knowing as God knows us and as God intends us to know.

Being born spiritually, as Jesus explained to Nicodemus, reverses this order of death. Life returns in our spirit immediately. Life grows in our soul and in our mind progressively. Life ultimately occurs in our bodies in resurrected likeness.

Two minds are disclosed many times in Scripture. Paul knew these two minds as few others. He also knew that in one mind there was life and in the other was death. Initially his mind fiercely fought against life as found in Christ. When he experienced the renewing of his mind, he became as strong an advocate for the mind of Christ as he had been strong in his hostility toward Him.

> *For the mind set on the flesh is death, but the mind set on the*
> *Spirit is life and peace, because the mind set on the flesh is hostile*
> *toward God (Romans 8:6, 7, NASU).*

The settings of two minds are contrasted. One is the mind set on the flesh, which is self-ruled. The other mind is set on the Spirit, which is Christ-ruled. Self-rule is death. Christ-rule is life and peace.

These contrasting minds are amplified in the writing of Paul that we saw in the testimony of God. God's mind is described. Our mind is reviewed.

Without God's mind becoming part of our mind, our mind is inadequate to comprehend essential knowledge.

Again, He contrasts our two kinds of minds. One mind is natural and cannot comprehend. *"But a natural man does not accept the things of the Spirit of God, for they are foolishness to him; and he cannot understand them, because they are spiritually appraised"* (1 Corinthians 2:14, NASU).

Self-rule is death.
Christ-rule is life and peace.

The other mind is the spiritual mind taught by the Spirit of God. *"For to us God revealed them through the Spirit; for the Spirit searches all things, even the depths of God. For who among men knows the thoughts of a man except the spirit of the man which is in him? Even so the thoughts of God no one knows except the Spirit of God. Now we have received, not the spirit of the world, but the Spirit who is from God, so that we may know the things freely given to us by God"* (1 Corinthians 2:10-13, NASU).

The Difference Between the Brain and the Mind

The mind is not the brain, and the brain is not the mind. There is an important distinction—the brain is like the womb, in which we were given life and became a person. Our lives are not the womb. We came from our mother, but we are not our mother.

Minds form in the remarkable schematics of neurons, electrons, and dendrites in the cells of the brain. But our minds contain another aspect of us—our eternal destiny. Astute scientists know the mind has similar qualities to the brain, interacting with the brain and yet unique.

The mind will function forever. The brain will die with the death of the body. I will discuss some of this later. For now, realize that the formation of the mind is an important part of our being at ease.

Our mind contains our identity. We are a spirit with a soul living in a body. In Adam the spirit dimension of life died. In Christ the spirit dimension is made alive. That is why the two births are necessary. The first birth is natural. The second birth is spiritual.

Our natural birth contains the spiritual death of Adam. Our spiritual birth contains the spiritual life of Christ. We are born the first time into the spiritual death of Adam. We are born the second time into God's life and likeness returned in Christ.

In that birth, we die with Christ to our former self-ruled life. Birth in the Spirit with God occurs with death in our self-rule. We are new creations. The old person we were is replaced with a new person in whom Christ's incarnation is repeated.

If this is turning into thinking overload for you, simply relax. The reality comes not from *thinking toward God* but from *allowing the thoughts of God to come to you*. The true rest God shares comes when we make His thoughts ours. As we welcome God's thoughts in our mind, spiritual reality occurs. Waiting on the Lord is like waiting for the movie to begin. Don't go charging off to the projection room to hurry the process.

Scientists are now recognizing the existence of our mind in addition to our brain. "The Brain Behind the Mind" is the title of a chapter in the book *The Hidden Face of God*. The author, Gerald Schroeder, is an often-quoted physicist.

> Within the brain we perceive the consciousness of the mind, and via the mind we can touch a consciousness that pervades the universe. At these treasured moments our individual self dissolves into an eternal unity within which our universe is embedded….
>
> The mind is our link to the unity that pervades all existence. Though we need our brain to access our mind, neither a single synapse nor the entire brain contains a hint of the mind. And yet the consciousness of the mind is what makes us aware that we are humans; that I am I and you are you.
>
> The most constant aspect of our lives is that we are aware of being ourselves. Even in the illogical jumble of a dream, filled as it may be with fantasy, the constant is that we are ourselves.[62]

What a blockbuster thought! Even in our dreams that contain fantasy, we are always ourselves—not superman or superwoman. We know ourselves!

Dr. Schroeder, who works both in physics and biology, is very honest in his pursuit of knowing how the physical and spiritual relate. He acknowledges that science cannot give complete answers to the development of the mind as compared to the brain. He also knows that the mind is eternal.

> But the mind is very much greater than a layering of the holistic feelings of self and awareness onto the observable facts recorded by the brain. True, the conscious mind arises from the brain. Destroy

the cortex and you destroy consciousness. Destroy the brain and the palpable mind goes with it into oblivion.

But the physical organs of the brain may not be only the circuitry that makes the mind humanly perceptible. In that case, a form of the consciousness may remain. Smash a radio and there's no more music to be heard. But the radio waves are still out there. We just don't have the apparatus to change the electromagnetic radiation into mechanical sound waves. The brain does for the mind what the radio does for music.[63]

Thus it becomes imperative that we get the "trees" of our brain aligned with the thoughts of God, as well as our mind thinking in unison with the mind of God. No wonder Dallas Willard could suggest that people who think they want to go Heaven might find they can't stand it. Thoughts *about God* that are in reality *opposite from God* would make a mind uncomfortable, to say the least, and, at most, totally miserable.

Our Spirit Interacting with the Brain Creates the Mind

Our reality detector is in our spirit. It is the spirit's interaction with the brain that creates the mind. The mind is a combination of the thoughts generated by the brain as well as the thoughts or intuition of the spirit.

Francis Collins turned from atheism when he recognized the fact of the moral law, or moral compass. Knowing from his own experience that every person has the compass to know good and bad, he concluded that God had created the compass.

Francis Collins turned from atheism when he recognized the fact of the moral law, or moral compass.

The relationship between our body, soul, and spirit has greater implications than we probably yet know. When the soul stopped believing God, the body stopped believing the soul. The correlation between what we are experiencing in our soul, mind, will, and emotions, and what we experience in our body, is well documented.

Our Spirit Is God's Light for the Whole Body

The spirit of man is the lamp of the Lord, searching all the innermost parts of his being (Proverbs 20:27, NASU).

Our spirit is intended to be God's light, or presence, to search all our being, including our body. The inward light of God through our spirit engages our body as well as our mind.

Knowing God is the difference in all we know. Peter Kreeft writes:

The soul makes the difference between life and death in the body, and the spirit makes the difference between life and death in the soul.... Life is not a thing, like the body, but the life of that thing. Similarly, a soul without a spirit is a dead soul, and the difference between a dead soul and a living soul is not a soul difference.[64]

The difference is the presence of God's life-giving spirit. A living soul is gaining life from the Spirit, or the life, of God. Our body is alive because our soul is still furnishing the activity of our mind, will, and emotions essential to our body's functions.

Dead souls think (dead thoughts) and feel (dead feelings) just as living souls do, but they have no life. If you want to see dead souls, or at least dying souls, just walk through certain city streets.[65]

C.S. Lewis knew the difference between the spirit of man saying yes or saying no to God. "There are only two kinds of people in the end: those who say to God, 'Thy will be done,' and those to whom God says in the end, 'Thy will be done.'"[66]

The term "walking dead" is not a cliché. Walking without God's life through His spirit means that, instead of choosing life, we have chosen death. If we walk alone without God, we are part of the walking dead. Adam and Eve were the walking dead among the trees to hide from God.

Dallas Willard was guiding the work of an important book answering hard questions when his graduation from this life occurred. Through the gifted skills of his daughter, Becky Heatley, this book was completed. From his speaking, his lectures, his papers, and recordings of interviews he gave, Becky completed the second mile several times over. Her summary is classic: "In bringing these pieces together, I felt like a tailor who has been blessed with a bolt of cloth and a perfect pattern. The fabric and pattern come entirely from Dallas; only the stitching is mine."[67]

If we walk alone without God, we are part of the walking dead.

In *The Allure of Gentleness,* Dallas describes the choice of some, who do not want God to be part of their life.

> Many people simply do not want to be with God. The best place for them is to be where God is not, and that is what hell is…. For those people, being with God is the worst thing that could possibly happen to them.

> He has allowed us to avoid him here on earth in some measure if we want to, but if you go to Heaven, God's the biggest thing on the horizon. You're no longer going to be able to avoid him…. That is why I sometimes say that the fires of Heaven burn hotter than the fires of hell.[68]

Death had not come to their bodies, but death in the spirit occurred when, in their spirits, they turned from God. Their souls gradually experienced death's advance, and likewise death would eventually come to their bodies.

Dallas Willard's amazing thought that he might be dead for some time physically before he knew it should alert us to another possibility. We might be alive physically and live a long time spiritually dead and never know it! Henry David Thoreau thought that through to the conclusion that he did not want to come to the end of life and discover he had never lived.

> *For those who are according to the flesh set their minds on the things of the flesh, but those who are according to the Spirit, the things of the Spirit. For the mind set on the flesh is death, but the mind set on the Spirit is life and peace (Romans 8:5-7).*

> *However, you are not in the flesh but in the Spirit, if indeed the Spirit of God dwells in you. But if anyone does not have the Spirit of Christ, he does not belong to Him. If Christ is in you, though the body is dead because of sin, yet the spirit is alive because of righteousness. But if the Spirit of Him who raised Jesus from the dead dwells in you, He who raised Christ Jesus from the dead will also give life to your mortal bodies through His Spirit who dwells in you (Romans 8:9-11, NASV).*

We know either life from God with accompanying peace or a life without God. God's spirit gives life to our spirit, to our soul, and to our body.

We might be alive physically and live a long time spiritually dead and never know it!

The very power that raised Christ from the dead is in us giving life to our mortal body. In the metaphor of the human-body clinic we have partially toured, every part our body is affected by every other part, especially our mind and our spirit. Getting the connection between our body being at ease and our mind being at ease with God is an essential reality. The spirit gives life to the soul and the body.

We Get Mostly New Bodies Every Five Years—And Completely New Ones Every Seven

The training of Dr. Swenson in both medicine and physics offers great insight: " … the human body is a million times more complex than the universe."[69]

The universe is both a dwelling place for God and for us. Our bodies are also a dwelling place for God as well as for us. David, the psalmist, understood the majesty of creation as God's workmanship. Further, he understood that man was given management under God for all creation.

> You made him ruler over the works of your hands; you put
> everything under his feet (Psalm 8:6, NIV).

We are seen as temples (1 Corinthians 6:19), and we contain Christ's presence in us with the accompanying glory of God (Colossians 1:27).

From dust—His creation—God made the human body. Our body contains 10,000,000,000,000,000,000,000,000,000 atoms. If I counted right, that is 1 followed by 28 zeros. God took the smaller base of His creation, the atom, and added components to create a cell. God gathered atoms for Adam as he gathered the dust to form man. Swenson writes, while quoting an explanation from David M. Baugham, MD:

According to isotope studies, 90 percent of our atoms are replaced annually. Every five years, 100 percent of our atoms turn over and become new atoms…. We are continually being recreated from dust and returning to dust …

The fundamental particles that comprise us have been floating around since the beginning. They roost within us for a while, and then move on down the road to inhabit our neighbor. Some of the atoms that resided in our childhood frame are now probably doing their similar work within a body in Mongolia....

We share our physical existence with our neighbors, however remote.... Through shared sneezes, sloughed skin, the jet stream, flowing rivers, and a myriad of other mixing devices, God brings us together constantly.[70]

If we really comprehend sharing our physical existence through sharing our skin, there would be no place left for racial prejudice. Skin we wear today may have belonged to people of another race toward which we have harbored a prejudice. May God's design of shared skin be a guide motivating us to share life flowing out of God's love.

The ingenious design of our bodies being replaced through God's scheduled maintenance should make us aware that He has always counted our bodies of great value. His promise to give new bodies to those in Christ is already being demonstrated in part with the replacement of our cells. The knowledge that this replacement activity occurs so effortlessly should make us believe God with even more confidence.

Every person at or near my age (I am 80) has had the cells in their bones replaced ten times already considering the approximate rate of replacement every seven years. The rest of our body cells have already been replaced 14 times at the rate of every five years. That should make us aware that the replacement bodies we are receiving now, biologically, are an example of the supernatural replacement bodies that await us. They are bodies shared from the supernatural power of Christ's resurrection.

Should that make us more at ease or less at ease? More, since it verifies our eternal existence. Much more if we know God and know that He is in charge! Beyond our present level of comprehension and knowledge are the complete provisions of God for our eternal, enjoyable engagements with Him in managing the family estate.

There was life before life. God's life was shared in created life. There is life before death, and as a result, there is life after death.

There was life before life. God's life was shared in created life.

There was death in life when Adam chose against life. There was life in death as Christ died, reversing the choice of Adam. In the power of the resurrection of Christ, we have the right to be restored to God.

God has set before us life and death. Life is in God, whose love is truth. Death is in a false god whose fear is a lie.

Everyone has a relationship with God, whether known or unknown, wanted or unwanted. That relationship will extend eternally. Knowing God and wanting God makes us at ease. Not knowing God and not wanting God makes us ill at ease.

God wants our companionship whether we respond or not. Whatever our response, we are related to God forever. He is eternal, and even if we refuse His overtures of love and grace, we are related to Him forever—in either refusal or denial.

Those farthest from God are still related to Him because they choose to deny Him. They will know eternally that they have forfeited a relationship with God. They will also know it was their decision and not God's.

Being at ease with God leads to being at ease with ourselves. Once we are at ease with God *and* ourselves, being at ease with others follows. We can't love our neighbors as ourselves until we love ourselves in the way God already loves us.

From God's love comes our love for ourselves and for others. God's love is the most important element of life. Knowing His love makes life the many-splendored experience that He intended.

The Best Thing About the Best Days of My Life

These are the best days in my life. They are not the best days because of my physical strength, my accomplishments, or my assets. They are the best because of an ever-widening understanding of God's limitless provision through His attending presence within the kingdom of the heavens.

These are the best days in my life. They are not the best days because of my physical strength, my accomplishments, or my assets.

The best thing about these days is experiencing the rights of repentance. Repentance is the major benefit I have found in this stage of life.

Early in my life, repentance had fallen among thieves and was stripped of its true meaning. It meant to me a turning *from* my worst instead of turning *to* God's best.

Then I realized that repentance is embracing the best. With the best comes freedom from the worst. Repentance is the best thing about the best days of my life.

A whole lot of repenting goes on in the kingdom of God. The kingdom of God is so astounding to "orphanic thinking," a term coined by my friend Dudley Hall, that mind revisions are neverending.

At 80, I find myself repenting more now than when I was a gangly teenager who had just come to know Jesus Christ as my savior. I never would have thought of Him being my older brother as well as my Lord back then. Neither did I think that His father was as much my Father as His. That reality required a level of repentance that calls for daily maintenance with the renewing of my mind.

Our proper response to the revisions of the mind through repentance is ...

THANK YOU!

CHAPTER ELEVEN

Getting Around to Thinking Straight

It is hard to imagine today the brilliant minds Adam and Even must have had. With little or no self-consciousness, they were totally aware of God's majesty and His reflection in the majesty of creation.

Thinking would have been easy, because no conflicts—or breaks in the circuitry connecting truth and reality—existed for them. They enjoyed full view of both the visible and invisible. Their awareness included the chronicles of the known as well as access to the yet-to-be-known.

With organic computers, access to all knowledge was theirs. They could know without ever straining to do so.

One of the promises God makes to us is that He is providing for us to "know" what is needed: *That you may know the hope to which He has called you, the riches of His glorious inheritance in the saints, and his incomparably great power for us who believe"* (Ephesians 1:18, 19, NIV).

Knowing is part of our return to the new order of kingdom life. The way Jesus introduced the kingdom must not be taken lightly.

Jesus introduced the kingdom coming to earth with the bold assertion that a change in the way we think is essential. He called for repentance, or rethinking, of every issue. Without thinking that reflects the reality of God's presence, there can be no kingdom awareness.

God's four-hundred-year silence between Maliachi, the last book in the old testament and Matthew was broken with the message: *"Repent, for the kingdom of Heaven is at hand"* (Matthew 3:2). That messenger, John the Baptizer, introduced Jesus to the world: *"Behold the Lamb of God that takes away the sin of the world."*

The first message Jesus gave was exactly the same as the message of the one who introduced Him. From that time, Jesus began to preach, saying, *"Repent, for the kingdom of heaven is at hand"* (Matthew 4:17).

Both men heard what God said and declared it. Both called for repentance—something so revolutionary was being offered that nothing short of a new way to think and process reality would connect them to this invasion from Heaven. It was a kingdom of Heaven, or Heaven's order and plan, on earth.

Thinking is an issue that God presented in the messages of John and Jesus as the key to gaining access to God's kingdom of the heavens. Repentance was the method, and it was a reversal of the decision made by Adam. He thought—or repented—his way *from God.* Jesus offers the right to think—or repent—our way *back to God.*

Thinking with God was not a new idea. Isaiah understood this. Isaiah welcomed the idea of thinking with God. So he shared what God said to him: *"Come now, let us reason together, says the Lord: though your sins are like scarlet, they shall be as white as snow; though they are red like crimson, they shall become like wool. If you are willing and obedient, you shall eat the good of the land"* (Isaiah 1:18, 19, NIV).

He thought–or repented–his way *from God.* Jesus offers the right to think–or repent–our way *back to God.*

Isaiah understood that God wanted to "talk it out." I find it very assuring that God wants to talk. He invites us to join Him to reason or talk out the issue of our sin. Though we are stained with sin, God's stain remover makes us white as snow. God makes that offer to everyone.

Again, as seen by Moses and reviewed earlier, the ball is placed firmly in our court: "If you are willing and obedient." This is God's offer.

God has always wanted His thoughts to become our thoughts. A comprehensive review of thinking with God came from Isaiah. God's thinking as revealed to Isaiah is displayed in large parts of what Jesus taught.

*The poorest could afford to think with God, as understood by
Isaiah: "Come, all you who are thirsty, come to the waters; and
you who have no money, come, buy and eat! Come, buy wine and
milk without money and without cost" (Isaiah 55:1, NIV).*

These are like the poor in spirit that Jesus addressed. They have nothing—nothing but the desire to hear what God thinks. Those whose self-image is the poorest of the poor can access God as quickly as anyone.

Isaiah said that the desire to hear God is enough. You can come and buy without money. There is no price, and thus no money is required. God furnishes everything—the desire, the money, the purchase, and the food and drink to satisfy and make you healthy. It is all His and you get in on it.

He used King David, an icon of greatness, as an example of one who got what he didn't deserve: *"Pay attention, come close now, listen carefully to my life-giving, life-nourishing words. I'm making a lasting covenant commitment with you, the same that I made with David: sure, solid, enduring love"* (Isaiah 55:3, *The Message*).

God's Thoughts Can Be Our Thoughts

Our way of habitual wrong thinking leads us to think wrongly about what the Bible says. We often use Isaiah 55 to picture God thinking at a level that is completely unattainable: *"My thoughts are not your thoughts and my ways are not your ways"* (Isaiah 55:8).

I grew up hearing that the gap between my thoughts and ways, from God's thoughts and ways, would never be bridged. But God was saying that *without Him* the gap exists. With God's thoughts becoming ours, we can think *with* Him.

Here is how He described His thoughts and ways coming to us out of Heaven:

> *For as the rain and the snow come down from heaven and do not return there but water the earth, making it bring forth and sprout, giving seed to the sower and bread to the eater, so shall my word be that goes out from my mouth; it shall not return to me empty, but it shall accomplish that which I purpose, and shall succeed in the thing for which I sent it (Isaiah 55:10, 11).*

With God's word coming like rain and snow from Heaven, we have His ways and thoughts. Our part is to do the only thing we ever do when rain or snow comes, and that is to receive it. Rain and snow come from His love for us. We do not generate the needed life-sustaining moisture—we receive it. We get to join God in thinking the way He thinks. That is called repentance.

The Value of Thoughts from God

North Texas has been in a prolonged drought for several years. We all rejoiced as it ended recently (during the period in which I was writing this book). It was predicted at one time that some of the smaller cities would out of water within months. Millions of dollars were spent to find an alternate source for essential water.

Good thoughts are as essential for life as water. Isaiah understood the correlation between our need for God's thoughts and our need for water. No value can be assessed of God's thoughts. Life and death are determined by their supply reaching us.

Dr. Caroline Leaf's exhaustive research leads to understanding the influence of every thought we entertain:

> Every time you have a thought, it is actively changing your brain and your body—for better for worse....
>
> No system of the body is spared when stress is running rampant. A massive body of research collectively shows that up to 80 percent of physical, emotional, and mental health issues today could be a direct result of our thought lives. But there is hope. You can break the cycle of toxic thinking and start to build health patterns that bring peace to a stormy thought life.[71]

Every thought contributes to our health—positively or negatively. Further, Dr. Leaf describes the advance that has occurred in the science of thinking in the past several years:

> When I first started to research the brain more than twenty years ago, the scientific community did not embrace the direct link between the science of thought and its effect on the body.
>
> The common wisdom of the time was that the brain was like a machine, and if a part broke, it couldn't be repaired. It was believed that the brain was hard-wired from birth with a fixed destiny to wear out with age. Adding this belief to the assumption that we were bound to a fact predetermined by our genes made the horizon of hope seem bleak.[72]

But she continued to explore this "horizon of hope" and found this remarkable reality:

Now a revolution is sweeping through the field of brain science like never before. The greatest part for me as a scientist is that it all lines up with God's precepts. I am so excited that we get to be part of one of the most thrilling science adventures of mankind—understanding the "true you." I want to … encourage, rather than shatter, your hopes and help you to realize you have an amazing brain filled with real physical thoughts that you can control.[73]

This gift of hope means that our thoughts can become God's thoughts. God did not offer a replacement couple for Adam and Eve; He offered *replacement thoughts* so they could change their minds.

Our knowing is not a stab into a darkened abyss. Knowing is getting in on God's way of thinking and joining Him by adjusting our thoughts to agree with His.

Dr. Leaf offers valuable insights about her own way of thinking with God.

As a scientist and a follower of Christ, my starting point is always the Bible, and Scripture tells us God made humans in His image … over and above the animals. Therefore, humans are not a high form of animal (Genesis 1:27, 28); humans are unique (Psalm 139) and have a *divinely implanted sense of purpose* (Ecclesiastes 3: 11)….

Unlike any other part of creation, humans are gifted with what I call the "I-Factor"[—]the ability to think and choose for oneself. God made humans beings uniquely. In all creation there is nothing like us…. We are not robots…. We're surprising, capricious, constantly changing beings who are capable of a seemingly endless spectrum of choices.[74]

God's Highest Honor is Wanting to Spend Time with Us

Fellowship with God is the highest honor that He can bestow upon us. When accepted, it enables us to experience as well as enjoy God the Father in the way Jesus did.

That which we have seen and heard we proclaim also to you, so that you too may have fellowship with us; and indeed our fellowship is with the Father and with his Son Jesus Christ (1 John 1:3).

"Spirituality" is not something we ought to be. It is something we are and cannot escape, regardless of how we may think or feel about it. It is our nature and our destiny.[75]

Instead of God hiding from Adam and Eve, they began hiding from Him. Perception is reality to the one who holds it, but without God it is a flawed perception. Reality starts with "In beginning, God." Thus our perception is guided by God's perception shared with us. It is more than our knowledge of Him—it is His knowledge transferred and shared with us.

Losing sight of God led them to resist the sight of God. Hiding from God leads to a perception that God is hiding from us. His existence is not determined by our recognition of His presence. God is present with us whether we see Him or not.

Losing sight of God led them to resist the sight of God. Hiding from God leads to a perception that God is hiding from us.

God is not in hiding. We hide from Him behind the trees of our wrong thoughts, wounded experiences, and deceitful information coming from the same voice that convinced Adam and Eve to believe a lie.

No doubt God wants us to see him. That is a part of his nature as outpouring love. Love always wants to be known. Thus he seeks for those who could safely and rightly worship him. God wants to be present to our minds with all the force of objects given clearly to ordinary perception.[76]

Seeing God in Nature: His Arrangement of Creation's Furniture

God's displays in nature can't be missed. Dallas Willard further compares God's arrangement of these objects as being similar to our arrangement of furniture. "The arrangement of the furniture in your apartment is a manifestation of your will. It is as you have provided for and want it to be, though you are not always thinking of that arrangement and 'willing' it. It is also a continuing revelation of you to all who know you well."[77]

We would be amused and amazed if people came to our homes and took pictures of our furniture and even commented on the remarkable beauty and design—all while ignoring us. To see God's masterful design and not want to know *Him*, as one superior to the artistry of His creation, is the greatest error we can make.

Picture-taking of God's creation without ever knowing the creator is to miss knowing the originator of such workmanship. Our culture admires creativity and builds museums to house great works of art.

God has chosen a greater display of His genius than even the earth can hold. The billions of galaxies stretching out beyond us contain and exhibit a part of this marvel of His power as well His love. Yet God visits the museum of earth and even gives us personal tours and explanations for His choices and His plans for the future.

He wants us to know Him. He wants us to think like He thinks—to see . things through His eyes with His understanding. *Seeing Through Heaven's Eyes* is one of the better books on God's perspective of life. I urge you to get Leif Hetland's extraordinary vision of "Seeing God the Way Jesus Sees Him"; "Seeing Ourselves the Way the Father Sees Us"; "Seeing Others the Way the Father Sees Them"; and "Seeing the Future the Way the Father Sees It."[78]

Leif did not always see as clearly. As God showed him His love, a gift of sight brought him new understanding. You will read and exclaim: "Wow, what a sight!"

God likes His creation now as much as when He declared each day's work good. It could be that He likes it even more now, having maintained it these many years.

During one of my early reads of Dallas Willard's classic, *Divine Conspiracy*, I found myself—vicariously—enjoying a beach with Dallas in South Africa. Then Dallas insightfully shared that the one who made the beach enjoyed it along with him.

> While teaching in South Africa … a young man … took me to see a beach near his home in Port Elizabeth. I was totally unprepared for the experience. I had seen beaches, or so I thought. But when we came over the rise where the sea and land opened up to us, I stood in stunned silence and then slowly walked toward the waves. Words cannot capture the view that confronted me. I saw space and light and texture and power that seemed hardly of this earth.
>
> Gradually there crept into my mind the realization that God sees this all the time. He sees it, experiences it, knows it from every possible point

of view, this and billions of other scenes like and unlike it, in this and billions of other worlds. Great tidal waves of joy must constantly wash through His being.

It is strange to say, but suddenly I was extremely happy for God and thought I had some sense of what an infinitely joyous consciousness he is and of what it might have meant for him to look at his creation and find it "very good."[79]

For the first time, I realized that the beach creator can enjoy it more than the beachcomber. In turn, He desires to share his enjoyment, as He did with Dallas.

God is at ease and enjoying all of his vast creation, starting with our small plot of land called earth and extending to the billions of planets and galaxies stretching beyond our ability to see. Isn't it time for us to learn the meaning of being at ease as well?

From the current creation, Heaven and earth, God is preparing His combined workmanship—a new Heaven combined with a new earth. Our eternal endeavors will be based from this convergence of Heaven and earth.

Our response of belief that God shared the vast expanse of His creation with us and that He will enjoy it with us is …

THANK YOU!

CHAPTER TWELVE

Jesus: The Friend of Thinkers, Good and Bad

Adjusted thinking was the first requirement Jesus announced that accompanied a kingdom coming from Heaven. Then He began to describe as well as demonstrate His kind of thinking.

Jesus shared God's thoughts, actions, and examples:

And he went throughout all Galilee, teaching in their synagogues and proclaiming the gospel of the kingdom and healing every disease and every affliction among the people. So his fame spread throughout all Syria, and they brought him all the sick, those afflicted with various diseases and pains, those oppressed by demons, epileptics, and paralytics, and he healed them. And great crowds followed him from Galilee and the Decapolis, and from Jerusalem and Judea, and from beyond the Jordan. Seeing the crowds, he went up on the mountain, and when he sat down, his disciples came to him. And he opened his mouth and taught them (Matthew 4:23–5:2, ESV).

He compared this kingdom demonstration to a net being cast into the sea. *"Again, the kingdom of heaven is like a net that was thrown into the sea and gathered fish of every kind"* (Matthew 13:47, ESV).

From that sea of need came a sea of people to Jesus. His fame formed the net that allowed Him to draw them to Himself so they could learn of His Father's provision.

A multitude gathered trying to get as close to Him as possible. On this particular day, He chose a place farther up the incline so others could both see Him and hear Him. With a lake below them and the land stretching upward, a kind of amphitheater was created.

What He said was—and is—so revolutionary that, after thousands of years, many teach it exactly opposite from His true meaning. Probably not many understood it that day either.

I don't think many of us get it today. For years, I was one who taught an inverted order, or upside-down order, to what Jesus was saying the kingdom of God is like. My upside-down thinking came from the inverted process of thinking I was taught.

You will probably guess that it was Dallas Willard who challenged my thinking about what Jesus was teaching. At first, I was reluctant to embrace the implications that Jesus was not telling us what to *do* but was sharing what God *had done* for us.

Blessings Coming from God

Look at Dallas's insightfulness for yourself.

> The Beatitudes, in particular, are not teachings on how to be blessed. They are not instructions to do anything. They do not indicate conditions that are especially pleasing to God or good for human beings.
>
> No one is actually being told that they are better off for being poor, for mourning or being persecuted … or that the conditions listed are recommended ways to well-being before God or man…. They are explanations and illustrations, drawn from the immediate setting, of the present availability of the kingdom through a personal relationship to Jesus. They single out cases that provide proof that, in Him the rule of God from the heavens truly is available in life circumstances that are beyond all human hope.[80]

We call this famous teaching the Beatitudes. These verses are about God being who He is so He can teach us who we are. Jesus is telling his followers they do not need to do anything to earn kingdom benefits. Kingdom benefits had been earned for them and were presented for them to take home from that hillside, based simply on their belief in Him.

Doing what the kingdom family of God does would come from mankind being who God was inviting them to be. Jesus gave clear teaching, in other discourses, on what they would be doing.

Their doing would come from *being*, just as in God's first creation. They would become new creations in Him. God's grace account was full and they could receive a gift of eternal life found in Him and in God's kingdom

Sit down with Jesus for a time and listen to Him. Look around you at the crowd he saw. It was made up of people who had not prepared themselves for this event. The range of thoughts, lifestyles, and needs was as vast as the crowd itself.

But they were not so vast that Jesus did not know them. He looked into eyes that opened the windows of souls in deep depression, and He saw faces that mirrored despair. Some eye windows revealed deep sorrow, some apprehension about tomorrow—the range was extensive.

Some of these windows of the soul revealed thoughts of great perception and insight. Whether these thinkers were the good, the bad, or the ugly, Jesus was there to be their friend. He is a friend of thinkers—thinkers of the worst kind and thinkers of the best kind.

He looked into eyes that opened the windows of souls in deep depression, and He saw faces that mirrored despair.

Listen to what came from His mouth:

Blessed are the poor in spirit, for theirs is the kingdom of heaven.
Blessed are those who mourn, for they shall be comforted.
Blessed are the meek, for they shall inherit the earth.
Blessed are those who hunger and thirst for righteousness, for
they shall be satisfied.
Blessed are the merciful, for they shall receive mercy.
Blessed are the pure in heart, for they shall see God.
Blessed are the peacemakers, for they shall be called sons of God.
Blessed are those who are persecuted for righteousness' sake, for
theirs is the kingdom of heaven (Matthew 5:3-10, ESV).

A blessed life was offered to everyone on the mountain that day. Jesus did not offer a proposition that said, "If you do this you will get … " Instead, He offered a proclamation that was good news.

The proclamation was that everyone who wants to take part qualifies for the kingdom. His first two examples of who could believe the good news were "the poor in spirit" and "those who mourn."

Their qualifications for being part of the kingdom of God were found in the One speaking to them. A kingdom already present and operative was being described.

They heard that they could take the kingdom home with them. As amazing as this news was, it was clear that His offer was to the least likely. To the poor in spirit, living at the lowest level of self-worth, He said, "Yours is the kingdom of Heaven."

Imagine those thoughts reaching some who were living at the lowest possible level of self-worth. In their sense of worthlessness, they had never thought of owning more than the clothes on their backs, or maybe a simple shelter, let alone owning a kingdom. Some thought of themselves as worse than "homeless"; they were *worthless!*

To the poor in spirit, living at the lowest level of self-worth, He said, "Yours is the kingdom of Heaven."

Among the poverty-laden thinkers of that crowd were those who mourned. Mourning came from self-abuse as well as the abuse of others. They mourned in the depression of the "dark night of the soul." The darkness had been so intense they may not have known they had a soul. How souls were supposed to function was even less clear.

Light had come, but a lot of darkness needed to be replaced. Some were in such deep depression that their thoughts were labored and confused. It was like hearing thoughts so muffled that there was little clarity. He told even the most impoverished thinkers that He was their friend—whether they were good or bad.

As a friend of thinkers, Jesus said, "Let's start where you are. If your thinking is so convoluted you can't tell up from down or right from wrong, you can be changed. These attitudes that come from being part of God's way of thinking can be yours. You can have what God intended—a place in the kingdom and the rights that belong to His sons and daughters."

Jesus declares that our self-image shouldn't be determined by our behavior or by the behavior of others toward us. Our self-image and our self-worth are found in the offer of the blessed life. Only one standard can determine the blessed life—that is the standard of God. What God thinks of you is the way to think of yourself—not what you think He must or ought to think of you.

God's Thoughts and Their Thoughts

Jesus planted thought seedlings from Heaven into their thinking. A new row of dendrites (trees) were about to be developed in their brains. Thoughts that never before existed began to grow. He told them what they were thinking of themselves, as well as what God the Father was thinking of them.

What Did God Think?

He thought the kingdom of Heaven was theirs. *"Blessed are the poor in spirit, for theirs is the kingdom of heaven."*

He thought comfort was theirs. *"Blessed are those who mourn, for they shall be comforted."*

He thought they would inherit the earth. *"Blessed are the meek, for they shall inherit the earth."*

He thought their desire for things to be right would be realized. *"Blessed are those who hunger and thirst for righteousness, for they shall be satisfied."*

He thought mercy would be their companions. *"Blessed are the merciful, for they shall receive mercy."*

He thought they would see Him and enjoy Him. *"Blessed are the pure in heart, for they shall see God."*

He thought they would be recognized as His sons and daughters. *"Blessed are the peacemakers, for they shall be called sons of God."*

He thought they would be treated as some treated His Son because they were part of the kingdom of Heaven. *"Blessed are those who are persecuted for righteousness' sake, for theirs is the kingdom of heaven."*

They Were Essentials, Not Discards

While probably only part of this amazing new way of thinking was soaking in because it was too much and too soon for them to comprehend, they heard Him say, *"You are the salt of the earth; you are the light of the world."*

They may not have known everything He was saying, but they did know that both light and salt were absolutely essential for life. Their everyday experiences had told them that salt and light were basics to preserving food and growing food. Salt flavored and preserved and was part of the needed chemistry of their bodies.

Light was essential in the growing season for food to mature and find its way to their tables.

If they were salt and light, they were not discards. Should they lose their salt qualities, they would forfeit the life God intended.

Jesus told them: *"You are the salt of the earth, but if salt has lost its taste, how shall its saltiness be restored? It is no longer good for anything except to be thrown out and trampled under people's feet"* (Matthew 5:3).

So, being discarded would be their choice, not God's. God would honor their choice, but His choice was for them to be valued as salt and light.

As essentials, they had worth. Their worth was determined by the thoughts coming *from God*. He had determined their value and was offering them participation in a colony of life coming from Heaven. A kingdom from Heaven was so mind-expanding that their minds threatened to snap instead of expand.

But somehow they got that part—they were somehow essential to this kingdom operation. They were salt and light.

A whole lot of repenting was going on. Thought circuitries were being rewired and changed so fast their faces could hardly keep up with the change of moods they were going through. From the pits of abject, impoverished thought, those who believed Him embraced a kingdom inheritance that included joint ownership of the earth and titles of "children of God," with all the accompanying rights and authority.

When you open your life through repentance or a change of thinking, you qualify for the kingdom right here and right now. This kingdom is yours if you will turn your thoughts from being independent and indifferent toward God to being willing to receive from Him by believing Him.

Our best thinking occurs when we are willing to change our thinking in favor of God's.

His most precious gift is yours in the offering of His Son. Faith in what the Son of God can *do for you* is what God the Father *wants from you*. There was a full, complete payment of Christ in the way He lived without sin, in the way He died to pay for our sin, and in the way He rose victorious even over death.

As Jesus moved through the various thoughts the people on that hillside entertained, He told them that they could even inherit the earth! The thought that earth's joint ownership was offered by a loving Father who would make them His heir and joint heir with His Son … this was a thought that had never before entered their minds!

Ideas were knocking at the door of their thought life that had never before asked for entrance. The only way those thoughts could be part of them was through the repentance process He had introduced. They could change their thinking and embrace God's offer.

Our best thinking occurs when we are willing to change our thinking in favor of God's.

Our proper response to believing all God wants to share with us is …
THANK YOU!

CHAPTER THIRTEEN

God-Shaped Thoughts

The crowd on the hillside that day was really no different from the crowds—and us as individuals—today. Jesus thought thoughts that came from Heaven because He heard what His Father was thinking.

People in the crowd, however, were thinking thoughts that came from flawed sources and experiences.

As a gifted student of man's thinking as found in philosophy, Dallas Willard knew well the thoughts of people throughout history. He concluded that our thinking today is not really that different from the crowds Jesus addressed.

> You can be sure that nothing fundamental has changed in our knowledge of ultimate reality and the human self since the time of Jesus….
>
> Many will be astonished at such a remark, but it at least provides us with a thought—that nothing fundamental has changed from biblical times—that every responsible person needs to consider at least once in his or her lifetime, and the earlier the better. And as for those who find it incredible—I constantly meet such people in my line of work—you only need ask them exactly what has changed, and where it is documented, and they are quickly stumped.[81]

Dallas further comments on some of our contemporary thoughts:

"Rudolf Bultmann, long regarded as one of the great leaders of twentieth-century thought, had this to say, 'It is impossible to use electric lights and the wireless and to avail ourselves of modern medical and surgical discoveries, and at the same time believe in the New Testament world of spirits and miracles.'"

Dallas wisely knew how to reject such flawed thinking of people without rejecting them: "To anyone who has worked though the relevant arguments, this statement is simply laughable. It only shows that great people are capable of great silliness.

Yet this kind of 'thinking' dominates much of our intellectual and professional life at present, and in particular has governed by far the greater part of the field of biblical studies for more than a century."[82]

Jesus, the Ultimate Thinker

Then with laser-sharp perception, this highly respected thinker among the thinkers of academia as well as Christendom offers this summary of the thinking capacities of Jesus:

> And can we seriously imagine that Jesus could be Lord if He were not smart? If He were divine, would He be dumb? Or uninformed? Once you stop to think about it, how could He be what we take Him to be in all respects and not be the best-informed and most intelligent person who ever lived?

> That is exactly how His earliest apprentices in kingdom living thought of Him. He was not regarded as perhaps a magician, who only knew "the right words" to get results without understanding, or who could effectively manipulate appearances. Rather, He was accepted as the ultimate scientist, craftsman, and artist.

> The biblical and continuing vision of Jesus was of one who made all of created reality and kept it working, literally "holding it together" Col 1:17 — . And today we think people are smart who made light bulbs and computer chips and rockets out of "stuff" already provided! He made "the stuff."

> Small wonder, then, that the first Christians thought He held within himself "all of the treasures of wisdom and knowledge" (Col 2:3).

This confidence in his intellectual greatness is the basis of radicalism of Christ-following in relation to the human order. It sees Jesus now living beyond death as "the faithful witness, the first-born of the dead, the ruler of the kings of the earth … the first and the last, the living One," the one who can say "I was dead, and behold, I am alive forever more, the master of death and the world of the dead" Revelation 1:5, 18 — .[83]

This affirmation of Christ as a thinker affirms the fact that "it takes one to know one." Thank you, Dallas, for giving us this appraisal of the One who influenced you to think appropriately and to teach us the skills of aligning our thoughts with His.

In these days of writing, I have imagined myself on the hillside listening to Jesus bring this "talk," as our contemporaries define it. The more I have listened, the more I have seen of this kingdom of limitless expanse, solutions, and excellence. From the one who held within himself "all of the treasures of wisdom and knowledge" came these insights with transformational life.

May I encourage you, dear friend, to spend as much time as possible and as many times as possible sitting with Him and letting Him teach you.

Let Him Tell You Who You Are

He saw the crowd, but he saw far more. He saw *you* in the crowd. He saw you before the foundation of the world. Many of His statements were answers for people there that day. But they now can become answers to your questions today.

Notice that His focus was not on who He was, but on who they were! Many of them didn't yet know who He was. He would tell them at the right time and in the right way.

He saw *you* in the crowd. He saw you before the foundation of the world.

We cannot know who He is until He lets us see. It is equally true that we do not know who we are until He tells us. He told his followers then who they were, and it is His desire to tell you now who you are.

This marvelous unfolding of an offer they had never heard before is about you as well as them. But it was also about you as relates to Him. He is

where you are so you can be where He is. Don't miss this important truth—
the kingdom of Heaven is yours. Think with Him now.

Thoughts that come from the downloading of God's way of thinking in-
tegrate all of life. The One who knows all things presents kingdom reality.
These thoughts or attitudes do not necessarily follow an order, but they support one another.

They all offer a provision of the Father for His family. The first one begins
with the provision of the kingdom being yours. The last one gives the same
provision of the kingdom being yours. The thoughts in between all relate to
the various aspects of life. While they do not cover all of the issues of life, they
deal with the basics, or foundational issues.

Seeing God Is Normal Spiritual Reality

Within this instruction is the provision that the pure in heart will see God.
Seeing God does not normally come from a physical vision. It can and does
for some. But seeing God is seeing His illumination or revelation of any issue
needing His clarification.

Having a vision of Jesus as Dallas Willard did, as reviewed in Chapter Four, is not the only meaning of seeing God. Seeing God is consciously
knowing that God is with us—with or without supernatural sight. Believing
Him in our mind, through the Spirit, makes Him as real as a vision.

Such kingdom sightings are sightings that God Himself brings to us.
When God comes, He comes as light, for God *is* light! When God announced,
"Let there be light," He was, in effect, saying, "Let me be present."

For there to be sight, there must be light. Seeing God includes seeing
with the illumination of God's outshining presence. You, too, become a light
when you are a God-seer. As a God-seer, your gift of sight comes from the
gift of light—God's own presence. The fact that He is light makes the one
seeing Him light as well.

> "This is the message we have heard from him and proclaim to
> you, that God is light, and in Him is no darkness at all. If we say
> we have fellowship with Him while we walk in darkness, we lie
> and do not practice the truth. But if we walk in the light, as He is
> in the light, we have fellowship with one another, and the blood of
> Jesus his Son cleanses us from all sin" (1 John 1:5-7).

Seeing God Comes with God-Shaped Thoughts

Jesus was not saying that those who are pure in heart are an elite group that attains the right to see God. He was saying that everyone has that right as part of being in God's kingdom family. Within this blessed life of the kingdom, seeing God is the normal way of life.

The question is whether a pure heart earns the right to see God—or whether seeing God results in a pure heart! Seeing God is being aware of His presence. Everyone on the hillside that day was looking at God. What percentage of the crowd knew who they were seeing we do not know.

Philip, a disciple, would later acknowledge he wanted to see God the Father. Jesus gave this classic statement, telling him that he was seeing God:

> *Philip said to Him, "Lord, show us the Father, and it is enough for us." Jesus said to him, "Have I been so long with you, and yet you have not come to know Me, Philip? He who has seen Me has seen the Father; how can you say, 'Show us the Father?' Do you not believe that I am in the Father, and the Father is in Me? The words that I say to you I do not speak on My own initiative, but the Father abiding in Me does His works"* (John 14:6-10, NASU).

Jesus was saying, "You are asking me to show you whom you are already seeing." But of course Philip did not know whom he was seeing without the instructions of how to think it through.

We have the same void in our thought life. Practicing the presence of God is the directing of our thoughts to recognize God's presence at all times. He is present, and we just don't know whom we are seeing.

Receiving a Pure Heart

Early in my life I had no expectation of seeing God, yet I yearned for His presence. If only a pure heart could do that—my own heart was far from pure, as evidenced by some of my thoughts. Little did I know that my thoughts do not create a pure heart. God gives us a pure heart by putting His spirit in us.

Ezekiel could see the day God transplanted His heart through the gift of Christ living in us. *"Moreover, I will give you a new heart and put a new spirit within you; and I will remove the heart of stone from your flesh and give you a heart of flesh. I will put My Spirit within you and cause you to walk in My statutes, and you will be careful to observe My ordinances"* (Ezekiel 36:26, 27, NASU).

The early church faced the question of who qualified to be part of God's family. Jews and Gentiles were two totally different cultures. The question was: how could two groups that were so different become followers of Jesus?

It was a story of the good church crowd and the wild bunch, the well-schooled in religion and the unlearned in God's ways. It was a contrast of rigid standards and the epicurean way of living it up with no standards.

The early church faced the question of who qualified to be part of God's family.

Peter found out the "wild bunch" were welcome to God's family. It took a vision to rewire his brain. But he understood the new way of thinking, and he liked the new members of the family. So he addressed the part of the church whose minds had the old wiring.

> *After much discussion, Peter got up and addressed them:*
> *"Brothers, you know that some time ago God made a choice*
> *among you that the Gentiles might hear from my lips the message*
> *of the gospel and believe. God, who knows the heart, showed that*
> *he accepted them by giving the Holy Spirit to them, just as he*
> *did to us. He made no distinction between us and them, for he*
> *purified their hearts by faith"* (Acts 15:7-10, NIV).

Peter declared, "He made no distinction between us and them, having purified their hearts by faith." Notice that they did not purify their own hearts. Their hearts were cleansed by God when, through faith, they trusted Christ as the one who reconciles us to God. It was faith in God that resulted in a clean and pure heart. When we let this renew our minds, we will get it also.

John said it this way: *"Beloved, do not imitate evil but imitate good. Whoever does good is from God; whoever does evil has not seen God"* (3 John 11, ESV).

John knew those doing evil did so because they had not seen God. Had they seen God, they would have a changed heart that wanted to do good.

God wants to be seen as Dallas Willard so clearly defined in the earlier quote. Don't try to earn the right to see God. Receive that right by believing Him!

You *can* see God. In Him, you find a pure heart transferred to you.

Our proper response for all God is giving us is …

THANK YOU!

CHAPTER FOURTEEN

Selecting Plants for the Garden of Thoughts

All the thoughts we plant in our garden of thought come from either a climate of love or a climate of fear. Love's climate offers truth as a healthy plant. Fear's climate offers the lie of a diseased plant. God's thoughts are plants bearing his DNA of love. Thoughts without God's DNA are always based on fear.

The teachings of Jesus about how God thinks were so radically different that He had to quickly explain He was not contradicting the law and the prophets. What he taught did not mean that the law and the prophets were wrong.

He did not destroy the law, but rather fulfilled it and made it work. He did not refute the prophets, but gave clarity to their words and showed the fulfillment of their proclamations.

Jesus contrasted the traditional way of thinking, replacing it with the way God thinks. Six times He said, "*You have heard it said … but I say to you!*" (Matthew 5:21, 22,as one of those times).

Hearing Tradition or Hearing God

That refrain was heard with regard to six issues of well-known teachings of Jesus' day. All the teachings were right, but their practice missed the mark. (Read through Matthew 5:21-48). A different way of seeing each issue was being offered by Jesus, and the new way was quite different from what they had previously heard. We deal with the same "you have heard it said … but

I say to you" issues today. Much of what we hear is tradition instead of the sound of God's voice to us.

Best practices in their religious world were being raised to a new standard. Jesus said, "*Your righteousness must exceed the righteousness of the scribes and the Pharisees*" (Matthew 5:20).

That refrain was heard with regard to six issues of well-known teachings of Jesus' day. All the teachings were right, but their practice missed the mark.

Jesus taught a righteousness that started from within the person. It was not the performance of righteousness for the sake of approval from people.

Scribes and Pharisees were regarded as the best at the outward practice of religion. Yet Jesus said that God starts with the heart, or the thinking, of the person.

His new way worked then, and it works now because of the enabling power and presence of God at work within us. Each one of these issues relates to the Lord being able to guide our thinking.

Love Becomes the Foundation for All Good Thinking

Love becomes the essence of the way we are to relate to all the issues of life. Each issue draws from love—and not fear—as we agree with God and draw love from Him. Love is released in us as the Holy Spirit makes God's nature real to us (see Romans 5:5).

These are higher standards. Is God setting us up for failure? Of course not! He is showing us a way of life that is supernatural rather than dependent upon our best efforts. Our best efforts come short of God's ways. We are to receive God's best efforts and let them guide ours.

In these teachings, Jesus was informing us that thinking is at the core of our relationship with God as much as our actions.

What We Think Is What We Are

Jesus said that to hate with thoughts that want to remove the person from earth is to have murdered that person in the heart. To entertain the thought of having sex with a person other than our spouse is committing adultery in the heart. So kingdom reality, spiritual reality, starts in the heart or mind, where our thoughts occur.

Does condemnation now follow since we have a standard impossible to meet within ourselves? Again, of course not! Paul knew this victory as a work of God within him, leading to righteousness, not condemnation. Here is revelation that came to him:

> There is therefore now no condemnation for those who are in Christ Jesus.

> For the law of the Spirit of life has set you free in Christ Jesus from the law of sin and death.

> For God has done what the law, weakened by the flesh, could not do. By sending his own Son in the likeness of sinful flesh and for sin, he condemned sin in the flesh,

> In order that the righteous requirement of the law might be fulfilled in us, who walk not according to the flesh but according to the Spirit.

> For those who live according to the flesh set their minds on the things of the flesh, but those who live according to the Spirit set their minds on the things of the Spirit.

> To set the mind on the flesh is death, but to set the mind on the Spirit is life and peace.

> For the mind that is set on the flesh is hostile to God, for it does not submit to God's law; indeed, it cannot.

> Those who are in the flesh cannot please God.

> You, however, are not in the flesh but in the Spirit, if in fact the Spirit of God dwells in you. Anyone who does not have the Spirit of Christ does not belong to him.

> But if Christ is in you, although the body is dead because of sin, the Spirit is life because of righteousness (Romans 8:1-10).

How God Sees You Is the Way to See Yourself

Look carefully at the comprehensive list of how God sees us and how we are to see ourselves. These are God's thoughts. We are to set our minds on God's thoughts—not thoughts from any other source.

You are not under the gloomy cloud of condemnation—you are in Christ, the light of the world! There is no condemnation (verse 1)!

These are God's thoughts. We are to set our minds on God's thoughts–not thoughts from any other source.

The law of the Spirit of life sets us free to experience God instead of loading us up with more to do (v. 2).

Righteousness, which God requires, is already achieved and released in us, so we walk with the Holy Spirit as a companion (v. 4).

We walk by setting our mind either on what we think, our ability—or on what God thinks, His ability (v. 5).

Set the mind on the Spirit and there is life and peace. A spirit setting in the mind brings God's peace and life (v. 6).

You are not in the flesh. You are not on your own. You are in the spirit. Think like it. Act like it. The Spirit is life because of righteousness already achieved in Christ (vv. 9, 10).

So the proper question here is: "What am I thinking?" The solution is to *think* before I think and choose to think with God.

We Set Our Mind, or Our Mind Sets Our Life

We have the exclusive control of our will. We set our mind on God's revealed ways or on an alternate deceptive substitute. Your remote control never leaves your hands. No one else can choose for you. God gave us the dial to adjust in repentance to what He thinks and is saying.

Resetting the dial of the mind in repentance is required as often as we move it to consider some other "wacky" thought.

The Replanting of Our Garden

Once we acknowledge that God's thoughts truly are not our thoughts, and that our ways are not His ways, we are at a place to get in on His thoughts. Isaiah said God's thoughts come to us from Heaven in the way that rain and snow come to bless the earth. Reviewing this again as a means of replanting our garden of thought is very significant.

For my thoughts are not your thoughts, neither are your ways my ways, declares the Lord.

For as the heavens are higher than the earth, so are my ways higher than your ways and my thoughts than your thoughts.

For as the rain and the snow come down from heaven and do not return there but water the earth, making it bring forth and sprout, giving seed to the sower and bread to the eater,

So shall my word be that goes out from my mouth; it shall not return to me empty, but it shall accomplish that which I purpose, and shall succeed in the thing for which I sent it (Isaiah 55:8-11).

God's words, or God's thoughts, come from His mouth like the snow and rain come from Heaven. God sends them and we receive them. From the essential moisture they offer comes needed water to cause seeds to grow, resulting in bread for the hungry. The thoughts of God are like rain and snow to accomplish what God has sent them to do. God sends them— we receive them by believing Him.

The result is that the garden comes alive in us. The garden comes alive around us. In fact, Isaiah saw a big garden.

For you will go out with joy and be led forth with peace; The mountains and the hills will break forth into shouts of joy before you, and all the trees of the field will clap their hands.

Instead of the thorn bush the cypress will come up, and instead of the nettle the myrtle will come up, and it will be a memorial to the Lord, an everlasting sign which will not be cut off (Isaiah 15:12, 13, NASU).

Mountains and hills are part of the landscape that creates the picture of a great garden. When God's thoughts are welcomed, they make us aware that the garden of God's creation is alive with a sound from Heaven.

God's words, or God's thoughts, come from His mouth like the snow and rain come from Heaven.

The sound of music comes from Heaven. Mountains and hills sing as trees of the field clap their hands, applauding the peace in a garden adorned with beauty. Instead of the thorns and thistles of dangerous thought, we have productive trees of healthy thought.

This is a picture of the planting inside us. New thoughts are planted and begin to grow. Old thoughts are replaced. In this new planting, we are gardeners guided by God. Our choice of what is planted is determined by where we set our mind.

Guarding Our Garden of Thoughts by Capturing Our Thoughts

Dr. Leaf reviews the process of how thoughts are formed in her book *Who Switched Off My Brain?* "As the electrical information from your five senses pours into your brain, your brain is gathering electrical impulses through your peripheral nerves (the lines of communication between your brain and your body). These senses become the doorway into your intellect, influencing your free will and your motions."[84]

Light is a key to our inward garden just as light is a key to the garden planted in soil of the earth. Plantings in the soil of the mind require light as well. Plantings that come from flawed sources want the dark. Darkness fears the light just as the first parents feared God after their brain crash.

Our ability to monitor the incoming information and decide what we intend to keep and what we refuse is a gift from God. We are instructed to guard our minds. The instructions are specifically to take every thought captive. That means taking control of every thought. Accept the healthy thought. Refuse the diseased thought.

> *For the weapons of our warfare are not of the flesh but have divine power to destroy strongholds. We destroy arguments and every lofty opinion raised against the knowledge of God, and take every thought captive to obey Christ, being ready to punish every disobedience when your obedience is complete (2 Corinthians 10:4-6, ESV).*

We are to check the list against the knowledge of God, which is the knowledge coming from the thinking of God. Every thought is to be taken captive or controlled. The controlled thought is examined against the thinking God gives us. This captive thought is then placed in submission or obedience to Christ.

The decisions we make for laying out a garden of healthy thoughts takes place physiologically in our thalamus. "The thalamus is the meeting point for almost all the nerves that connect to different parts of the brain. You can think of the thalamus as an air traffic controller. There isn't a signal from your environment that does not pass through the thalamus. It connects the brain to the body and the body to the brain, and it allows the entire brain to receive a large amount of important data from the external worlds all at once."[85]

The landscape of our garden of thoughts is gathered from three sources—God's thoughts, our thoughts, and the thoughts from others. I am including in the thoughts of others the father of lies, who offered thoughts to Adam and Eve leading to their fall. They switched their minds to a lie from Satan and away from the truth spoken by God. This resulting reset of their minds plunged them into the confusion of no longer knowing who they were, where they were, or who to believe.

All thoughts are derived either from the Father of truth or the father of lies. Thoughts from the Father of truth always contain life-giving love. Thoughts from the father of lies always contain death-giving fear. Plants that we accept and establish in our garden may be healthy or they may be diseased. God's thoughts carry life, health, and vitality. Our unhealthy thoughts originating within us or coming from outside us will send runners and give root to more unhealthy thoughts.

Unhealthy thoughts may come to us from many sources. Often the delivery of the corrupted way of thinking will be through people.

They are usually people being influenced by the one who deceived Adam and Eve. They may be well-meaning people. Yet they have received a thought coming from a source already diabolically distorted. Contained in this distorted twisting of truth is a lie carrying diseased thoughts, which in turn carry potential disease to our bodies.

Well-Meaning People May Be People Opposing God

Peter was a well-meaning person. When he heard Jesus declaring that He would be rejected, suffer, killed, and then raised from the dead, Peter had thoughts enter his mind that were so disturbing that he rebuked Jesus. He delivered the thought, but Jesus knew the source, or origin, of the thought.

> *Peter took him (Jesus) aside and began to rebuke him. But turning and seeing his disciples, he rebuked Peter and said, "Get behind me, Satan! For you are not setting your mind on the things of God, but on the things of man" (Mark 8:32, 33, ESV).*

Notice that Peter spoke to Jesus when he rebuked him, but Jesus did not speak to Peter. He spoke to Satan, who had flashed a thought in Peter's mind so skillfully that Peter took it for a good thought coming from his own mind. Then He addressed Peter: "You are not setting your mind on the things of God." The mind of the well-intentioned can be quickly moved to a wrong setting.

Peter's alignment of his thoughts with Satan's thoughts must not be taken lightly. In the presence of the embodiment of truth found in Jesus, Peter offered a contradictory rebuke of Jesus. His source of thought came from the one who is the embodiment of lies, Satan. Jesus rebuked the source. We cannot take lightly this account so that we may let it guide us past these weapons of mass destruction.

The mind of the well-intentioned can be quickly moved to a wrong setting.

Startling indeed is the fact that the man to first hold the keys to the kingdom could choose to believe the thoughts he spoke. Contradicting the living Truth of Christ, who had just shared the long-held thoughts of God, is deception at the highest margin. Peter was opposing God's eternal plan to redeem and restore life and all creation to His original purpose.

Jesus did not come to this earth to win an argument. He was not here to outthink and out-debate those who opposed God's thoughts. He was here to win their hearts with love-filled thoughts. So He did not argue with Peter. He spoke to Peter's source of deception.

Love is the greatest authority on earth; it is God's nature expressed. All power and authority in heaven and earth was embodied in Jesus. It was this authority He drew from to address the issue. Jesus commanded Satan to get behind him. He then instructed Peter to reset his mind.

Did his thinking improve quickly? Hardly. When the events started which Jesus described, he wielded a sword and took an ear from a Roman soldier trying to stop the abduction. The soldier's head was the target; Peter simply missed and got an ear instead. Then he watched Jesus place the ear back on the soldier and willfully yield to the soldiers of Rome.

Events unfolded with unimaginable speed. More unimaginable were the manipulations of religious practice and governmental corruption. The greatest miscarriage of justice ever witnessed occurred. Lies filled halls where truth was supposed to reign.

That spirit of lying spread across a city now shrouded with an evil presence. In one man, truth was heard. Without defense of Himself, but with affirmation that He was king of a kingdom not of this world, He spoke love's truth.

Peter was not able to accompany this One whom he knew and declared to be the Christ, Son of the Living God. Out in a courtyard with that layered evil presence hanging over the city, he lied three times by denying that he knew Jesus. He had even been warned by Jesus that he would deny Him before a rooster crowed to announce the morning.

The Father of Lies Develops People of the Lie

Peter knew the truth and told a lie. Not once but three times. He had become one of the people of the lie. He had deserted the people of the truth.

People of the Lie is the title of a book written by a courageous man, M. Scott Peck, MD. I read it years ago and reread it during this writing. Peck's role as a psychiatrist led him to conclude many people make up a populace he calls "people of the lie."

Among his patients suffering mental dysfunction he observed a pattern: the pattern of lying to themselves and lying to others. As a scientist of thought, he wanted to know the source. Could there be an evil presence or an evil one influencing these damaging maladies? His studies in psychiatry had not offered evidence of a source for evil. As a new Christian he was wanting to know the truth.

Patients whose recovery was either very slow or never realized shared this common experience; they were people believing lies and telling lies to themselves and others. Seeking to gain insight and thus offer hope to people he cared about, Peck wanted clinical evidence to establish a case for evil. He dared to advertise for patients to be part of his research—people who might be demonized. Some really weird people showed up at first. And early in the quest there was no verification of anther personality, a spirit, within their own characteristics. Then he found patients being guided supernaturally by demons manipulating their thoughts.

While his immaturity as a Christian and his little experience with the alternatives of good and evil are evident, Peck serves us well to have documented the fact of angels opposite—fallen angels, or demons. Their service is to another fallen angel, Satan. Peck in his book quotes the insights of C.S. Lewis's identification of a spiritual battle for our minds and thoughts. "There is no neutral ground in the universe: every inch, every split second is claimed by God and counterclaimed by Satan."[86]

Here are some of his conclusions: "The only power that Satan has is through human belief in its lies." … "In fact, the best definition I have for Satan is that it is *a real spirit of unreality.*"[87]

Notice that Peck does not give Satan the definition of a person by using a personal pronoun. Instead, he refer to Satan as "it."

His own conclusions leave room for more understanding. But he is also hitting the target of truth to identify lies and truth as being the opposite poles of spiritual reality. What we believe, and thus embrace in our thoughts, makes the difference.

Peter is an example of this same battle for the mind that you and I face. *Who I am, where I am, and who to believe* are daily questions we all face. Knowing the truth by believing the truth sets us free, as Jesus proclaimed.

> *"If you abide in my word, you are truly my disciples, and you will know the truth, and the truth will set you free" (*John 8:31, 32, ESV*).*

Truth was not a concept apart from Jesus any more than it is a concept apart from God. Jesus was truth, just as God is truth. Truth is not only the character of a thought, but the character of a person as found in God and His Son. Character determines the deeds revealing the truth found in a person. God's character is always impugned by our unbelief. Our unbelief is saying God is not a truth-teller because of some character flaw.

John understood the implications of our not believing God. In unmistakable language he says our not believing the Father of truth is the same as calling God a liar:

> *Whoever believes in the Son of God has the testimony in himself.*
> *Whoever does not believe God has made him a liar, because he*
> *has not believed in the testimony that God has borne concerning*
> *his Son (*1 John 5:10, ESV*).*

The Way Back to God's Love Is the Truth

Our response to God as One who loves in truth requires our own truthfulness to our selves, to others, and to Him. Lying to our selves is usually the beginning of our lying to others. Peter lied to Himself before he lied to others. Lies coming from fraudulent thoughts create lies coming from our lips. Eventually, lies will characterize our lives—we can become a person of the lie. The good news is the way back to the truth found in the person of Jesus is even easier than the step taken from Him. It was so for Peter. Not only did he walk away, he ran back!

We do not have lie detectors until truth deposits are received. We must know the truth—that truth is not an idea but a reality of God's character. Peter is a worthy case study because, even when he knew truth, he embraced a lie before turning to truth again. His return to truth and affirming trust of Jesus led to Jesus affirming His trust in Peter. It was that same mind, renewed by the indwelling Holy Spirit, that was trusted to speak the first message about the resurrected Christ. From the mouth that offered three lies came this bold declaration: *"Let all the house of Israel therefore know for certain that God has made him both Lord and Christ, this Jesus whom you crucified"* (Acts 2:36).

The same mind that received a thought from Satan and used it to rebuke Jesus affirmed Jesus as Lord and as God's anointed one. And Peter was speaking to a crowd capable of calling for his death as they had called for Christ's.

Fear and intimidation that once guided his life were gone. Courage and faith-filled confidence enabled him to share God's message of hope for every person willing to hear and receive. He shared how Christ had always been the offer of God to them, even being seen and foretold by their epic king, David.

God's offer was to share Himself fully with them. Three thousand accepted the offer. Understand that your mind is capable of such a transformation as well.

Every mind can be transformed by embracing God's thoughts.

Our proper response to the offer and experience of a renewed mind is … THANK YOU!

CHAPTER FIFTEEN

Paying Off or Paying Back

Forgiveness provided the turning point in human history. Through the power of forgiveness, God restored His family to Himself. God did not pay sin back—He paid it off. All of sin's charges were marked: "Paid in Full." God forgives us of our sin when we believe Him.

Sin does not separate us from God. That penalty is paid. Unbelief separates us from the gift of God Himself, the gift given to us in Christ. Christ took sin, when he was made to be sin, so we can take from Him the righteousness of God (2 Corinthians 5:21).

If forgiveness replaced the unforgiveness that generates anger, resentment and bitterness much less illness would occur. Jesus *taught us* to forgive on the hillside. He *showed us* how to forgive while on the cross. We will carefully look at the example that He provided.

Much of the illness in America would be cured if, instead of living with guilt, regret, fear, and anxiety that sin has created, we would accept the assurance of being forgiven. Our health assurance policy is paid in full. We are to have complete assurance, which enables us to step into the place of God's holy presence without even the hint of the sins we once committed.

One couplet of thought from the teaching of Jesus on the hillside illustrate how to think with God, and then how to pass on what God thinks:

Love your enemies.
Forgive those who sin against you.

Let's look again at the prayer that gives a foundation for such thinking and practice.

> *Pray like this: Our Father in heaven, may your name be honored.*
> *May your Kingdom come soon. May your will be done here on*
> *earth, just as it is in heaven.*
> *Give us our food for today,*
> *and forgive us our sins, just as we have forgiven those who have*
> *sinned against us.*
> *And don't let us yield to temptation, but deliver us from the evil*
> *one.*
> *If you forgive those who sin against you, your heavenly Father*
> *will forgive you.*
> *But if you refuse to forgive others, your Father will not forgive*
> *your sins (Matthew 6:8-15, NET Bible*).*[88]

Jesus connects our receiving forgiveness from the Father to our giving forgiveness to others, and He does so in an unmistakable linkage. The Amplified Bible uses this wording:

> *For if you forgive people their trespasses [their reckless and willful*
> *sins, leaving them, letting them go, and giving up resentment],*
> *your heavenly Father will also forgive you. But if you do not*
> *forgive others their trespasses [their reckless and willful sins,*
> *leaving them, letting them go, and giving up resentment], neither*
> *will your Father forgive you your trespasses (Matthew 6:14,*
> *AMP).*

Our need to get forgiveness is no greater than our need to give forgiveness.

Love Was Proven in Life Given in the Death of Christ

Forgiveness is God's greatest exhibit of love. God's proof of love is found in the exchange of life that occurred in Jesus' death on the cross. Christ is the perfect One died for our sins.

Our need to get forgiveness is no greater than our need to give forgiveness.

As sinners we take His perfection as a gift. That is the exchange of the cross. *"But God shows his great love for us in this way: Christ died for us while we were still sinners"* (Romans 5:8, NCV).

The energy of God's unconditional love offers us endless forgiveness. Forgiveness is a healing cure. It is a miracle that only God can perform. This miracle takes place inside us so it can be expressed by us.

Jesus did not offer a sugarcoated emotional experience to forget our sin. He dealt with the real issue, the real violation being canceled through God's power, and allowed us to be released for cleansing and the cancellation of sin. Jesus taught that the issue of forgiving others is an essential part of life when God's thoughts, which create His ways, become our thoughts and create our ways.

By thinking like God, Jesus forgave the crowd, who enjoyed putting Him to death. Forgiveness was an essential part of what He taught because it was a central part of how God thought. Jesus taught forgiveness knowing He would face the need to practice it.

Taking time to understand this supply of forgiveness and how to access it is vital.

Forgiveness God's Way

Life is contained within blood and it flows to us in Christ. The cleansing, as well as the transfusion of life, is found in Christ's blood.

> *Indeed, under the law almost everything is purified with blood, and without the shedding of blood there is no forgiveness of sins (Hebrews 9:22, ESV).*

> *Therefore, brothers, since we have confidence to enter the holy places by the blood of Jesus,*

> *By the new and living way that he opened for us through the curtain, that is, through his flesh,*

> *And since we have a great priest over the house of God,*

> *Let us draw near with a true heart in full assurance of faith, with our hearts sprinkled clean from an evil conscience and our bodies washed with pure water.*

> *Let us hold fast the confession of our hope without wavering, for he who promised is faithful (Hebrews 10:19-23, ESV).*

Full assurance of faith "with our hearts sprinkled clean from an evil conscience and our bodies washed with pure water" is part of the health assurance God gives us. Cleansing gives us a new record with God.

Confidence comes with cleansing to enter and enjoy God's presence. That confidence supplies full assurance of faith with accompanying hope.

Guilt, regret, fear, and anxiety are canceled by accepting the assurance of being forgiven. Our health assurance policy is paid in full. We are to have complete assurance to step into the place of God's holy presence without even the hint of the sins we once committed.

All the benefits of God's assurance policy are found in His presence. Our faith is full, our hearts are clean, our conscience is cleared, and our bodies are washed. Full coverage of health assurance was paid at the cross.

What Really Matters: God Fore-Knows and God Fore-Gives

Forgiving sin is not a casual occurrence, as if it doesn't matter that much anyway. Sin is a real affront and offense to God. A real crime is committed.

God's power to forgive is not based on a trivial incident, but on a high crime against His own holiness and character. Yet in spite of the atrocious affront, God chooses to wash the ugliness of the thought, or the act, from the record altogether.

N.T. Wright wrote: "Forgiveness does not mean, 'I didn't mind' or 'It didn't matter.' I did mind and it did matter; otherwise there wouldn't be anything to forgive at all."[89]

God did mind, and it mattered to Him—that is why God planned a way to forgive. Before the world was made, God's combined wisdom and love, in covenant agreement with His Son, provided forgiveness. The cross was not an emergency extinguisher to put out a fire suddenly threatening lives. It was the means by which life would be returned in the abundant, eternal form that God originally intended.

Adam and Eve had eternal life. They did not carry it to full term. God offered it again on the installment plan of blood being spilled and placed on the mercy seat each year. That was a cleansing *from* sin but not a forgiveness *of* sin. It rolled the debt forward for another year.

The blood sacrifice cleansed but did not cancel eternally—until Jesus died at the cross. At the cross, blood that carried a life transfusion was shed. Life—eternal life—was in Christ's blood.

Whoever lives and believes in Him never dies. Believing in Him is the means by which the needle is injected into our veins to give us a transfusion of life in which forgiveness of all sin occurs. That includes sins past, sins present ... and even sins yet to be sinned.

Does that offer a license for all the sinning we want? No, no! Quite the contrary, in fact: it offers something supernatural that changes our attitude and appetite for sin. What we wanted to do in unbelieving disobedience, we no longer want. What we didn't want to do in believing obedience to God, we now want to do.

The Place Where Fore-Giving Occurred

God could forgive because He "fore-knew." If sin took His family from Him, a way was already in place to bring His family back. What He fore-knew included a way to fore-give.

The right to a family would not be violated. But neither would their free will be violated. They could come back only if they received the offer of Himself in His Son.

History's Epic Moment Occurred on a Cross

The epic moment in world history was that moment when fore-giving occurred. From a suspended position between Heaven and earth, God's Son, weakened by the excruciating pain of execution and with the weight of sin's atrocities pressing down on Him, gathered the strength to speak to His Father.

Their covenant agreement had been made before the earth was formed— it would take place at a skull-shaped likeness known as Golgotha. At a time when no trees existed for crafting crosses, God could see this wooden instrument. From that instrument has come the most recognizable symbol in today's world—the cross.

Out of a father and son agreement, Jesus would die to reconcile anyone who was willing. *"Father,"* He called, *"forgive them, they don't know what they are doing."*

Instead of throwing their sin back at them, Jesus took their sin as if it was His. He did not have any of the sin they had. They didn't have any of the righteousness He had. Yet He took all they had so they could have all that He had. He forgave them because, from the Father's heart, He took the payment to pay off their assault against Him.

Instead of throwing their sin back at them, Jesus took their sin as if it was His.

Taking time to reflect on Jesus' words from the cross is a wise investment of time. To His request, and thus His pronouncement of forgiveness for those who put Him there, He added, " *... for they do not know what they are doing.*"

Was He making this a reason to convince the Father to grant forgiveness? I don't think so, considering other instances when He forgave without mentioning that He was doing so because they were not aware of what they were doing.

He was making a statement about all sin. All sin is an irrational decision. From the time of the first brain crash in the garden, people have engaged in information-deficient decisions.

Jesus knew well that a plot to kill Him had existed for most of His public years. From birth, when Herod gave the edict to kill all the male children two years old and younger, Jesus' life was at risk. Leaders with sources of information from government, religion, and education all conspired to put Him to death—Herod, Pilate, Annas, and Caiaphas. They were the ruling elite. They had a lot of information. But Jesus was saying of them, as well as of the crowd on Golgotha: "They don't know what they are doing."

Paul knew that to be true and wrote the following: *"None of the rulers of this age understood this, for if they had, they would not have crucified the Lord of glory"* (1 Corinthians 2:8).

Does not knowing what we are doing excuse us from the decision to do it? Of course it does not. Our responsibility extends to finding out what to do. If we lack wisdom, God has offered to supply it (James 1:5). Not knowing what we are doing does, however, qualify us for God's compassion.

With their minds furnishing them thoughts that were well-rehearsed, this crowd knew they wanted Jesus put to death. What they did not know was hidden from them. They could see Him, hear Him, and hear from others about Him—yet they did not know Him.

Like Mike May, they saw but could not grasp what they were seeing. Jesus understood that their immediate need was forgiveness. So He took it from the Father and gave it to them.

The Difference Hearing God Makes

Just a little over a month from that day, much of that same crowd listened to these words from Simon Peter: *"Jesus of Nazareth, a man attested to you by God with mighty works and wonders and signs that God did through him in your midst, as you yourselves know—this Jesus, delivered up according to the definite plan and foreknowledge of God, you crucified and killed by the hands of lawless men. God raised him up, losing the pangs of death, because it was not possible for him to be held by it"* (Acts 2:22-25).

This time they got it. They wanted Him because God gave Him to them. This time they believed He died forgiving them and rose from the grave through His power over death. They understood He gave His life for them and wanted to share His life with them forever.

What if Jesus had not cried out to the Father as He did? He could have cried, "Father, give them what they deserve. They know what they are doing; they chose to free a criminal and to kill me. Give them what they are giving me!"

Instead, He said, "Fore-give them." Fore-giveness came from the fore-known supply of God's provision. The fore-known supply was released.

God Decided to Forgive; He Lets Us Decide Whether to Accept

God does not have to decide if He is going to forgive you. You have to decide if you are willing to accept His forgiveness. Humility is the willingness to accept that which you do not deserve and will never deserve.

A part of that humility is to believe it is true for you because God said it. Because God said it, that settles it. But it is not settled in you until you believe it. That is why so much "dis-ease" exits in people's minds toward God. They are not really at ease with Him because they do not believe Him.

Had Jesus called for payback, the world, already plunged into darkness from the sun's eclipse because of the torture inflicted on its creator, could have ignited with flames of destruction. Instead, the forgiveness Jesus claimed from God's way of love-guided thought flowed out upon the earth.

The Supply Source for All Forgiveness

The cross is the supply source for all forgiveness. It is where the Father released it. The Father chose to demonstrate that payback is not His way of thinking or acting. Instead, the record was changed. "Paid in full pending acceptance," was marked on all accounts.

The crowd at the cross went home without receiving forgiveness until they heard the good news from Simon Peter. Likewise, God's forgiveness awaits our taking it by believing Him for who He is and what He says.

A thief being crucified with Jesus believed he could be forgiven. Forgiveness came quickly from Jesus. With that forgiveness came the promise he would have a place with Him that very day in paradise, a garden of God's provision (Luke 23:43).

Forgiveness Comes from Knowing Where to Get It

We don't have forgiveness to give if we don't know where to get it. That is why so many spend their lives hurt, wounded, and nursing bitterness. Instead of being at ease, they are often carrying dis-ease because of the violation of this essential practice.

Without forgiveness, offenses are passed from life to life. It is like a staph infection that attacks a hospital: The disease being treated is no longer the greatest threat.

A good friend of mine had a successful hip replacement. He was elated over the success of the surgery and the comparative lack of pain. Then a staph infection impacted his body and he nearly died. Just a few infected cells affected every other cell of his body.

The most deadly virus of all time, sin, was arrested and contained because Jesus took it all for Himself that day. At the same time, He called for the Father to prevent it from infecting the angry, taunting crowd. He would die so they could live. We too gain that life, because He gave His for us and to us. Passing it on is just as important as receiving it.

We either pay back or pay off the sins that are committed against us. Jesus could have resorted to the payback of retaliation. Instead, He chose to pay off the wounds inflicted on His body, as well as the insults and charges so false that they comprised the greatest injustice ever witnessed. The payoff of forgiveness stops the spread of the virus of revenge.

Forgiving as Jesus Forgives

How did Jesus forgive? He is our model. Many well-meaning counselors never take people to the real source of forgiveness.

All power and authority belonged to Jesus. He used it with the careful guidance of His Father by doing only what He was being told to do. That included the right way as well as the right time.

Jesus did not declare His forgiveness that day. Instead of pronouncing His own forgiveness for those who hung Him on a cross and further mocked and maligned Him, He claimed their forgiveness from the Father. Their pre-creation covenant was made active. From the Father, he claimed the forgiveness long guaranteed to everyone willing to receive it.

It is important to learn that we do not have to give what we have not received from the Father. We get it from the Father just as Jesus did. We may not feel like forgiving someone. That does not keep us from choosing to get from the Father what we don't feel at the time. Choose to forgive, and take it from God's heart to give to whoever needs it.

The Father had already chosen to forgive. That was why Jesus called to Him. Jesus knew what the Father thought. He was willing to accept the Father's example and make it His choice as well.

We can go the Father as Jesus did. From His heart for us, as well as for those who have wronged us, we can choose forgiveness. It is a choice and not an emotion.

Forgiveness from the cross did not take place in a quiet room of reflection. It took place in the awful trauma of emotional, physical, and spiritual pain.

It was a choice, and Jesus made it. Jesus did not act out of what He *felt*. He acted out of what He *knew*. From His mind, filled with the knowledge of His Father's love-filled mind, He called for the forgiveness that perfect love supplies.

The choice to forgive may or may not have accompanying positive emotion. We may not feel like it. Emotions may be shouting: "No, be angry, be bitter, and get even." Our minds may dredge up even more evidence for a case to continue the offense.

The choice to forgive may or may not have accompanying positive emotion. We may not feel like it.

The Father gave the volition of our choice-making capacity to us, and it is ours to use. Switch the dial of your will to God's setting. Choose to accept God's forgiveness of your wrongs and the wrongs of others.

Now, choose to forgive yourself, and with that forgiveness choose to forgive others. There may be no emotion, or there may be negative emotions protesting what you are choosing. You may be void of all positive emotions.

The much-needed love toward yourself and others, with the accompanying peace for healing the hurts of the past, may come slowly. Let me state emphatically: forgiveness is a choice, not a feeling. The choice includes choosing to believe God for what He gave you through His Son's shared life.

Forgiveness is a choice, not a feeling.

Forgiving God's Way

A woman named Corrie Ten Boom shared a helpful illustration of forgiveness based on choice rather than feelings. Several years ago, I was privileged to spend most of a week in the company of this amazing woman.

During that time a small group of us listened as she related story after story about her life and experiences in the companionship of her Lord. The story I am sharing from her book, *Tramp for the Lord,* I heard her tell during one of our sessions.

The Ten Boom family of Holland had offered God's love and protection to Jewish people when injustice and hate prevailed. During the Nazi Holocaust, when Germany occupied their homeland, the courageous Ten Boom family provided shelter, protection, and escape for Jewish people about to die.

When the family was reported and arrested, they all suffered horrible punishment. Corrie and her sister Betsie were imprisoned in Ravensbruck, the infamous place of cruelty and death. Betsie was one of those who did not survive the starvation and cruelty. Corrie did survive and brought a message of forgiveness and hope.

> It was a church in Munich that I saw him—a balding heavyset man in a gray overcoat, a brown felt hat clutched between his hands. People were filing up the basement room where I had just spoken, moving along the rows of wooden chairs to the door at the rear. It was 1947, and I had come from Holland to defeated Germany with the message God forgives.
>
> It was the truth they needed most to hear in that bitter, bombed-out land. And I gave them my favorite mental picture. Maybe because the

sea is never far from a Hollander's mind, I like to think that's where forgiven sins were thrown. "When we confess our sins," I said, "God casts them into the deepest ocean, gone forever. And even though I cannot find Scripture for it, I believe God then places a sign out there that says, NO FISHING ALLOWED."

The solemn faces stared back at me, not quite daring to believe. There were never questions after a talk in Germany in 1947. People stood up in silence, in silence collected their wraps, and in silence left the room.

And that's when I saw him, working his way forward against the others. One moment I saw the overcoat and the brown hat; the next, a blue uniform and a visored cap with its skull and crossbones. It came back with a rush: the huge room with its harsh overhead lights; the pathetic pile of dresses and shoes in the center of the floor; the shame of walking naked past this man. I could see my sister's frail form ahead of me, ribs sharp beneath the parchment skin. *Betsie, how thin you were!*

The place was Ravensbruck and the man who was making his way forward had been a guard—one of the most cruel guards.

Now he was in front of me, hand thrust out. "A fine message, Fraulein! How good it is to know that, as you say, all our sins are at the bottom of the sea!"

And I, who had spoken so glibly of forgiveness, fumbled in my pocketbook rather than take that hand. He would not remember me, of course—how could he remember one prisoner among those thousands of ladies.

But I remembered him and the leather crop winding from his belt. I was face to face with one of my captors, and my blood seemed to freeze.

"You mentioned Ravensbruck in your talk," he was saying. "I was a guard there." No, he did not remember me.

"But since that time," he went on, "I have become a Christian. I know that God has forgiven me for the cruel things I did there, but I would like to hear it from your lips as well. Fraulein … "—again his hand came out—"will you forgive me?"

And I stood there—I whose sins had again and again [been] forgiven— and could not forgive. Betsie had died in that place—could he erase her slow, terrible death simply for the asking?

It could not have been many seconds that he stood there—hand held out—but to me it seemed hours as I wrestled with the most difficult thing I had ever had to do.

For I had to do it—I knew that. The message that God forgives has a prior condition; that we forgive those who have injured us. "If you do not forgive men their trespasses," Jesus says, "neither will your Father in heaven forgive your trespasses."

I knew it not only as a commandment of God, but as a daily experience. Since the end of the war, I had a home in Holland for victims of Nazi brutality. Those who were able to forgive their former enemies were able also to return to the outside world and rebuild their lives, no matter what the physical scars. Those who nursed their bitterness remained invalids. It was as simple and as horrible as that.

And still I stood there with the coldness clutching my heart. But forgiveness is not an emotion—I knew that too. Forgiveness is an act of the will, and the will can function regardless of the temperature of the heart. "Jesus, help me!" I prayed silently. "I can lift my hand. I can do that much. You supply the feeling."

And so, woodenly, mechanically, I thrust my hand into the one stretched out to me. And as I did, an incredible thing took place. The current started in my shoulder, raced down my arm, sprang into our joined hands. And then this healing warmth seemed to flood my whole being, bringing tears to my eyes.

"I forgive you, brother!" I cried. "With all my heart."

For a long moment we grasped each other's hands, the former guard and the former prisoner. I had never known God's love so intensely as I did then. But even so, I realized it was not my love. I had tried, and did not have the power. It was the power of the Holy Spirit as recorded in Romans 5:5: " … because the love of God is shed abroad in our hearts by the Holy Spirit which is given to us."[90]

We Access Everything God Has When We Believe Him

We can access everything God has for us if we choose to believe Him. Corrie Ten Boom did that because her will overruled her emotions. We can join our will to God's will and act in faith as she did.

Taking what God is offering is the key. We take it for ourselves and know we are forgiven. We take it for others and pass it on as an act of our will. Passing it on may or may not have accompanying feelings of love and peace. Those feelings will follow, but the schedule may not be as quickly as Corrie experienced.

We can access everything God has for us if we choose to believe Him. Corrie Ten Boom did that because her will overruled her emotions.

Her contrast in the condition of those who forgave and those who harbored bitterness deserves highlighting in our minds: "Those who were able to forgive their former enemies were able also to return to the outside world and rebuild their lives—those who nursed their bitterness remained invalids."

The payoff comes from Christ to us. He paid for our sin, and there is plenty left in the payment fund for us to pay off others. Our funding for paying off others is endless. Our ability to pass on the payoff of our forgiveness was shared by Jesus in one of the final sessions He had with the disciples.

And when he had said this, he breathed on them and said to them, "Receive the Holy Spirit. If you forgive the sins of anyone, they are forgiven; if you withhold forgiveness from anyone, it is withheld" (John 20:22, 23).

Forgiveness Is a Good Business Practice

This truth about God's thinking and ways regarding forgiveness applies to every realm of life. Doug Russell is a businessman and personal friend with a very successful track record of taking struggling businesses and making them profitable. He did not do that without some failures. In the process of success and failure, he learned to ask the Father what He thought and to adjust his thinking accordingly.

Forgiving others was one of the adjustments he made. As he heard from God about how to react to both management and employees in his companies, he was struck with this Scripture (quoted above): *"If you forgive the sins of anyone, they are forgiven."*

Believing he was to practice this, he began to approach his employees differently. When they made bad decisions, violated rules, or were late or lazy, he started by praying for them and forgiving them. When he spoke with them to give an evaluation of their actions, he did it with forgiveness already granted.

As they realized he knew their wrongs and had chosen to forgive them, they were amazed. With gratitude, most of them accepted his offer of grace and his suggestions of to how to do their jobs right. Instead of multiple terminations, he saw multiple transformations. Efficiency and effectiveness in his companies accelerated.

The Forgiveness Factor Is Pivotal

The forgiveness factor is a most neglected factor. It was not only the turning point in history, it is a pivotal point in our lives and health. From the hill where Jesus taught to the hill where Jesus died, there is a connection to change every life.

On the hill where Jesus taught, He said we must learn to forgive. On the hill where He died, He showed us how to forgive. We take from the Father His way of thinking and acting and give it to others.

Before closing this chapter I want to refer you to one of the most important books on forgiveness I have read. I have read and re-read it and am doing you a service to urge you to read it as well: *Unconditional, The Call of Jesus to Radical Forgiveness*, by Brian Zhand.[91]

We do not live very long before we realize we need forgiveness for our wrongs. Neither have we lived much of life until we face the need of forgiving others. In forgiving we break the bonds tying us to the tyranny of injustice we have done or others have done against us. Forgiveness is a part of the ruling order of God's eternal kingdom. Both receiving forgiveness and giving it reveals God's decision to forgive—a decision made before a person with a wrong needing forgiveness even existed. This act offers us a new future born out of the new way to think about the reconciling way that God forgives.

We have already seen that life and death, blessing and curses were offered us in the capacity God gave us to choose. Blessings beget life. Curses beget death. When we forgive we bless. When we hold unforgiveness we curse. We are instructed to bless and not curse. Whatever the injustice to us, we are to bless. *"Bless those who persecute you; bless and do not curse"* (Romans 12:14, NASU).

Life and Death Are Contained in Thought

Life or death flows into our minds through the thoughts we receive. Life or death flows out from our minds in the thoughts we have for ourselves and for others. Forgiveness releases blessings to attend others. Unforgiveness releases a curse to assault others.

Curses were reversed at the cross when Jesus took the curse of the sin of the past and the curses of the mob around him and pronounced the blessing of forgiveness. Words of forgiveness came from His mouth because thoughts came from His Father to bless and not curse.

Arrogance and anger come for an enemy of corrupted thought. Humility and forgiveness come from the One who is love.

If we get real, we see that we have not known what we were doing in most of the wrongs we inflicted. Well, neither did those who wronged us. They suffer the same lack of knowledge. We don't know until the Father's way of thinking guides us. They don't know either, so forgive them and release them from the debt you think they owe you.

> **If we get real, we see that we have not known what we were doing in most of the wrongs we inflicted. Well, neither did those who wronged us.**

You have the funds of God's grace to grant them forgiveness, just as Jesus did. He got the payment from His Father. So can you!

Our proper response to God's forgiveness to us and His supply of forgiveness for others is …

THANK YOU!

CHAPTER SIXTEEN

Wasting a Good Day with Anxiety

Jesus said the greatest waste of time possible is that spent on anxiety. Bring all the anxiety you can find—use it all and it will accomplish nothing. God's way of thinking does not include anxiety.

As Jesus began to summarize the alternatives to our thinking, He contrasted two ways of life. We live life in His family knowing He is our provider, our protector, and our promoter; or we live life anxiously trying to either obtain or retain what we believe will satisfy us.

Concern for promotion and the attending position we can hold may or may not be part of anxiety, but concern about needed provision and protection can always be found.

Instead of being anxious about life, Jesus described how we should enjoy life. The time we spend in anxiety means there is that much less time for living life. Life is God's greatest gift, and He doesn't want it marred with injuries from our wrong thinking. Anxiety adds nothing to life—nothing is gained, repaired, or improved by it.

Anxiety brings only subtractions. It takes but never returns. It reduces without ever replenishing. Jesus said you can't use it to add to or alter your height. You can't use it to get food. You can't use it to make you look better. You can't use it to cause you to think well. You can't use it to overcome sickness.

Anxiety Is a Substitute God

Anxiety is really a substitute for God. We use our thinking about whatever concerns us instead of asking God to think with us. Anxiety contributes nothing and, all the while, God is waiting as our Father to care for us.

Jesus didn't say we wouldn't have hard times. We may experience difficult circumstances, but they will come attended with God's presence and provision. When hard times come, anxiety won't stare them down or drive them away.

Now, listen carefully in your heart to what Jesus said further on the mountainside that day. Let these words sink in. They contain life. They are words about living life instead of trying to manage it with anxious thoughts.

> *Therefore I tell you, do not be anxious about your life, what you will eat or what you will drink, nor about your body, what you will put on. Is not life more than food, and the body more than clothing? Look at the birds of the air: they neither sow nor reap nor gather into barns, and yet your heavenly Father feeds them. Are you not of more value than they? And which of you by being anxious can add a single hour to his span of life? And why are you anxious about clothing? Consider the lilies of the field, how they grow: they neither toil nor spin, yet I tell you, even Solomon in all his glory was not arrayed like one of these. But if God so clothes the grass of the field, which today is alive and tomorrow is thrown into the oven, will he not much more clothe you, O you of little faith? Therefore do not be anxious, saying, "What shall we eat?" or "What shall we drink?" or "What shall we wear?" For the Gentiles seek after all these things, and your heavenly Father knows that you need them all. But seek first the kingdom of God and his righteousness, and all these things will be added to you. Therefore do not be anxious about tomorrow, for tomorrow will be anxious for itself. Sufficient for the day is its own trouble* (Matthew 6:25-34).

All anxiety repeats the original mistake made in the garden. It is a decision based on faulty information that leads to a faulty conclusion. Anxiety is usually a baseless bit of information about a possible occurrence. Adam and Even took a baseless suggestion and placed their future on it. Instead of being like God, which they already were, or being more than God, they became less than ever because they were no longer ruled by God's Spirit.

In order for such skewed, anxious thinking to occur, we must step outside the time frame of the present. Instead of living in the present tense, we step into the future or the past. Most anxiety is based on peering into the future and trying to deal with the whens and what-ifs.

Anxiety is usually a baseless bit of information about a possible occurrence. Adam and Even took a baseless suggestion and placed their future on it.

The hypothetical moment of the "when" that anxiety says we will someday face never looks like we thought it would look. Jesus urged us to look at tomorrow and do ourselves a favor—let tomorrow take care of tomorrow.

We can only live today. Trying to live tomorrow is not only fruitless—it is utterly foolish. When tomorrows finally arrive, they are always *today*.

The Secret of Life Is Enjoying the Present in God's Presence

The secret to life is said by some to be "living in the present." That is partly true, yet it is incomplete. With whom do we share the present? If we are alone in the present and left to our own abilities, we have not found the secret to life. By tuning out the past and leaving the future for the future, we are in the right time zone. But our need of a Father to love us, to provide for us, protect us, and guide us is the essential element of life.

Life's supreme secret is enjoying God's presence in the present. We can know God is present to share in what we are thinking. We can practice God's presence by letting every thought include the reality of Him being with us in the present.

God's Absence Is Only in Our Brain

When there is no sense of His presence, the omnipresent, or "always present," One has not taken a leave of absence. Our consciousness or ability to see in our brain is where the fault lies.

If there is an empty space where we think God should be, the space exists only in the brain's comprehension. He is there. Acknowledge what He promised: *"I am with you always"* (Matthew 28:20).

Let the brain learn what the eyes of understanding are being offered in light of reality. The problem does not lie in His not being there—the problem lies in our lack of comprehending His presence.

It was Brother Lawrence who insightfully suggested that we practice the presence of God. He was not a trained theologian or a person of professional stature. He was a cook who knew his kitchen was a place where God lived simply because He knew God's presence. So he was a profound theologian who, instead of being a professional, was a possessor of stature as one of God's sons.

To practice the presence is to invite His presence to attend where we are at any given time. By taking the gift of thought, we welcome God to spend time with us as we think. God suggested, *"Come, let's reason together"* (Isaiah 1:18). Said another way, "Let's think this through together." To think with God leads to thinking like God thinks about the issues we face.

Jesus said that, instead of the anxiety of our own thoughts about "when," "how," "what if," and "how much," realize that *"your heavenly Father knows that you need them all"* (Matthew 6:3). Your Father knows. He knows the details. He knows our needs. He knows with a love that offers His endless supply.

A Bad Report–A Good Experience

"You have stage T2C Gleason score nine prostate cancer, and it is so advanced it may have metastasized," was the alarming report given to a couple, Lee and Lita, that Jane and I know well. We know and love them as two people with great qualities and character.

They are now retired and living their dream in their dream home near grandchildren. With skills few people have as a mechanic, though that was not his vocation, he built their beautifully appointed, state-of-the-art, virtually energy-free house.

The diagnosis of Gleason stage nine cancer was an inspection report of his body, his house on earth. It was possible the house would need to be vacated.

Their lives were in lockstep with each other from the time they met in high school. Always inseparable except for their jobs, they had become even more inseparable in their retirement. Now the unthinkable report contained the very real threat of parting. Anxiety was only a minor part of their range of emotions. Pain, death, and grief were all part of fear's anxious flood of the possibilities that awaited them.

As people of great character, they had played significant roles in the lives of other people in their community. He played a key role in security for the public schools of their city. She was involved in Family Court with cases involving families in crisis.

Anxiety was only a minor part of their range of emotions. Pain, death, and grief were all part of fear's anxious flood of the possibilities that awaited them.

Church life had been part of their early life together. But some events of church life that were displays of people's woundedness spread as wounds to them as well. Wounded people usually wound others, just as healed people usually heal others. So, church, to Lee and Lita, was a good organization, but not a part of their lives. They were followers of Jesus, but they were no longer part of the company business of church life.

My wife Jane loves this lady dearly. So, in her caring, perceptive way she began calling her regularly, encouraging her as well as her husband. At times, the grief of one so dear to Jane was poured out in streams of tears when words no longer came. They prayed and talked about God's love, God's care, and His power to heal. In prayer they claimed that.

The couple's local doctor became a source of referrals to the best oncologists and surgeons in the nation. They were recommended to M.D. Anderson Hospital in Houston. With that referral came access to some of the best-trained doctors in America.

A Most Unlikely Place for God's Presence

God showed up on their behalf in a most unlikely place and in a most unlikely way. With heavy hearts, they took their turn in the waiting room of the local hospital. Tests that would be run there and forwarded to Houston were occurring on schedule.

Filled with fear while waiting for Lee's appointment, Lita noticed a lady busily knitting as she too waited. After Lee was taken in for his appointment, the lady with a newly finished shawl moved over to Lita and, placing the shawl around her shoulder, said, "As I was knitting this shawl, I heard the Lord tell me to give it to you to wrap you in His love and to assure you He is with you in this time you are going through." Lita was so unprepared she could only say, "Thank you, you are so kind" … as she then lost her composure.

When she was able, she looked up and the nameless lady was gone.

Without a group for spiritual support around them, God had come in such a thoughtful, tender manner that His presence was unmistakable. Suddenly in that room far from the Bible Belt, where that kind of compassion would be more common, a lady who was part of God's family reached out to a lady she didn't know. And they still do not know each other.

Without earning the brownie points of church life, a couple became recipients of God's greatest gift, His love declared and demonstrated. God is not interested in brownie points. He is not putting us on a payment plan. He is a giver of grace and love that cannot be earned—only received. Don't mistakenly hear me saying that church life is not beneficial, but do hear me saying no one earns what only God's grace gives.

The event was real and surreal at the same time. They returned to their home knowing something special was taking place, yet not knowing how to really understand or define it.

In the days that followed, Lita learned in times of anxiety to get the shawl and place it around her as a reminder that she was covered with love and the care of God her Father. She and Lee often prayed together, at times sharing the shawl. It covered both sets of shoulders.

Both came to know God's love as a covering. God's presence began to be real, not only in the shawl symbol but in their thoughts and their visits with Him. His presence in the present gave them confidence as they counted down to the time for the surgery.

A Sudden Change–A Significantly Skilled Doctor

Lee's case had been assigned to a good doctor at M.D. Anderson. The earliest possible date was set for surgery. Airline tickets were bought for them and their two children. Suddenly they received a call that the doctor scheduled for the surgery was unavailable and that another doctor was being assigned for a later date. The hospital arranged the change of all the flights with no added cost.

Research revealed the newly assigned surgeon had a reputation as one of the most skilled practitioners in the nation. As they met him in the pre-op they were further aware God had guided this change. He was obviously experienced, caring, and thoughtful. Then he paused and said, "I like to pray with all of my patients for God to bless, guide, and heal. May I do that?"

"Yes, of course!" was their immediate response. A shawl had covered their lives expressing God's loving presence. Now prayer from the surgeon was connecting both them and the doctor to God's caring concern as well as His wisdom and skills in healing the body.

The difficult and delicate surgery could not have been more successful. The skill of the surgeon and the guiding hand of God was obvious in the test results and recovery that followed. Treatment brought the cancer down to undetectable levels. God continues to bless and guide Lee on his journey today.

A shawl had covered their lives expressing God's loving presence. Now prayer from the surgeon was connecting both them and the doctor to God's caring concern.

God guided His daughter to knit a shawl and then pointed out to her a person in need of knowing how much He cared and how real and present He desires to be to everyone. That shawl was placed about Lita's shoulders as carefully and lovingly as if an angel had taken a human form and used human hands to make the transfer.

Does God need to come to us with such an unexplainable supernatural demonstration? Yes He does, if He so chooses. And no, He doesn't, because His love is already displayed. Love is already pledged and declared to us in countless ways. That is enough. Yet, God often uses the supernatural to remind us of what is so easily forgotten. Keeping our thought life current is part of enjoying God for who He is.

God chose to show Himself to Lita and Lee. In doing so I can tell you and encourage you that he has a covering of love for you.

He used Jane in prayer. He used their daughter and their son. He used a nameless lady with a set of knitting needles. He used doctors and hospital staff members. He used cab drivers, airline pilots, airline crews, and all the "what's their names?" that make up God's great family.

God has a shawl for you to wear. Let Him place it about you in His way with His chosen words or deeds.

Our proper response to His covering of love is …
THANK YOU!

CHAPTER SEVENTEEN

The Power of Endless Life: What to Do with It

God likes this earth that He created. God likes Heaven. He plans to combine them in a new Heaven and a new earth.

Our distorted way of thinking includes thinking incorrectly about this earth. It is not a worn-out structure marked for demolition. Instead, it is a creation marked for remarkable refurbishment by combining Heaven and earth as one.

This picture and truth is vividly described by the apostle John, who was caught up into Heaven to get the real scoop on what God was thinking and will do one day.

> *Then I saw a new heaven and a new earth, for the first heaven
> and the first earth had passed away, and the sea was no more.
> And I saw the holy city, the New Jerusalem, coming down out of
> heaven from God, prepared as a bride adorned for her husband.
> And I heard a loud voice from the throne saying, "Behold, the
> dwelling place of God is with man. He will dwell with them,
> and they will be his people, and God himself will be with them
> as their God. He will wipe away every tear from their eyes, and
> death shall be no more, neither shall there be mourning nor
> crying nor pain anymore, for the former things have passed
> away." And he who was seated on the throne said, "Behold, I am
> making all things new." Also he said, "Write this down, for these
> words are trustworthy and true." And he said to me, "It is done!*

I am the Alpha and the Omega, the beginning and the end. To
the thirsty I will give from the spring of the water of life without
payment. The one who conquers will have this heritage, and I will
be his God and he will be my son" (Revelation 21:1-7).

Earlier in this book, we attended God's first press conference with Moses. Now we are privileged to enjoy this press release, one given to John in Heaven. It calls for careful thought because it requires reversing much of our thinking. This account is not about our leaving earth to go to Heaven. It is about Heaven coming here with us.

A new Heaven and a new earth are merging. This is an improved Heaven and an improved earth now combined. A prefabricated city is coming down, not going up.

Press Release: Heaven Is Coming Here!

This remarkable city is the centerpiece of what God announced in this press release. God is coming with the city that He calls His dwelling place. Note that He is coming to dwell with us to bring a dwelling He says is so elaborately created it is like a wedding gown.

He will be at home here with us. We will be at home with Him. The summary of this amazing press release is: *"Behold, I am making all things new."* He also said, *"Write this down, for these words are trustworthy and true."*

God is coming here! Heaven is coming here! Our "here" will be remade to look like His original masterpiece, but enhanced and enlarged to include a home for His family of sons and daughters. This is our inheritance. This is God's original plan, re-enacted, because His Son made a covenant with His Father and kept it.

In this disclosure to John, God makes clear this finished, eternal plan: *"And he said to me, 'It is done! I am the Alpha and the Omega, the beginning and the end. To the thirsty I will give from the spring of the water of life without payment. The one who conquers will have this heritage, and I will be his God and he will be my son'"* (vv. 6-7).

The eternal God had an eternal plan. He put eternity in our hearts, as we saw earlier. We are eternal beings. We choose to live forever with God or choose to live forever apart from God.

The power of endless life is a description of the life God offers us. Everyone is going to live forever. Some have eternal life. Some have eternal existence. But all live forever.

The phrase "the power of endless life" is found in the prefiguring of Christ's role for us and found in a unique man in Scripture. He is Melchizedek. I have never known a child named after him, but he is a person of great importance.

Some have eternal life. Some have eternal existence. But all live forever.

He pictures Christ as a priest who takes our case and makes everything right between God and us. The mystery of his life includes no mention of His father or mother and no record of the beginning of his life or the end of it (Hebrews 7:3).

His role was to live a life *"resembling the Son of God … he continues a priest forever"* (Hebrews 7:3). But this succinct description of the life he lives is a preview of Christ, *"who has come, not according to the law of a fleshly commandment, but according to the power of an endless life"* (Hebrews 7:16, NKJV).

Endless Life Is Shared in Christ

When we consider the power of an endless life, we discover in its endless continuity a power enjoyed that connects us to God and to His eternal plan.

Other translations read as, or similar to: "the power of an indestructible life." Such a life that is indestructible, or endless, means we enter that life through Christ. There is a world of difference, or, better said, a kingdom of difference, between the power of an endless life and an endless existence. Actually there are two worlds of difference. One is the world of fellowship with God as His child, and the other is a world estranged from the One who offered Himself to us.

Eternal life is the life of God returned to us in Christ. As I have emphasized, Adam and Eve had eternal life but failed to carry it to full term. Death came to them as a veil of separation, just as God had declared. Yet in Christ they too regain the promise of God for endless life.

The eternal Christ came with endless life in a human body once again. His life as God in a man gave Him the authority to die and conquer death. The authority of God's own Son, experiencing physical death and returning in a resurrected body, defeated death.

A succinct review of the eternal One who gave us eternal life at the cross is found in this passage in Colossians:

He is the image of the invisible God, the firstborn of all creation.
For by him all things were created, in heaven and on earth,
visible and invisible, whether thrones or dominions or rulers or
authorities—all things were created through him and for him.
And he is before all things, and in him all things hold together.
And he is the head of the body, the church. He is the beginning,
the firstborn from the dead, that in everything he might be
preeminent. For in him all the fullness of God was pleased to
dwell, and through him to reconcile to himself all things, whether
on earth or in heaven, making peace by the blood of his cross
(Colossians 1:15-20*).*

Christ knew the meaning of eternal life as no one else. He had an eternal experience with life. His definition of eternal life therefore must be valued as the most complete definition ever given. The Holy Spirit gives us the record of His prayer as He speaks with the Father. In prayer He gave this definition of eternal life: *"And this is eternal life, that they know you the only true God, and Jesus Christ whom you have sent"* (John 17:3).

Don't let the brevity of this definition of eternal life cause you to discount the significance of the truth. Jesus declared that eternal life is knowing the only true God. Stated as part of the prayer, Jesus is agreeing with His Father that knowing His Father is the only way to have eternal life.

He further makes it unmistakable that you cannot know His Father as the true God without knowing His Son, Jesus Christ. It is interesting that He does not refer to Himself as "knowing me" but as "Jesus Christ, whom you have sent."

Knowing God By Knowing Jesus Christ

We do not know God until we know Jesus Christ. God can come to us wearing a disguise—and often does. We may not know who He is at first. But that disguise will always come off when the discovery occurs that we know God by knowing Jesus Christ.

The true God is God who came in the person of Jesus Christ. Knowing Him as God, displayed in His Son, is the only way to know Him. Altering whatever concept we may have embraced is part of the repentance factor so essential to our being at ease with God and with ourselves.

Another perspective of this essential understanding is found in these words:

> *And this is the testimony, that God gave us eternal life, and this life is in his Son. Whoever has the Son has life; whoever does not have the Son of God does not have life. I write these things to you who believe in the name of the Son of God that you may know that you have eternal life. And this is the confidence that we have toward him, that if we ask anything according to his will he hears us* (1 John 5:11-14*).*

There is no way to misunderstand this statement: *"Whoever does not have the Son of God does not have life."* Not having the Son of God in your life means you do not have eternal life.

God is not leveling with you on this issue to offend you or threaten you. He is letting you know that if you don't have Christ in your life, you truly don't have eternal life.

Not having eternal life does not mean you are exempt from receiving this power of endless life. You can exercise this God-given right, as I have emphasized throughout this book.

God is not leveling with you on this issue to offend you or threaten you.

He wants you to know it is the lack of knowledge, or the brain blockage of not seeing Him for who He is, that causes this spiritual blindness.

This disclosure gets even clearer from John's letter: *"And we know that the Son of God has come and has given us understanding, so that we may know him who is true; and we are in him who is true, in his Son Jesus Christ. He is the true God and eternal life. Little children, keep yourselves from idols"* (1 John 5:20, 21).

Notice the emphatic repetition: *"He is the true God and eternal life."* In the true God, there is eternal life. Without the true God, there is eternal existence rather than eternal life.

An Idol Is a Man-Made Image of God

The truth that most needs to impact us is this warning: *"Little children, keep yourselves from idols."* This means that to walk away from the true God is to walk on with an idol.

An idol is a man-made image of God. The image may exist only as an image in the brain, but it is an idol as real as the one crafted from any metal, piece of wood, or a location considered sacred.

Our brain has remarkable capacities. Dr. Swenson reminds us that thoughts in our brain become pictures or images. "Our three-pound brain is the most complex arrangement of matter ever discovered in the universe. It contains ten billion neurons (possibly ten times as many as that) and has 100 trillion neurological interconnections that if stretched out would extend 100 thousand miles.... Each of us carries around a mental videotape cassette containing three trillion pictures."[92]

Among the three trillion pictures, the brain can contain idols we construct with our thoughts, which may very well be the image that hides God from us. Idols are man's image of God, which is the reverse of God's intention in creation—man bearing the image of God! We either have a god we make in our image, or we allow God to return us to an image He calls "a new creation" (2 Corinthians 5:17).

Jesus did not come to scare hell out of people. He came to love hell out of people. That love led Him to make clear the fact there is not only a Heaven, there is a hell.

Knowing the True God—And Enjoying Him Eternally

He warned about hell as the forfeiture of God's offer of Himself. To refuse God or shun one so remarkably perfect as His Son is to have missed life already.

If it were possible to go to Heaven without knowing God, it would not be Heaven at all. Eternal life is knowing the true God. Without knowing the true God, Heaven would be an eternity of being ill at ease, at the least, or a burning cauldron of anguish, at the worst.

Heaven with all of the vistas and experiences is primarily about being in the presence of God. That presence is here now if we are willing to learn to identify what we are seeing and experiencing. To be ill at ease with the presence of God now would mean spending eternity in an awkward, even anguishing awareness.

Among the many things Dallas Willard thought through was the fact that not everyone would like Heaven if they could get there. I referenced part of his insight in my introduction. Here is more:

> I am thoroughly convinced that God will let everyone into heaven who, in his considered opinion, can stand it. But "standing it" may prove to

be a more difficult matter than those who take their view of heaven from popular movies or popular preaching may think. The fires of heaven may be hotter than the other place.[93]

Dallas gives you a few minutes to check out the weighty possibility that people talking about wanting to go to Heaven might not like it at all! Then he adds:

> It might be helpful to think occasionally of how, exactly, I would be glad to be in Heaven if I make it…. I often wonder how happy and useful some of the fearful, bitter, lust-ridden, hate-filled Christians I have seen involved in church or family or neighborhood or political battles would be if they were forced to live forever in the unrestrained fullness of the reality of God—and with multitudes of beings really like him.

> There is a widespread notion that just passing through death transforms human character…. But I have never been able to find any basis in scriptural tradition or psychological reality to think this might be so…. What would one *do* in heaven with a debauched character or a hate-filled heart?[94]

Dear reader, God has given you the right to decide. He honored you with a choice. You now can honor Him with your choice to believe Him for what He has done for you as well as to believe Him for who He is—the true God as revealed in Jesus Christ, His Son.

Write out your own declaration that you believe Him and trust Him with your life. Or speaking aloud, tell Him that you believe Him and trust Him with your life. This will begin a learning curve of getting to know Him. Following Him involves steps—one step at a time.

Knowing God–And Enjoying His Presence

Knowing Him comes with following Him and knowing His presence with you. Find others who know him and follow Him. His family has family gatherings. Gather with them to learn and to reach out to others.

What one would do in Heaven with a "debauched character or a hate-filled heart" is a very important issue. But an even greater issue is: what will *anyone* do in Heaven?

Our proper response to the power of endless life is …

THANK YOU!

CHAPTER EIGHTEEN

Don't Save Eternity Until Later

Living out of God's limitless supply of love, found in the power of endless life, starts now! Eternity is an extension of God's life being both shared with us and extended through us to all of His creation.

We were created to be co-managers with Him of all of His creation. Our love-starved, performance-obsessed culture knows little about love or eternity.

We ride on a planet awaiting further development. Our planet in turn rides the orbits of space, but it is tiny compared to some of its neighbors. Our universe shares space in a galaxy that is like a pebble along the beach.

We are being trained for management of the entire family estate. God may be adding to it regularly. That information has not been discussed with the family here, but it will be at the right time.

The misconceptions of religious tradition have planted thoughts in our mental files that are far from reality. Such is true of our limited concept of Heaven.

Heaven Is Not a Long Vacation

A popular concept many hold is that Heaven is an escape to a long vacation made up mostly of an unending church service. Yet in my sixty-plus years of being what is called a professional pastor, I have never known pastors who wanted to take their vacation in a long church service. *They* don't even like too many services here!

And auditioning for the eternal choir does not appeal to many. So, what are we going to do forever?

It will take forever to complete the plans that God has for us to be part of the management of all of creation. Our family management team needs to get used to long-range planning, eternal-range planning. We need to adjust our thinking to never-ending skills and engagements, not just work to make enough to be comfortable until we retire.

Working with God is working with love. Loving God includes loving work. If work now is just a job we must keep to survive, we have missed the essence of life as He intended it.

Enslavement to work as our provider is a form of slavery instead of joint ownership with God and His family. Nearly half of our waking life is spent at work. Without God's presence and counsel, we just have a job. *With* God's presence and counsel, we have management in a family business.

We Are Working with God, Not for God

None of God's family is unemployed, because the kingdom of God has no unemployment. We are all working with God in the family business. *"For we are God's fellow worker"* (1 Corinthians 3:9, NASU).

Taking God into our work results in God taking work to a new level of enjoyment and purpose. It may not even be a job we like. Choosing to take God to work with you is not about telling everyone you are a Christian, but being God's family member in what you do.

God Shares Management of His Big Estate

God has a big family. He has a big estate. He has big plans for developing what only His creative DNA enables us to do with Him.

We know our galaxy as the Milky Way. Our planet, known as the blue planet, shares the stars or suns in this special neighborhood with other planets. Mars is half our size, but Jupiter is so massive that one thousand Earths could fit inside.

Now fasten your thinking seat belt. Swenson writes: "The universe contains at least a hundred billion other galaxies. Each is peppered with about a hundred billion stars…. These galaxies are spread across the expanse of the universe yet not evenly … in other areas however there are clusters of galaxies together and even superclusters."[95]

A lot of real estate owned by the family will need attention. Vast Texas-sized ranches will look like tiny cups growing a plant in a science lab.

Our role is to step into the management of the family enterprise. It is a big estate. Don't plan on driving across it in a day. You will have seen a tiny fraction of it after just the first year.

Life Ought to Work: Effectively, Efficiently, Meaningfully

Everyone has enough of God's DNA as a carryover from creation to have a sense that life *ought to work*. In fact, every culture and every religious system on earth is saying things ought to work.

We intuit that systems we use ought to be effective, efficient, and meaningful. That is why we keep inventing and perfecting. DNA from a creator gives us creativity. Only fear keeps people from pursuing intuitive desires to create something not existing before. That is Godlikeness in our makeup, whether we are children or just friends of the family. And friends of the family can become members of the family by believing Him. Enemies of the family can become members by the same believing experience! Saul of Tarsus, whose life we have reviewed, was such an enemy. As Saul he was every bit as strategizing a terrorist as any today.

Enemies of the family can become members by the same believing experience!

Saul's story is that an enemy became a family member, with full rights belonging to every child of God through spiritual likeness in Christ.

Enemies of the family can become members by the same believing experience!

We see things and do not know how to identify them, just as Mike May did not know what he was seeing. Intuitively, that causes us to want in on it. Well, guess what? God wants us in on it forever. It will take forever to see it all, to understand it all, and to enjoy it all.

But don't expect to find something so big you can go off by yourself without God and others. You will do it with God and with others whom you already know and love. Others you will get to know will be equally enjoyable and stimulating.

All Creation Is Longing for New Management

Our world is waiting for new management. New management is being prepared. Life is about being prepared to live and manage the creation of God forever. Here is the way Scripture puts it. Now get this, because it is the *Better Homes and Gardens* edition of what God plans for the housing developments of eternity.

> *For the creation waits with eager longing for the revealing of the sons of God. For the creation was subjected to futility, not willingly, but because of him who subjected it, in hope that the creation itself will be set free from its bondage to decay and obtain the freedom of the glory of the children of God. For we know that the whole creation has been groaning together in the pains of childbirth until now. And not only the creation, but we ourselves, who have the first-fruits of the Spirit, groan inwardly as we wait eagerly for adoption as sons, the redemption of our bodies (Romans 8:19-24, RSV).*

Notice this statement: *"The whole creation has been groaning together in the pains of childbirth until now."* This is not the groaning of death. Creation is waiting for a birthing experience. It is the beginning of a new day—not the ending of the old.

All Creation Is Ill At Ease

All creation is ill at ease. Creation's lack of ease comes from the labor pains of giving birth to a new way of management.

The labor pains of longing for new management is better understood when we reflect on the memory of our cells. The labor pains of seeking to birth new management includes our bodies, the highest order of God's creative genius. Our cells with the codes reflecting God's genius call for the same good management.

The groaning or laboring for the birthing of God's intended management is the desire for sons of God to take their intended place. Creation is not groaning for ecologists to guide nature's management. In case you are an ecologist and think I have dishonored you, please understand I have great respect for you. Nor is creation straining with groans for pastors or religious professionals to take the lead. In fact, no professional is being called for. The hopeful anticipation is for sons of God, those who are hearing God's affirmation of who they are, where they are as relates to why they are here, and who can be believed for answers to all of life's issues.

Through hearing God, sons of God have access to God that no one else can experience. These sons may not be distinguished professionals, but they are longed for—not for professionalism but for likeness: likeness to God in thought, character, and behavior. God's family—members without letters of academic achievement—turned the world upside down in the first century because they could hear God and confound the wise. It is likeness to God in His children that creation yearns to see birthed. Our bodies may be the first to know the difference when one of God's children is managing the medical clinic known as the human body.

A body created with cells from God's encoding finds itself in a schizoid, or conflicted state, when the thinking in the mind contradicts the creator. Cells outside the brain know their created role. Cells within the brain are part of choosing what to think and do. Neurons with cellular roles in the mind entertain thoughts that are in opposition to the rest of the body's codes, resulting in both mental and neurological lack of ease. We have the choice. That gift is ours to realign our cells engaged in thought with the cells coded throughout our body.

All of creation's intricate systems know new management is needed. Only sons and daughters of earth's creator will be familiar with methods and practices that created the first garden. As sons and daughters we will take our place in having dominion, or management, under the guidance of the Father.

Previews of This New Management

As early as Isaiah, God spoke of a new garden that was planned for this earth. Look at this reality:

> For the Lord comforts Zion; He comforts all her waste places and makes her wilderness like Eden, her desert like the garden of the Lord; joy and gladness will be found in her, thanksgiving and the voice of song (Isaiah 51:3).

Ezekiel also saw the same plans God had drawn up to restore the garden:

> And they will say, "This land that was desolate has become like the Garden of Eden, and the waste and desolate and ruined cities are now fortified and inhabited." Then the nations that are left all around you shall know that I am the Lord; I have rebuilt the

ruined places and replanted that which was desolate. I am the Lord; I have spoken, and I will do it (Ezekiel 36:35, 36).

Our family membership and our management with the Father, His Son, and the Holy Spirit means that everything can be made to work the right way again. All nature has been waiting for the sons of God to get back to management. Orphanages cannot and will not bring things to the order God intends. Creation knows the difference.

Orphanages create a kind of class structure or caste structure in which the elite manage and the rest follow orders. Creation is not waiting with eager anticipation for more orphans to have a try at management. There is no eager longing for more of the same—the wait is for those who carry God's life in them and think with God's thoughts.

Sons and daughters are made new creations with the DNA of God's Spirit. God shares Himself in Christ, who shares with us the family enterprise, His eternal purpose. The real managers engage because they are heirs, and thus already owners.

Owner/Managers Enjoy Work

In the convoluted thinking of our day we have created a view of work and creative productive engagement that says to only do as much as is required so we can have time off. We work like wage earners instead of owner/managers. Time off is getting to the weekend or getting to retirement. A restaurant chain exists that capitalizes on the mistaken concept of work, and they make it their brand: TGIF—Thank God It's Friday.

Teaching ophthalmologist Dr. Michael Siatkowski told me: "I always tell my residents who complain about work that God never made work as a punishment but as a blessing. They have a choice to work from this perspective, and if they do, they will see and learn things never imagined that will change their life."

Striving for retirement as soon as possible is the same escapist way of thinking. Work and productivity are healthy. Our best days are ahead of us, never behind us. God yearns to share life with us, enjoy life with us, and teach us His creative and productive ways of engagement.

The Limitless Wonder of the Mind

A friend of mine grew up in a fairly dysfunctional home. The most positive thing about his home was there was an attempt to honor God. Yet the image his family had of God led to religion as a duty that made God seem harsh and demanding.

In my friend's heart as a child were thoughts about God that were pure and perceptive. He knew God loved him and had more for him than he could imagine. From childhood, his mind was wired for high voltage. He was equipped to think with God and ask God to show him His ways and His secrets.

At the age of six, he watched a thunderstorm out the window of his home in a Texas coastal city. The energy of that storm led this six-year-old to conclude that there is more energy in this world than we know about or understand.

So, standing there at the window watching the storm, he asked God his Father to show him some of the sources of energy waiting for discovery. Years went by before his prayer as a boy was answered.

God knows when it is time to share His plans. He knows who is ready to hear Him and to receive what He has to say.

In the very center of downtown Fort Worth, in a small apartment, God began to show him a source of energy that already exists and is waiting to be released. It was a matter of placing the existing energy in exacted space in order to release what God had already provided.

God knows when it is time to share His plans. He knows who is ready to hear Him and to receive what He has to say.

Several years later, after he saw this remarkable principle and how it would work, he built the working model. I have seen this energy demonstrated in a laboratory test. This invention has the potential to change the energy supply for the entire world. Because I have signed a letter of non-disclosure, I am not at liberty to share more unless the public release of this remarkable invention occurs before the printing of this book.

This kind of creative, breakthrough provision is why it will take forever to explore all that this universe houses. My friend, a gifted, remarkable man, was wired for high voltage. We are all wired with a God-determined voltage that is much higher than what we are using.

The mind of Christ is yours to enjoy and use for interaction. Learning to think with God about every issue is a key to everything you face.

Endless Life Offers Endless Fulfillment

The power of endless life gives us a sense of continuity and the satisfaction of endless fulfillment. The sense of life ending, and with it the enjoyment of this earth taken from us, offers nothing but regret that something so magnificent would cease.

The good news is that it will not end, nor will the earth cease to be. What lies ahead is a restoration of everything. Earth will be restored as a new earth. Heaven will be restored to the earth, so the new heaven and the new earth will be joined as one. That is previewed in the kingdom of heaven Jesus presented as open and operative with His presence.

You are not going to face the end of your life. Your life won't end. You will face the transition of your life, but that is *not* the end. Dallas Willard punctuated this truth by saying, "You are never going to cease existing, and there is nothing you can do about it."[96]

We Are Never Finished with Life or Life's Work

Years ago, when a week's vacation occurred, my temperament was to fully enjoy only the first four days of it. After the fourth day, I was more than halfway to the end. So the fifth day was really worth only a half-day of vacation time, in my mind, since I was already partly engaged in re-entry thoughts.

By the sixth day, my regret that the time of relaxation was all but gone made it seem that most of it was already gone. By the seventh day, it *was* gone. I was already packed, just not out the door. I was still physically present at the vacation site, but in my mind I was already back to the very routines I had enjoyed being away from for four of the seven days.

Many people face death like that. At about the time they become the most productive, life is about over. When they are the most at ease with themselves and those around them, they realize it is getting much closer to the time to leave.

Leaving a place so lovely and people so enjoyable is like leaving a most meaningful time in which the projects we worked on and the dreams we dreamed aren't all complete.

What about the things we were working on here? What about the plans we had to see cities transformed and nations find their place in God's protective provision? The fact is, death should be viewed as a graduation, not a termination. To die is gain, not loss. (See Philippians 2:21 for this truth.) Graduation for this school of training occurs in death. A graduation occurs because we have reached a stage of being ready to enjoy life in a greater, more fulfilling way.

Seeing What God Sees: The City of Life

We will be part of seeing Eden and the garden as described by Isaiah and Ezekiel and even more clearly by John in the Revelation. He saw a city as a centerpiece of the combined Heaven and earth.

Its size boggles the mind. It is 1,400 miles in length, width, and height. If it was centered in North America, it can be estimated that it would stretch from Canada to Mexico and from just beyond the Rocky Mountains to the Appalachians.

Because it is a cube, there are as many levels in height as in breadth. Depending on the height of the ceiling of each "floor," you can imagine the endless space included.

The beauty of the city gets the most attention. Every imaginable part of creation blushing with beauty is described. The most succinct description of that beauty is summarized in these words: *"It shone with the glory of God, and its brilliance was like that of a very precious jewel"* (Revelation 21:11).

The beauty of the city gets the most attention. Every imaginable part of creation blushing with beauty is described.

Then comes the description of the city's focal point. At the center of the city is a river. The name of the river is taken from God's original act of creation. This city is named to commemorate what God had in mind as He made the masterpiece of creation and breathed into him the breath of life.

Life Is the Centerpiece of the City of God

God had life in His mind. The Water-of-Life River flowing with the endless, eternal energy of God's life is in the middle of the city's boulevard.

Along the sides of the river is a tree named in the original garden. It is the tree of life. The description is not of *trees* being located on each side of the river of life, but as *the tree*. This may suggest the tree is like a canopy covering the flow of life beneath it.

The Water-of-Life River flowing with the endless, eternal energy of God's life is in the middle of the city's boulevard.

The most basic need for physical survival is water. Our bodies reflect that essential element of survival. Remember that Dr. Swenson informed us that sixty percent of our body is water. At the center of the new garden in this gigantic city is an endless water supply of life.

The tree of life, taking the needed moisture from the river of life, is covered with leaves for healing. The healing of the nations is found in the tissues of these leaves. Healing from all the hurts and all the pain of the nations for all of time is provided. Every nation will be part of this gigantic municipality of the redeemed from all the ages.

Fruit on the tree of life is described as being grown on a monthly schedule. Instead of a crop of fruit every year, or maybe twice a year, this tree has fruit year-round.

You may read the word picture of what I am describing from the original words written by John in Revelation 22:1, 2. My suggestion is that you read it in several contemporary translations. It contains a verbal description of a flowing river with a covering of a tree. Both the river and the tree contain life.

The name of this city could appropriately be The City of Life, though the Bible does not give it that name. God's life creates the boundaries and the functions of this remarkable government of family order.

The family members will not leave the presence of God in this city of life. No city limits signs will be posted. There will be limitless life and a limitless awareness of God's magnificent being.

We will dwell in a city developed and owned by our Father and jointly owned for further development with our family. Family enterprises and expansions will call the best from us and mean endless fulfillment. The power of endless life will be the power supply of this city, where God's very presence will reside.

God's presence with us in God's new garden creation will enable us to be eternally at ease.

Our proper response to His gift of the power of endless life is …

THANK YOU!

CHAPTER NINETEEN

The Lord's Prayer Becomes Our Prayer

The digital age has enabled us to hear each other as never before. Smartphones have linked us to each other and whatever pursuit we choose from the almost limitless applications available.

There are almost as many cell phone users in today's world as there are people, nearly 6 billion according to a U.N. Telecom Agency report. Probably a third of those are the sophisticated smartphones that are small computers offering almost limitless information.

Even the Bible can be accessed in the handheld computers we often see pressed to someone's ear. A pastor friend of mine was leading a Bible study and asked a young man to read from another translation from his smartphone. "My Bible has lost its power," was the young man's reply.

Technology has created a social network that Leonard Sweet reviews in his book, *Viral.* This informed professor, an expert on sociological trends, believes that the current communications technology will enable us to see the greatest spiritual awakening since the first century.

The Greatest Communications Network Is Prayer

Yet an ever-greater network of communication often goes unused. We need to know that God can hear us and that we can hear Him. God's provision gives us access to Him anywhere and anytime without any dropped service or power loss. Access to God belongs to us. We see that in Jesus' basic teaching about how the Father thinks and how we can converse with Him.

Learning to think like God thinks leads us to be at ease as we listen to God as well as when we talk to God. God's acceptance of us in Christ and our acceptance of Him in us leads to our being at ease in all of God's ways, including prayer.

God's provision gives us access to Him anywhere and anytime without any dropped service or power loss.

Prayer is probably the most unused communication tool we can enjoy. Our biggest problem seems to be reversing the usual method of prayer that most employ. Prayer is not about speechmaking or getting God to hear us as much as it is about us hearing God and responding.

"But everyone must be quick to hear, slow to speak" (James 1:19, NASU). The ratio of our two ears to our one mouth verifies that the need to hear is far greater than the need to speak. That is especially true in prayer.

How to Pray Without Ceasing

One of the more challenging instructions I faced for much of my life was this verse: *"Pray without ceasing"* (1 Thessalonians 5:17). If prayer required a certain posture, a certain allotted time, a certain manner of speaking, then I knew this was an unrealistic, unattainable goal.

One day I suddenly realized that praying without ceasing is possible because there is never a time we are not listening. Even in sleep we are listening, just not consciously. Our conscious listening occurs continuously. We may not be listening for God, but choosing to do so easily connects us to His frequency of thought.

Prayer is thinking with God. God's thoughts include wanting to know our thoughts in prayer. Getting God's thoughts is what makes prayer, prayer.

His Prayer Becomes Our Prayer

A familiar prayer Jesus gave us is known as The Lord's Prayer. But if we accept it as the gift He intended, it becomes "Our Prayer." It is ours when we receive this remarkable insight into what the Father wants to talk about.

In this prayer, Jesus offered the talking points He knew the Father enjoys discussing. Yet it is our prayer as well, because God is our Father. If it was not our prayer, Jesus would have begun, "My Father." Instead, He again chose to share his relationship with the Father with us and used the plural pronoun "our" instead of the singular pronoun "my."

That reality is huge. We have this prayer as part of our family heritage and privilege.

Let's let our Father guide us in thinking with Him as part of prayer:

"Our Father who is in heaven" is God's address. But His address does not limit His location. Knowing the Father of Heaven is to know that He is as present here as He is there. He is at home with us here, and He makes us at home with Him there.

King David knew the meaning of the presence of God. His kingdom reign was a preview of the kingdom of One coming out of his family tree on earth. Christ's heritage on this earth included His right to reign from the throne of His father David (Luke 1:23).

That consciousness of His presence was so pronounced that David knew he could not be isolated from God's presence. The space I am carefully allotting to this point is very important.

You can't get away from God. If you are on the run, you should give up. He comes, calling you out from the tree behind which you are hiding—just as He did Adam.

Listen to this illumination from God's light of truth from David:

Where shall I go from your Spirit? Or where shall I flee from your presence? If I ascend to heaven, you are there! If I make my bed in Sheol, [the depths of the earth] you are there! If I take the wings of the morning and dwell in the uttermost parts of the sea, even there your hand shall lead me, and your right hand shall hold me. If I say, "Surely the darkness shall cover me, and the light about me be night," even the darkness is not dark to you; the night is bright as the day, for darkness is as light with you.

For you formed my inward parts; you knitted me together in my mother's womb. I praise you, for I am fearfully and wonderfully made. Wonderful are your works; my soul knows it very well. My frame was not hidden from you, when I was being made in secret, intricately woven in the depths of the earth. Your eyes saw my unformed substance; in your book were written, every one of them, the days that were formed for me, when as yet there were none of them.

*How precious to me are your thoughts, O God! How vast is the
sum of them! If I would count them, they are more than the sand.
I awake, and I am still with you* (Psalm 139:7-18).

As you can see, I have taken a lot of space in print to tell you that there
is no space between you and God! He is always there *with* you. He is always
there *for* you. He is there to offer Himself and all that belongs to Him. Yet,
He will always honor your decision. If you don't want Him with you, you will
likely never have consciousness of Him.

Wherever you look you should expect the scene to contain the presence
of God. He is there!

Where Would God Go If You Told Him to Go Away?

Because God is everywhere, whether you recognize Him or not, he will not
leave you. If you don't want Him with you, and you tell Him to go away,
where would He go? He would not go where He is already! Since He is already
everywhere, He will remain everywhere.

What you do with God's presence is still your choice every bit as much
as it was Adam and Eve's choice in the garden. It is yours to enjoy or yours
to ignore. If only Adam and Eve had asked, "Father, what do you think?" For
"*Our* Father in Heaven" means He is ours here and now, having sent part of
Himself and part of Heaven with His Son to this earth.

Honoring the Name of God

John Piper is one who scanned the meaning of the hallowed name of the
father and got it right. With helpful insight, he points out that Jesus is teaching us to pray, not to proclaim.

> "Hallowed be thy name" is a request, not a declaration. It is part of the
> prayer, not a public pronouncement. We are not saying, "Lord, your
> name *is* hallowed!" We are praying, "Lord, cause your name to be
> hallowed!" John Piper wrote:

> That is, cause your word to be *believed*, cause your displeasure to be
> *feared*, cause your commandments to be *obeyed*, and cause yourself to
> be *glorified*. You hallow the name of God when you trust him, revere
> him, obey him, and glorify him.[97]

The significant insight that this is a "request," not a "declaration," carries weight that cannot go overlooked. Getting His name right by calling Him Father is not the only point. Equal to knowing He is our Father is the fact His name is to be honored and revered by us first, and then by all who witness His presence. Hallowing or honoring His name starts with believing Him. We dishonor Him by refusing to believe Him.

This is made very clear in John's epistle:

> *If we receive the testimony of men, the testimony of God is greater, for this is the testimony of God that he has borne concerning his Son. Whoever believes in the Son of God has the testimony in him. Whoever does not believe God has made him a liar, because he has not believed in the testimony that God has borne concerning his Son. And this is the testimony, that God gave us eternal life, and this life is in his Son. Whoever has the Son has life; whoever does not have the Son of God does not have life (1 John 5:9-12).*

When we do not believe God, we still believe someone or something. We may believe our own flawed thinking. We may believe other people, whose thinking is just as suspect. Or we may believe the suggestion of the deceiver.

If we quote God without believing God, we behave no better than Adam and Eve. A father of lies convinced them to accept a deceptive offer. In doing so, their actions said the deceiver was the truth and God the liar.

Think this through: *"Whoever does not believe God has made him a liar."* Most of us are shocked to think that when we push back against what God has said, our unbelief dishonors God as if we call Him a liar.

Does this threaten God? Does that mean that God is out for revenge? No, it means God is out to change our thinking. If God were out to even the score, the whole world would have long since been vaporized.

Who loses when we won't believe? We lose, and others lose as well because we have not allowed the purpose of God to be extended through us.

God loses the joy of not being allowed to share Himself with us. Understand that your right to choice is the right to honor or dishonor God. Believe Him and you honor Him. Not believing Him is rank dishonor—as if He were a liar.

In asking for the hallowing of God's name, we are asking for our honor of Him to be evident in our believing. We believe Him and sign our names to His truth. He is the true God!

Your Kingdom Come

As God's son and likeness, Jesus provides the essence of God's greatest desire—to express and share Himself and His kingdom now and eternally. He wants our expectancy as we ask for that which He is eager to give. In His kingdom we find His presence and His way of working in synchronized harmony with the earth and our ways.

His eagerness to give His kingdom is partly because we can't mess it up. It is an unshakeable kingdom—one that is indestructible (Hebrews 12:26-29). God's kingdom is His ruling presence. He shares the rule with us as sons and daughters, but He never relinquishes control.

His eagerness to give His kingdom is partly because we can't mess it up. It is an unshakeable kingdom–one that is indestructible

In case you are wondering what His kingdom coming would look like and where it would go, here are some sightings:

And Jesus went throughout all the cities and villages, teaching in their synagogues and proclaiming the gospel of the kingdom and healing every disease and every affliction. When he saw the crowds, he had compassion for them, because they were harassed and helpless, like sheep without a shepherd (Matthew 9:35, 36, ESV).

"The kingdom of heaven is like treasure hidden in a field, which a man found and covered up. Then in his joy he goes and sells all that he has and buys that field. Again, the kingdom of heaven is like a merchant in search of fine pearls, who, on finding one pearl of great value, went and sold all that he had and bought it" (Matthew 13:44-46, ESV).

"Let the children come to me; do not hinder them, for to such belongs the kingdom of God. Truly, I say to you, whoever does not receive the kingdom of God like a child shall not enter it." And he took them in his arms and blessed them, laying his hands on them (Mark 10:14-16, ESV).

*"But if it is by the finger of God that I cast out demons, then the kingdom of God has come upon you" (*Luke 11:20, ESV*).*

*"Fear not, little flock, for it is your Father's good pleasure to give you the kingdom" (*Luke 12:32, ESV*).*

The kingdom comes where people are in need of God's supply. God's love and compassion contain God's supply of supernatural provisions. That means dis-ease is replaced with the order, or the ease, of God's ways. Though it was not the only evidence, healing was a clear demonstration of kingdom benefits.

God's Will on Earth, Just As in Heaven

God's will is the execution of His perfection and love. Heaven is ruled with the will of God. God's throne marks His right to rule. God's rule is God's forever role.

God rules because His perfect love extends all power and authority in Heaven and on earth. The kingdom of Heaven coming here includes the ruling presence of God in every sphere of influence on this earth.

God desires to extend His rule to every realm of our life. Wherever life exists, God offers to share Himself with ruling excellence. All of His creation will ultimately know His ruling presence.

When we choose God, we are choosing what He chooses—His will. Choosing God's choice for us means we believe Him for who He is as well as what He does. God's will in Heaven, being operative here, begins in us. We choose His will as ours here, now!

Because God has all power and because He loves with a perfect love, we can be assured His will is superior to any alternative. If He loved with perfect love but lacked all power, He could not provide what His love desires for us.

Give Us Today Our Daily Need

The gift of our bread is our daily need. Bread represents the basic need for sustaining our life. God has supplies. We have needs. He promises to supply our every need.

Paul knew this reality as part of his life experience. He shared this promise with us: *"And my God will supply every need of yours according to his riches in glory in Christ Jesus"* (Philippians 4:19).

God has supplies. We have needs. He promises to supply our every need.

Before a need exists, God's supply is waiting to fill it. That is the daily provision God has made for our well-being. The supply originates in God's abundance, or riches of His presence, found in the glory of Christ Jesus. Paul knew this provision on a daily basis.

Today, you may claim from the Father your need. We have already seen that our time zone with God is the present. Anxiety about the past, the present, or the future contributes nothing to life.

God was with us in the past whether we honored Him or recognized Him at all. He will be with us in the future, but His eternal presence is not experienced in either the past or the future, but in *today*—right now. Having God's presence today means we have God's provisions for this very time of need.

Paul had learned this today-time-zone was an "eternal now." He said, *"The life I now live, I live by the faith of the son of God"* (Galatians 2:20). God's presence now means our future is God's presence.

From His presence comes His provision. Our asking is not for things, but for His presence. With His presence, He supplies our needs from His own abundance. Our needs being met are epiphanies containing His presence. UPS or FedEx could deliver the supply, but they originate in God's own loving presence and carry that presence with them.

We ask for bread and discover what Jesus said:

Jesus said to them, "I am the bread of life; whoever comes to me shall not hunger, and whoever believes in me shall never thirst. But I said to you that you have seen me and yet do not believe. All that the Father gives me will come to me, and whoever comes to me I will never cast out. For I have come down from heaven, not to do my own will but the will of him who sent me. And this is the will of him who sent me, that I should lose nothing of all that he has given me, but raise it up on the last day. For this is the will of my Father, that everyone who looks on the Son and believes in him should have eternal life, and I will raise him up on the last day" (John 6:35-40, ESV).

We ask for bread and bread is given. The bread does not have the label of the local bakery. It was the same bread that Jesus ate every day, the bread of the Father's provision found in His presence.

He explained what it meant to eat this bread: *"For I have come down from heaven, not to do my own will but the will of him who sent me. And this is the will of him who sent me … that everyone who looks on the Son and believes in him should have eternal life, and I will raise him up on the last day."*

Ask for today's bread for today's need. Accept it as being yours. Eat it with thanksgiving. God has supplied. You have received. He has come, personally, to meet your need. Each day He is your daily provision.

The Forgiveness of Forgiving

Claiming forgiveness is needed for two reasons. We must know we are forgiven if we are to be at ease with God and ourselves. It is equally true that we must forgive others so we are at ease with both ourselves and with them. Failure to forgive does more damage to us than the ones whom we refuse to forgive.

Jesus tied our forgiveness from the Father to the forgiveness we share with others. We ask Him to "forgive our sins as we forgive those who sin against us." The experience of receiving forgiveness is inseparable from our need to grant forgiveness to those who wrong us.

God's grace and mercy that forgives us cannot be enjoyed without us granting the same grace and mercy to others. We are not forgiving in order to earn forgiveness for ourselves. We are forgiving because we have experienced this gift and choose to pass it on.

Jesus claimed God's forgiveness on the cross, as I have emphasized already. He claimed it for the undeserving. That forgiveness is ours to receive by believing a gift from God's heart of compassion and mercy.

> ## We are not forgiving in order to earn forgiveness for ourselves. We are forgiving because we have experienced this gift and choose to pass it on.

To take forgiveness and not pass it on is to miss the meaning of being forgiven. The meaning of our forgiveness cannot be separated from our willingness to share forgiveness with others.

If we do not grant forgiveness, we do not know or enjoy true forgiveness. To know experientially God's forgiveness of our sins will always result in a desire for others to share in this discovery of His mercy and acceptance. Knowing forgiveness leads to sharing forgiveness.

God forgave you. Believe Him. Now, forgive yourself. Grant forgiveness to those who have offended and hurt you.

The crowd that crucified Jesus did not ask for forgiveness. But whether someone asks or doesn't ask, grant what they need. You have the need to forgive them as much as they have need to be forgiven.

Their hurtful ways may have been intentional or unintentional, but that is not the issue. You have a clean slate with God. Now, pass on this gift you have received.

Lead Us from Temptation

Temptation is a strategy to divert our attention from God's ability to supply our needs, and it is an issue we always face. Jesus' experience in temptation becomes a clear example. He was already affirmed by the Father as a Son who was completely pleasing. The temptation was to question what was already clearly confirmed.

Every temptation is an attempt to take our focus away from what God thinks. Temptation wants to take our focus from what God thinks of us and can do for us and suggests we think and do things independently from Him. It wants us busy doing things for Him instead of doing things with Him.

"For we are God's fellow workers" (1 Corinthians 3:8, 9, ESV). Our work is not *for* God, but *with* God. Working with God means we do whatever we do conscious of His leading, enabling, and empowering presence.

Had Jesus accepted the temptation to draw people to God with a sensational leap from the temple that required an angel to catch Him, He would have worked *for* God. Instead, He worked *with* God, letting God's presence with and in Him draw people. He did not tempt God, but yielded to God.

The enemy's subtle way of tempting us is usually with some "noble idea" such as what he presented to Adam and Eve. No more noble idea can be entertained than to be like God. But being like God comes from His workmanship, not our working at making ourselves into His image. We are clay. He is the potter who shapes our likeness into His.

Asking to be led means we are yielding ourselves to the guidance of our Father. Just as He led His Son Jesus, He leads us. The knowledge that there is temptation for God's children, starting with Adam and Eve, means we are asking to be guided past the danger zone of temptation.

Our lives are not governed by chance, by our ingenuity, or by the collective abilities of others. Our Father, who is wise beyond comparison and loving beyond measure, guides us. Our Father wants us to ask for His leadership so that the temptation to take our focus from Him does not occur.

God will use circumstances; the reasoning of our renewed, sound mind; and other people, both in His family as well as friends of His family—but He desires to guide our lives daily by speaking to us as we speak to Him.

As this prayer becomes our prayer, we can enter the value of these insights as if we were entering into the estate of our Father, just as the prodigal son did by entering the house with the father. Jesus gave us our right to address God as "our Father." Praying through it on a daily basis does not create a familiarity that lessens its ever-expanding relevance and assurance.

It was often part of the daily discipline of Dallas Willard to spend time praying through this limitless reservoir of wisdom and understanding.

Spend time often on the hillside with Jesus and listen to Him tell you how the Father thinks. Spend time often with the Father talking to Him about what He likes to talk about.

You are learning to think like the Father. Spend time with the Holy Spirit—let him guide you in prayer, knowing He is a prayer expert.

As He shares this prayer with you, you are now listening as well as talking to Him about what He most desires. He is "our Father," and this is "our prayer" given by His Son to guide a conversation led by the Holy Spirit. Be at ease!

Our proper response is …

THANK YOU!

CHAPTER TWENTY

Replanting Thoughts: Repentance

God has always intended for us to be like Him. In Christ He offers us access to our intended selves again.

> *He came to his own people, but they didn't want him. But whoever did want him, who believed he was who he claimed*
>
> *and would do what he said, He made to be their true selves,*
>
> *Their child-of-God selves. These are the God-begotten, not blood-begotten, not flesh-begotten, not sex-begotten (John 1:11-13, The Message).*

For us to be "our true selves, our child-of-God selves," as Eugene Peterson identifies, we let Christ live in us. He enters through our will or heart.

As usual, Dallas Willard thought that truth through to life. "The will, or heart, is the executive center of the self. Thus the center point of the spiritual in humans as well as in God is self determination, also called freedom and creativity."[98]

He further assists us in understanding we are spiritual, whether we want to be or not. "'Spiritual' is not just something we ought to be. It is something we are and cannot escape, regardless of how we may think or feel about it. It is our nature and our destiny."[99]

With further insight, Dallas reflects on thought: "But any positive characterization of the spiritual must also mention that, besides having power, persons, or selves, and their experiences are consciously directed upon various subject matters that concern them. That is, persons think, and their thoughts pick out or select specific objects past present or future. This is the activity of the mind. It is the cognitive aspect of the spiritual being a person is. No physical thing has it."[100]

Thinking About Thinking Forever

Our mind embodies the spiritual. Our brains will die, but our minds will think forever. Jesus told the story of a man who died and went on thinking. It was a story of contrasts as retold by Luke. One man had about everything—except a relationship with God. The other man had little except his relationship with God. Both died. Both continued to think.

> **Our brains will die, but our minds will think forever. Jesus told the story of a man who died and went on thinking.**

Jesus said that the man with everything except God cried out in hell for someone to go to earth and warn his five brothers. He was concerned that his brothers were following the same patterns of thought and life he had pursued. In torment, he wanted them to hear from someone from the dead lest they join him.

The answer God gave was that if they will not hear Moses and prophets who have already spoken, they won't believe the One risen from the dead (Luke 16:23).

What we think has eternal consequences. We will think forever. That is why knowing how God thinks and thinking with Him is so important.

While it is true that we need to let Christ live in our hearts, our wills, and our spirits, it is even more true that we need to let Him live in our thoughts. In our thoughts we allow the inner quality of life God intended to germinate and grow.

Thoughts, remember, are trees to choose from, as Dr. Leaf explains:

The surprising truth is that every single thought—whether it is positive or negative[—]goes the same cycle when it forms. Thoughts are basically electrical impulses, chemicals and neurons. They look like a tree with branches. As the thoughts grow and become permanent, more branches grow and the connections become stronger.

As we change our thinking, some branches go away, new ones form, the strength of the connections change, and the memories network with other thoughts. What an incredible capacity of the brain to change and rewire and grow. Spiritually, this is renewing the mind.[101]

Thoughts Affect the Entire Body

Healthy thoughts are as important as healthy bodies. In fact they become an important part of the determination of our body's health. "Thoughts are not only scientifically measurable, but we can verify how they affect our bodies. We can actually feel our thoughts through our emotions…. In fact, for every memory you make, you have a corresponding emotion attached to it, which is stored in your brain, and as a photocopy in your body's cells."[102]

The linkage of our current health crisis in America to a thinking crisis is found in these important statements from research by Dr. Leaf.

> In fact, your thoughts create changes right down to the genetic levels, restructuring the cell's makeup. Scientists have shown the restructuring is how diseases are able to take hold in the body. On the flip side, when we choose non-toxic thinking, we step into a whole new realm of brain and body function. "Feel good" chemicals are released that make us feel peaceful and also promote healing, memory formation and deep thinking, which increase intelligence when combined together.

> Healthy, non-toxic thoughts help nurture and create a positive foundation in the neural networks of the mind. These positive thoughts strengthen positive reaction chains and release biochemicals, such as endorphins and serotonin from the brain's natural pharmacy. Bathed in these positive environments, intellect flourishes and with it mental and physical health.[103]

Thoughts Can Take You Captive

No wonder Scripture tells us to take every thought captive (2 Corinthians 10:5). If we don't, we may discover that thoughts have taken us captive. Understanding that thoughts determine whether we are at ease or in a state of dis-ease means we can take charge of our garden of thoughts.

An old nursery rhyme suggests we ought to be asking how our garden is doing. "Mary, Mary, quite contrary, how does your garden grow?" Once we know that our garden is overrun with weeds, briars, and other irritating plants, we understand why the plants of beauty and health-giving qualities are stunted, if not gone.

Dr. Leaf offers this hopeful conclusion from her two decades of research: "You can take back control of your body and mind! It is possible to lead an emotionally happy and physically healthy lifestyle simply by learning to control your thought life."[104]

Setting our mind is like setting out plants in our garden. What we grow is what we plant. *"Set your mind on things above"* (Colossians 3:2).

"Those who live by the spirit set their mind on things of the Spirit" (Romans 8:5). Our minds are set by our will. We are responsible for the thoughts that are entitled to live and grow there.

What we allow to grow among the plantings in our mind, which Dr. Leaf calls the "trees of your mind," leads to either stress or being at ease.

Our lack of being at ease results in graduated degrees of stress. Most stress is short-lived and quickly leaves. When stress is repeated, the plants of thought are getting a deeper root system. Fully developed stress-filled thoughts become damaging to our mind as well as our body. Again, Dr. Leaf assists us in this self diagnosis by identifying the three areas of our body most affected by stress that develops beyond the causal and short-lived phase: They are "the heart, the immune system and the digestive system."[105]

Our lack of being at ease results in graduated degrees of stress.

Out of her volumes of research, Dr. Leaf offers a recommended reading list of 366 books and scientific articles.[106] From these recognized publications, she draws specific conclusions, such as this important and pointed recommendation:

> You must confront repressed unforgiveness, anger, rage, hatred and any other form of toxic thinking. You have a medical need to forgive others and you also must forgive yourself.[107]

If we have no other motive to forgive others and pay off the charges we hold against them than our medical need, that would be enough. But, of course, there are many other needs connected to forgiveness.

The way to get forgiveness as well as pass it on is clear. God has it—we take it for ourselves, as He intends, and pass it on to others.

In Chapter Six, we looked at the testimony of God. His testimony is this: everything that belongs to Him is ours. Therefore whatever is needed for replacing the plants in our garden of thought, He is ready to supply.

Poisoned plants like poison ivy or poison oak can be replaced with healthy plants. While both poison ivy and poison oak look like beautiful vines, they are very dangerous.

Plants of thought in our mind may appear very attractive and innocent. Yet upon further analysis, they comprise dangerous elements to our well-being. "What you don't know can't hurt you" is one of those dangerous thoughts ever popularized by repetition. The fact is, what you don't know can *kill you.*

All of the poisoned plants of our thought life originate in fear. All the healthy plants in our garden of thought come from love.

Two Sources of Thought: Love or Fear

Dr. Leaf makes this insightful assertion as to the origin of our emotional reactions:

> There are only two types of emotions, each with their own anatomy and physiology: love and fear. Out of the love branch come emotions of joy, trust, caring, peace, contentment, patience, kindness, gentleness, etc. Fear-based emotions include bitterness, anger, hatred, rage, anxiety, guilt, shame, inadequacy, depression, confusion, etc.[108]

From these two sources of emotional reactions, love and fear, all of our thoughts and resultant behavior emanate. Love from God provides affirmation of His presence and protection. Fear provides anticipation of a pending threat. The quote of C.S. Lewis I used early in this book is an insight into the "terror" of being left out, or of impending loss.

It is probably easier to understand love's supply of positive emotions than fear's supply of negativity. Bitterness, anger, hatred, and rage, the emotions that Dr. Leaf lists—these are all acts of self-protection. That is also true of her entire list. Each is formed with contempt for a person, idea, or thing, to protect against what has already happened to us and/or will potentially happen.

Fear becomes a defense mechanism to guard us because we have lost the consciousness of God's presence with His attending provision and protection. On the hillside, Jesus spoke to this issue. His words rock our world of hearing without believing God. He points out the contempt we use against others as we label them with names, making them an object of our disdain, instead of the person God sees. Contempt strips them of personhood. Every enemy we have labeled comes from a source of fear in which the person is no longer more than an object worthy of hatred.

Jesus said we are to love our enemies. To do so we must see as God sees them. They may be wrong in their thoughts and ways, but they are a person for whom Christ gave His life. They can be loved to life. But they will only be hated to death.

This transforming power in Christ is clearly seen in the story of Ben Carson, from Chapter Five. Anger created by the fear of being hurt again by the taunting of a bully caused him to drive a knife blade at the stomach of the mouthy youth. But for a belt buckle becoming a shield to snap the blade, Ben Carson could have been another crime statistic. He affirmed that anger never attended his life again after the three hours he spent alone with God.

A broken knife blade led him to consult God about his anger. Following his freedom from anger, God guided him in his training to hold many finely honed blades in the scalpels he used performing world-renowned surgery. God's thoughts became his thoughts.

Every fear-induced thought can be replaced with a love-induced thought. We do not need to live with infected thoughts carrying the fear-contaminated flow of reasoning. Fear is just the opposite of what God thinks. God has never once been heard to say, "Well, I was afraid of that!" There is no fear in love—God is love!

Every fear-induced thought can be replaced with a love-induced thought.

God's offer remains: *"Come, let us reason together"* (Isaiah 1:18). Since God is love, He offers only love-filled thoughts. All fear comes out of our taking up the subtle suggestions of an enemy of God in our thoughts.

The same enemy who deceived Adam and Eve, with insidious thoughts that concealed his true intent with the "noble suggestion" of being like God, is the one who seeks to deceive us. *"For God has not given us a spirit of fear, but of power and of love and of a sound mind"* (2 Timothy 1:7, NKJV).

Examine Each Thought and Take Control

Since all thoughts are derived from either love or fear, it is essential that we come to grips with why it is so important to examine and take charge of each thought. We either accept the offer of love or the offer of fear—an offer of God or a spirit of deception.

Dr. Leaf points out the potential impact to our entire well-being as a result of thoughts that originate from fear: "In fact, research shows that fear triggers more than 1,400 known physical and chemical responses. This activates more than 30 different hormones and neurotransmitters combined, throwing the body into a frantic state."[109]

In contrast, she also describes the difference when love-filled thoughts are developed: "When we experience love emotions, our brains and bodies function differently… Science and the Bible teach us not to fear."[110]

Again she comments on the irrational nature of fear; these thoughts are from her book *The Gift in You*:

> It is really very interesting that scientists call this a "learned fear" because fear is not a natural part of how we were created. Fear is a distorted love circuit. We were created for love and all that goes with it, but we have learned fear.
>
> What we need to remember is this: A thought has an emotional component attached to it like a "chemical signature." Every time we think, we make chemicals that produce feelings and reactions in the body. Clusters of electrical thoughts with these chemical messengers create our attitudes. We express our attitudes—love or fear—through what we first think and then through the choices we make, which dictate what we say and do. When you add either love or fear emotions to a thought cluster and give it a unique flavor, then it becomes an attitude.[111]

Dr. Leaf also highlights the essential part that love plays in our mental makeup:

> Although we have discovered how powerful fear is, it is important to remember that love is much more powerful and our brains were made to operate in love. Each of us has our own familiar electrical chemical balance where we feel at peace. It is almost like an idle rate that runs on the love attitude….Even though you may not be able to choose your circumstances, you have the choice to operate in fear or love.[112]

As we have seen, two trees were named in the original garden. From the tree of life (knowledge of God), God's love is supplied, enriching each person who receives this abundant supply. From the tree of knowledge of good and evil (knowledge without God), comes fear, causing those who fed on it to live impoverished, ill-at-ease lives.

Dr. Leaf's exhaustive research must not be overlooked. She has identified two sources of thought that influence all of our thought life. Her book *The Gift in You* has two pages depicting the tree of love and the tree of fear. I could not agree more with her insightful conclusions.

Love-birthed thoughts are healthy. Fear-birthed thoughts are diseased. Getting our thoughts from God carries the guarantee that they are authentically filled with love and void of fear.

Love-birthed thoughts are healthy. Fear-birthed thoughts are diseased.

Garnering our thoughts from sources other than God leaves us vulnerable to fear-contaminated plants that will infect other plants.

We Choose Life or Death By Choosing Our Thoughts

God's offer of life or death as revealed to Moses still stands (Deuteronomy 30:19). His instructions reveal His desire for us: *"Now chose life."*

In the same way that we can choose life or death, we can choose our thoughts as well. If we want thoughts that originate in God's love and offer of life, we choose them. This is the benefit of choosing God's thoughts:

"That you may love the Lord your God, listen to his voice, and hold fast to him. For the Lord is your life, and he will give you many years" (Deuteronomy 30:20, NIV).

God's offer of Himself is found wherever we may turn. I repeat: wherever we look, we should expect to see God. He is there. We just don't understand how to recognize Him until we allow Him to teach us to see properly. The neurons of our spiritual mind must be activated by our desire for Him.

Listen to this declaration of His presence and His love:

What then shall we say to these things? If God is for us, who is against us? He who did not spare His own Son, but delivered Him over for us all, how will He not also with Him freely give us all things? Who will bring a charge against God's elect? God is the one who justifies; who is the one who condemns? Christ Jesus is

He who died, yes, rather who was raised, who is at the right hand of God, and who also intercedes for us. Who will separate us from the love of Christ? Will tribulation, or distress, or persecution, or famine, or nakedness, or peril, or sword?

But in all these things we overwhelmingly conquer through Him who loved us. For I am convinced that neither death, nor life, nor angels, nor principalities, nor things present, nor things to come, nor powers, nor height, nor depth, nor any other created thing, will be able to separate us from the love of God, which is in Christ Jesus our Lord (Romans 8:31-39, NASU).

God is for us—not against us.
He gave us His son to give us all things
Jesus gives us His life and took a place of power to pray for us.
Nothing can separate us from His love.

This list of possible barriers—death, life, angels, principalities, the present, the future, any powers, height, depth, or another created thing—cannot separate us from the love of God, which is in Christ Jesus, our Lord (vv. 37-39).

Students of Scripture know that, in Paul's letter to the Romans, he repeatedly asked for the response of the reader. He does it here in the opening verse: "What then shall we say to these things?" (He also asked the same basic question in Romans 6:1, Romans 7:7, and Romans 8:3.)

God Now Asks, "What Do You Think?"

In the book of Romans, God offers some of the most revolutionary thoughts the mind can entertain. Then He asks, "What will you say?" or, "What do you think?" These thoughts are weighty, with life-carrying issues, but God does not cram them into our thoughts. He lets us receive them or refuse them.

Let me ask you what you are thinking in light of these realities. What will you say to what God has said? Do you find yourself pushing back against God or pushing into God?

Once a thought occurs, we either embrace it or refuse it. In both embracing and refusing, we take the thought captive. Capturing thoughts is a right given by God.

The thought we keep is one we capture. The thought we refuse is also one we capture. Keeping what we capture or discarding what we capture is the issue. God's wants us to take charge of our thoughts instead of our thoughts taking charge of us!

Once a thought occurs, we either embrace it or refuse it. In both embracing and refusing, we take the thought captive.

Once the thought is captured or controlled by our will, we then choose to submit it or yield it to Christ. He is the standard for shaping our every thought, emotion, or impulse.

We destroy arguments and every lofty opinion raised against the knowledge of God, and take every thought captive to obey Christ (2 Corinthians 10:5, ESV).

For Christ to be part of our lives, our thoughts must provide an open door. Believing Him is the way we welcome Him in.

We hear God's voice. We see God's presence. Though we may not know whom we are hearing or whom we are seeing, God comes to all. If we allow Him to speak as well as show Himself to us, we come to know Him personally.

God's voice is heard in countless ways—God's presence is seen in many expressions. Because nature is one of the biggest and most obvious displays of God, no one can miss Him.

Thoughts make up the plants of our mind, which make up the garden inside us. We have spent much space in this book reviewing the garden God intended within us as well as around us.

The Landscape of Life Starts in the Garden of Our Thoughts

When the garden within Adam and Eve changed, the garden around them also changed.

Our thoughts make up the plants of the garden within us. When we think with God, our garden flourishes with lush plants. Thoughts that are not from Him create a garden of dangerous distortions and disease. Every thought matters because every thought contains life or death, blessings or curses, love or fear.

God created and planted His garden from His own thoughts. The exquisite beauty and perfection were expressions of Himself. He liked what He made and gave the "it is good" approval. Our garden of thoughts is ours to plant. From His thoughts we can have healthy life-giving thoughts coming from His indwelling presence—thoughts agreeing with His. These thoughts are ours to enjoy.

> *Fix your thoughts on what is true, and honorable, and right,*
> *and pure, and lovely, and admirable. Think about things that*
> *are excellent and worthy of praise…. Then the God of peace*
> *will be with you (*Philippians 4:8, 9, Holy Bible, New Living
> Translation*).*[113]

Our proper response to the God of peace sharing His thoughts with us as we create our own garden of thoughts should be …
THANK YOU!

CHAPTER TWENTY-ONE

If You Tell God to Leave, Where Will He Go?

Since God is everywhere, if you should decide to tell Him to leave, where would He go? Knowing God's whereabouts is our starting point for knowing who we are, where we are, and whose words we can believe.

The most basic issues of life are: *who we are, where we are,* and *who we can believe.*

By starting with God's identity and location, we can find ourselves. Quantum physics has provided evidence that the past, the present, and the future all converge in the experience of the eternal. While God does not need physics to prove anything, it is not insignificant that physicists and scientists have now become a strong voice in affirming the existence of God.

Gerald L. Schroeder, physicist, uses both physics and the Bible to locate God in the present:

> Creation of the universe from absolute and complete nothing marked the beginning of space, time[,] and matter. Theology has held that position for over three thousand years. Cosmology in the last decade or so has come to agree. These three parameters are characteristics of our universe not of the Creator. Just as the biblical God is not composed of space or matter, God is also not bound by time. God is outside of time. And being outside of time means to exist in an "eternal or unending now," an eternal present that includes past, present[,] and future simultaneously.[114]

The Meaning of God Being "Outside of Time"

We have proven that neither the physics of nature nor the genes of our bodies fix the future. We have seen that the Bible itself confirms that choice shapes the flow of events. If this is so, how does the Creator know our future even before we choose it?

The subtlety in the argument is that we are dealing with two frames of reference, one within and the one without the flow of time. For the Creator, being outside of time, a flow of events has no meaning. There is no future in the sense of what will "eventually" happen. The future and the past are in the present. An Eternal Now pervades, like a cloud coming at all times, not in the linear progression, but in simultaneity.

The concept of an Eternal Now is implied in the explicit four-letter name of God (Exodus 3:14). In the Hebrew, the spelling includes the letter of the verb "to be" in its three tenses: *I was, I am*, and *I will be*. The past, present, and future are all contained within the Eternal.

Physics Locates an Eternal Presence–God Is Here Now!

Einstein's discovery of the laws of relativity revealed the astonishing fact that dimensions of space, time, and matter are ever changing and always dependent upon the way in which they are observed. The only constant in our universe is the speed of light (approximately 186,000 miles per second in a vacuum). *[My comment inserted: Please note that God is light—He is the constant! — Jim Hylton]*

Einstein theorized and later experiments proved that the faster one travels relative to another object, the slower time flows for the traveler relative to the flow of time measured by the stationary observer. At the speed of light (the highest speed attainable in our universe), time ceases to flow altogether. The time of all events becomes compressed into the present, an unending now. The laws of relativity have changed timeless existence from a theological claim to a physical reality.[115]

Reader, if I have lost you along the way of this busy path of thought, please take a deep breath and consider what the MIT PhD in physics, Gerald Schroeder, acknowledges:

I don't pretend to understand how tomorrow and the next year can exist simultaneously with today and yesterday. But at the speed of light they actually and rigorously do. Time does not pass.

The biblical claim that the Creator, existing outside of time, knows the ending at its beginning is not because the future has already physically occurred within our realm of time, space, and matter. Einstein showed us, in the flow of light, the corollary of the Eternal Now: I was, I am, and I will be.[116]

This is a statement of monumental importance. Dr. Gerald Schroeder is a highly respected and oft-quoted scientist. His humility to say, "I don't pretend to understand how tomorrow and the next year exist simultaneously" is refreshing.

Even more significant is the fact that he believes what he does not fully understand. He believes because he chooses to trust the integrity of the One who said in Scripture: "I was, I am, and I will be."

It probably will not surprise you that I did not share all these points because I understand them all. I don't. But I do understand that science and physics are not enemies of God.

This treatment of the Eternal One is most refreshing to me. I will leave to the wisdom of God the understanding I do not yet have. When the right time to connect these issues in my understanding occurs, I will then know as God knows.

God Is Here Now—And He Will Be Forever!

"So where is God?" you may be asking. He is there with you in this exact minute, just as He is here with me as I write. That is true whether I am even residing on this earth by the time you read this.

Dallas Willard no longer has a residence on this earth in greater Los Angeles. But what he wrote in 1997 about God being with us comes from this convergence of time and eternity:

Nothing—no human being or institution, no time, no space, no spiritual being, no event—stands between God and those who trust him.

The "heavens" are always there with you no matter what, and the "first heavens" are always there no matter what, and the "first heaven," in biblical terms, is precisely the atmosphere or air that surrounds your body.... But it is precisely from the space immediately around us that God watches and God acts.[117]

God does not monitor you and your life from a distant location that represents the unapproachable or the unavailable. He is there now in all His qualities of proven love made accessible to us. Love causes Him to stay with you. His unfailing presence is because of His unfailing nature of love.

A man I know and admire, who has wrestled for years with thinking from a tormented mind, said to me recently: "I can affirm that God is everywhere. I found His presence in the torment of Sheol."

He was referring to the experience of the Psalmist: *"If I ascend to heaven, You are there; If I make my bed in Sheol, behold, You are there"* (Psalm 139:8, NASU). We can agree with God at this very minute: "There is no place where You are not present."

We Live and Move and Exist Because God Lives

With further insight on God's location, Dallas Willard chooses the discourse of Paul among the philosophers of Mars Hill as a reference:

> When Paul on Mars Hill told his Greek inquisitors that in God, "we live and move and exist," he was expressing in the most literal way possible the fact learned from the experience of God's covenant people, the Jews.

Dallas proceeds to address us concerning what we believe about this reality.

> In a church service we may heartily sing the grand old hymn,
> "O Worship the King … Whose robe is the light, whose canopy space.
> Thy bountiful care, what tongue can recite?
> It breathes in the air; it shines in the light;
> It streams from the hills; it descends from the plain;
> And gently distills in the dew and the rain."
>
> But do we actually believe this? I mean, are we ready automatically *to act* as if we stand here and now and always in the presence of the great being described by Adam Clarke, who fills and overflows all space, including the atmosphere around our body?[118]

Now let's look at ourselves in light of the reality that God is a spirit who is present in all of space as well as present in all of His creation. Dallas summarizes: " 'Spiritual' is not just something we ought to be. It is something we are and cannot escape, regardless of how we may think or feel about it. It is our nature and our destiny."[119]

And Dallas encourages us with more:

I am a spiritual being who currently has a body. I occupy my body and its environs by my consciousness of it and by my capacity to will and to act with and through it. I occupy my body and its proximate space, but I am not localized in it or around it. You cannot find me or any of my thoughts, feelings, or character traits in my body. Even I cannot. If you wish to find me the last thing you should do is open my body to take a look—or even examine it closely with a microscope or other physical instruments.

That very unity of experiences that constitutes a human self cannot be located at any point in or around this body through which we live, not even in the brain. Yet I am present as agent or causal influence with and about my body and its features and movements. In turn, what my body undergoes and provides influences my life as a personal being. And through my body[,] principally through my face and gestures, or "body language" but also verbally, I can make myself present to others.

Now, roughly speaking, God relates to space as we do to our body. He occupies and overflows it but cannot be localized in it. Every point in it is accessible to his consciousness and will, and his manifest presence can be focused in a location as he sees fit. In the incarnation he focused his reality in a special way in the body of Jesus. This was so that we might be "enlightened by the knowledge of the glory of God in the face of Jesus Christ." (2 Corinthians 4:6).[120]

I have taken this much space to review such important insights so I can underscore the fact that we are *not our body* and not our physical arrangement of cells. We *are spirit* because God shared His likeness.

The marring of that likeness through the choice made in the garden is reversed as we choose the gift of Christ's life. In Christ, we become a new creation, a creation of God's likeness.

Therefore if anyone is in Christ, he is a new creature; the old things passed away; behold, new things have come. Now all these things are from God, who reconciled us to Himself through Christ and gave us the ministry of reconciliation, namely, that God was in Christ reconciling the world to Himself, not counting their trespasses against them, and He has committed to us the word of reconciliation.

Therefore, we are ambassadors for Christ, as though God were making an appeal through us; we beg you on behalf of Christ, be reconciled to God. He made Him who knew no sin to be sin on our behalf, so that we might become the righteousness of God in Him (2 Corinthians 5:17-21, NASU).

This truth could not be more clearly stated! We are reconciled to God because God made Christ who had no sin to be sin for us. Our sin was placed on Christ, who was sinless. Christ's righteousness is placed on us, restoring us to God's likeness.

We are *not our body* and not our physical arrangement of cells. We *are spirit* because God shared His likeness.

Abraham experienced this same gift from God: *"For what does the Scripture say? 'ABRAHAM BELIEVED GOD, AND IT WAS CREDITED TO HIM AS RIGHTEOUSNESS'"* (Romans 4:3, 4, NASU). (The capitalization is mine; I believe this is so important that we must shout it!)

Paul knew this reconciling role of Christ that makes us one with God and thus at ease with God. He thought just the opposite until his own encounter with God in Christ. Discovering that God had taken a body and lived in time and space in Christ was a revelation to Paul, one that had no equal.

That revelation through a personal encounter commissioned him with the role of being an ambassador, or personal emissary, of Christ. This knowledge included the fact that all are meant be ambassadors displaying Christ in us. Paul then declares the passion of his life: *"We beg you on behalf of Christ, be reconciled to God"* (2 Corinthians 5:20).

Knowing God for Who He Is

But we can't be reconciled or at ease with God without knowing who He is. Paul thought he knew, only to discover that in refusing Christ he had missed God altogether. Many occupy that same mistaken place in our culture today, whether secular or religious.

Gerald Schroeder makes such a claim, that the error of the atheist may not be that different from the errant thinking of the one who thinks they know God.

The god an atheist does not believe is usually not the God of the Bible. Unfortunately, the god of the "believer" is also often not the God of the Bible.[121]

His definition of a "believer" would probably be different from mine, but his insight is not only shocking—it is well taken. Religion is always a security blanket, but it easily becomes a substitute for knowing God. It can be a haven for hiding from God, just as Adam hid in the trees of Eden.

Jesus was killed by people who thought they knew God. Yet the God they didn't know offered them eternal forgiveness and total restoration to life as He intended it! This was the God who raised Christ from the dead, exhibiting His true nature as well as His tender mercy, to give Christ back to them in risen authority over all things, including death.

Pope Francis Wants Everyone to Know Christ Personally

Pope Francis recently expressed a desire for all people, including the 1.8 billion Catholics around the world, to know Christ personally. During an unusual meeting with a pope, both in length and subject matter, a few evangelical leaders emphasized their concern for people to experience the living Christ.

Two of those who were present at this meeting are my friends, Kenneth Copeland and James Robison. Kenneth got the invitation from Pope Francis to bring a group of evangelicals.

James shared with Pope Francis his desire for all people to experience Christ. He told the pontiff that his own wife, Betty, had been an exemplary church member. She had even taught a Sunday school class—without experiencing Christ personally.

The spiritual leader of the Catholic Church affirmed the same desire for all his constituents around the world. James Robison and Pope Francis exchanged a high five, a way of acknowledging their agreement that everyone *needs* to know and *can* know Christ personally.

Knowing God By Knowing Christ

Paul held this same burning desire in his heart for all people. From his Jewish heritage he carried a compassion for those like himself to know that God was in Christ. He carried an equal yearning for people of every background, whether Jewish or not, to know God.

When he arrived in Athens, Greece, his heart went out to people who even honored "an unknown God." This was a city where giants of thought had influenced the world. Socrates, Plato, and Aristotle saw parts of the reality of the spiritual world. They had contributed some stones to the foundation of thought that would assist truth to be received, truth as it lived in Christ.

Paul's background gave him a basis for appreciating the "Golden Age of Greece," especially the city where these breakthrough thinkers lived and taught.

Jesus chose the word Plato used to describe the goodness of the human soul that knows God for His true goodness. Such is the goodness of the kingdom of God that Jesus presented in a portion of his talk on the hillside (Matthew 5:20-48).

The Greek word *dikaiosúnee* first appeared in the reasoning of Plato in his famous writings, *Republic*. The word today means *righteousness*.

Dallas Willard points out that "it retains a note of emphasis upon the relationship of the soul to God."[122] Further, Dallas defines it as "what that is about a person that makes him or her really right or good. For short, we might say 'true inner goodness'"[123]

The Greek word *dikaiosúnee* first appeared in the reasoning of Plato in his famous writings, *Republic*. The word today means *righteousness*.

The famous discourse Paul gave to the people of Athens is worthy of our time. He spoke in the marketplace of ideas. Limitless ideas were offered daily on Mars Hill for those who wanted to buy them.

He concluded this remarkable coverage of ideas by using the word righteousness, or *dikaiosúnee*, as the standard that God used to review the life of every person. He is saying that we should expect a final exam at the end of life before the graduation exercise of leaving our body. The test standard God will use is the standard of righteousness. Passing or failing the exam will be based on goodness, or *dikaiosúnee*.

Yet, here is the stunning thing: God's goodness becomes our goodness as a gift from Christ. Paul wrote: *"Because He has fixed a day in which He will judge the world in righteousness [dikaiosunee] through a Man whom He has appointed, having furnished proof to all men by raising Him from the dead."* (Acts 17:31 NASU)

Righteousness Will Be the Standard to Judge the World

God will judge the world in righteousness. Jesus shared that quality of righteousness, as I have noted. God uses it as His standard, and He looks for it in our lives.

How does it become part of our lives? Jesus made it clear the kingdom of God is to be found in us. "Nor will people say, 'Here it is,' or 'There it is,' because the kingdom of God is within you" (Luke 17:21, NIV).

God is good by nature. He wants us to know goodness, or righteousness, as part of our nature, not part of our religious performance. Paul knew this when he said: *"For the kingdom of God is not a matter of eating and drinking, but of righteousness, peace and joy in the Holy Spirit, because anyone who serves Christ in this way is pleasing to God and approved by men"* (Romans 14:17, 18, NIV).

The requirements to eat and drink properly in ceremonies of religious discipline were widely observed during Paul's day. He said we should not be more concerned about outward rules and habits first, but about inward "goodness"—righteous and inward peace—through God's inward presence.

It has become popular in some circles today to quote the litany:

"God is good, all the time. All the time, God is good!" This is a great truth, but until God is good *inside us*, we have not experienced the true meaning. Until God is good in us, we have no success in being good all the time, as He is.

God not only occupies the space around us, as science and physics verify, but He desires to return to the space within us as previously experienced in the garden. Upon making man, He breathed into him the breath of life and man became a living soul. That breath of life creates the inner peace and ease with God as the Holy Spirit manifests the kingdom in us.

"Christ in you is the hope of glory" (Colossians 1:27). "Christ in you" is Christ living His life from within us. He is not housed in our heart as a religious cubicle to be active maybe three Sundays out of the month. He lives from within where the kingdom of God is experienced and expressed through our life.

Idols Like a Forest of Trees

In a culture where ideas had been turned into idols, false gods stood like a forest of trees covering the prominent hill. In that forest of idols, Paul gave one of the most important presentations of the true God ever offered.

Taking time to review his knowledge of God is worth every minute and every bit of space it will take because of the eternal view it affords:

> *So Paul stood in the midst of the Areopagus and said, "Men of Athens, I observe that you are very religious in all respects. For while I was passing through and examining the objects of your worship, I also found an altar with this inscription, 'TO AN UNKNOWN GOD.' Therefore what you worship in ignorance, this I proclaim to you. The God who made the world and all things in it, since He is Lord of heaven and earth, does not dwell in temples made with hands; nor is He served by human hands, as though He needed anything, since He Himself gives to all people life and breath and all things; and He made from one man every nation of mankind to live on all the face of the earth, having determined their appointed times and the boundaries of their habitation, that they would seek God, if perhaps they might grope for Him and find Him, though He is not far from each one of us; for in Him we live and move and exist, as even some of your own poets have said, 'For we also are His children.' Being then the children of God, we ought not to think that the Divine Nature is like gold or silver or stone, an image formed by the art and thought of man. Therefore having overlooked the times of ignorance, God is now declaring to men that all people everywhere should repent, because He has fixed a day in which He will judge the world in righteousness through a Man whom He has appointed, having furnished proof to all men by raising Him from the dead" (Acts 17:22-31, NASU)*

Paul started by declaring that the unknown God is knowable. God's very nature is to be known and enjoyed as He intended.

He is the God who created all things, the world and everything in it. Nothing exists He did not make.

His creation is where He lives. Buildings are not his dwellings. Renowned architecture, seen from their vantage point, included the Parthenon and majestic temples built for named gods like Zeus.

God does not give us a to-do list so we can serve Him. He is in need of nothing. He wants us for ourselves, not our service.

As the giver of life, he gives life to every person by giving us breath. All life is sustained by Him just as life began in Him.

He is not far from anyone! He is where we are, and when we move He is where we move. We live, we move, and we have our being because of Him.

We Are God's Children—All Have a Home Who Choose

All people are the children of God. Notice carefully Paul is addressing God's children. *"'For we also are His children.' Being then the children of God, we ought not to think that the Divine Nature is like gold or silver or stone, an image formed by the art and thought of man."* Some are children who ran away from home. Some have made their home in stately buildings. Wherever they are without knowing the true God, they can come home. The story of the prodigal son that Jesus told makes it clear God is a father who wants every child to return home. But it is the child's choice.

He is not far from anyone! He is where we are, and when we move He is where we move. We live, we move, and we have our being because of Him.

God has a schedule. An appointed day is coming when God will give the final exam referred to as the judgment. He even gives us the answers to the questions on the exam before we arrive for the test. (As just an example of that gift, we saw in Chapter Five how God gifted Ben Carson with the answers while a student at Yale University.)

God will judge the world by the standard of *dikaiosúnee*, His inner goodness exhibited as well as distributed in Christ, and given to us in Christ. Christ in us is the hope of glory.

Our proper response to His presence now is …
THANK YOU!

CHAPTER TWENTY-TWO

What's the Matter with God?

"God remains humanity's greatest disappointment," Dallas Willard stated in his book, *Hearing God*.[124] He explains the notions people have about God that are not disclosures from Him. Thus, they reach a false conclusion and become disappointed with their version of Him.

Some who truly know God do the same thing. Years ago, the late David Wilkerson followed his bestselling book, *The Cross and the Switchblade*, with a shocking book titled *I Am Not Mad at God*.

With candor, he shared the disappointment he experienced due to a false anticipation that made him angry with God. Many times people who are used by God as co-laborers start to use God to achieve their agenda instead of His. David Wilkerson was refreshingly honest and returned to co-laboring on an even larger scale.

"What is wrong with God?" is like the question asked by Mike May: "So what is wrong with my eye?" (We reviewed his story in Chapter Two.)

"There is nothing wrong with your eye," Dr. Goodman said. "In fact, it's an almost perfect eye. Optically, I'd say you're 20/40."

"I am not sure I understand," May said.

"I'm not an expert on this," Goodman said, "but I'm pretty certain the problem is your visual cortex."

"My brain?"

"I think so. I mean, I can see your entire optical system, and it's excellent. An eye seeing as beautifully as yours should be able to read all the way down the chart. That leaves the brain."[125]

Our Brain Can Make God Look Bad

The only thing "wrong" with God is in our brain and our resulting mind, not with God Himself. God's image found in our brain and mind can be distorted. God lovingly seeks to correct that image if we are willing to make His thoughts our thoughts and His ways our ways.

God being seen as humanity's biggest disappointment occurs at the level where we use religious language without the accompanying reality. Years ago, James Robison met then-California Governor Ronald Reagan. The purpose of his visit was to see if the governor would consider being a candidate for President of the United States.

The only thing "wrong" with God is in our brain and our resulting mind, not with God Himself.

James wanted to know if Governor Reagan knew Jesus personally or theoretically. With an unusual approach, he asked Reagan: "Is Jesus Christ real to you?"

The man who would become a familiar figure to America and the world tilted his head slightly, as he often did, and mused: "Well, I was raised by my mother. She was the most important person in my life. Jesus is more real to me than my mother was."

The difference in Jesus being real, in God's presence being real, in God's love being real, is the difference between a theory and reality. Without the reality in our own consciousness, we may know only the clichés of correct verbiage.

Many are ill at ease because of this lack of conscious reality. Ronald Reagan could say, "Jesus is more real to me than my mother was." That reality is what God intends for all of us.

We can never be at ease until we know who we are, why we are here, and whom we believe. If life ends, who we are and why we are here—these cease to be big issues. Life will be over sooner or later. But if we are going to live forever, whether we like it or not, that has long-term implications. If we are going to think forever, while being ill at ease now, we would be ill at ease forever.

God Rests ... So Can We

God wants His thoughts to become our thoughts. He is at rest, as evidenced since the day He completed creation. Had Moses heard the story of the press release of creation that he was supposed to deliver, and then hurried off to break the story, he might have missed the most important part.

The most important part was: *God rested*. His family rested with Him. The need of the Sabbath rest that He modeled for the family is not about one day or one week, but an attitude of life for every day. We can join God in being at rest.

One of the most insightful men who ever downloaded the thoughts of God was Saint Augustine. He lived between 354 and 430 A.D. and influenced much of western thought.

His famous quote, from *Confessions I*, is a classic understanding of God being our only ultimate source of rest: "You have made us for yourself, and our hearts are restless until they rest in you."[126]

Restlessness ceases when we join the one who is resting. A famous pastor in Boston years ago paced back and forth in his study. He was asked, "Pastor, what is wrong?" His reply reflects what most of us often think: "I am in a hurry and God is not." When we are in a hurry and find God is not, we should join Him in rest instead of expecting Him to join us in stress.

Since God is resting in being himself, we can join Him by resting in who we are as He intended.

An Atheist Found God Looking Back at Him

God uses unusual tools to make Himself known to us today. Scientists are now saying that the god whom atheists believe doesn't exist is the one that doesn't exist. The god thought to not exist *doesn't* exist, because God is here speaking for Himself. Scientists have found God looking at them, as Francis Collins acknowledged.

The god thought to not exist *doesn't* exist, because God is here speaking for Himself.

Let's look at this summary of Collins's journey toward atheism, from his *The Language of God*:

I practiced a thought and behavior pattern referred to as "willful blindness" by the noted scholar and writer C. S. Lewis.... Reading the biography of Albert Einstein, and discovering that despite his strong Zionist position … he did not believe in Yahweh, the God of the Jewish people, only reinforced my conclusion that no thinking scientist could seriously entertain the possibility of God.... And so I gradually shifted from agnosticism to atheism.[127]

He decided to pursue medicine, and during his medical school days at the University of North Carolina, Collins spoke with patients whose faith in God captured his attention. "What struck me profoundly about my bedside conversations with these good North Carolina people was the spiritual aspect—faith provided them a strong reassurance of ultimate peace, be it in this world or the next."[128]

Confronted with the evidence that people were experiencing a God he had deleted from his personal hard drive, Collins went to see a Methodist minister. Wisely, he followed a suggestion to read *Mere Christianity* by C. S. Lewis. He was impacted by the truth that "moral law" is a moral compass in all people, whether verbalized the same, or obeyed or not.

This truth of moral consciousness rocked his world.

Encountering this argument at age twenty-six, I was stunned by its logic. Here, hiding in my own heart as familiar as anything in daily principle this Moral Law shone its bright white light in the recesses of my childish atheism, and demanded a serious consideration of its origin. Was this God looking back at me?

And if that were so, what kind of God would this be? Would this be a deist God, who invented physics and mathematics and started the universe in motion about 14 billion years ago, then wandered off to deal with other, more important matters, as Einstein thought? No, this God, if I perceived Him at all, must be a theist God, who desires some kind of relationship with these special creatures called human beings, and has therefore instilled this special glimpse of Himself into each one of us. This might be the God of Abraham, but it was certainly not the God of Einstein.[129]

I recommend reading Collins's excellent book, but will spare you wondering how he came to know God. He continued to read C. S. Lewis and gives the full quote of the famous call to a commitment to Christ by Lewis. Here is the essence of what Lewis stated: "I am trying here to prevent anyone saying the really foolish thing that people often say about Him: 'I am ready to accept Jesus as a great moral teacher, but I don't accept His claim to be God.'"[130]

His question, "Was this God looking back at me?" had been answered in his mind. By then, he was looking back at God.

> A full year had passed since I decided to believe in some sort of God, and now I was being called into account…. The next morning I knelt in the dewy grass as the sun rose and surrendered to Jesus Christ.[131]

What Kind of God is God?

When Francis Collins stopped using his "willful blindness" and concluded there is indeed a God, the question he raised ….becomes the issue for all of us: "What kind of God would He be?"

Is He a God who loves us? Is He a God who stays on duty attending to our needs? Is He a God with the power and resources to meet our needs?

Is He a God who can be trusted? Is He a God easy to be with? Is He a God who would lead us to take part in meeting the needs of others?

Is He a God who would enable us to love as He does? Is He a God who would trust us to co-manage His ingenious creation? Is He a God whose grace supplies a childlike, wide-eyed look at life?

If the answer to these questions is yes, there is nothing wrong with God! So where is the disconnect between God and us? Why are we ill at ease? Why is our management of life and our planet going badly at times?

Is He a God who can be trusted? Is He a God easy to be with? Is He a God who would lead us to take part in meeting the needs of others?

Why is there a health crisis in America when we have the best resources to promote good health? Why does the world contain terrorist bombs with the timer set to an unknown schedule? Why do half of the couples that pledged love break the pledge in divorce court? Why does fear stalk the lives of people in the streets of America instead of love?

God's creation does contain a language of God, as Francis Collins described. All of His creation is a dictionary of His words. Without letting Him speak for Himself, we may totally misconstrue what we are hearing in the echo of His voice in creation.

Science can help us hear! Matter really matters. In fact, everything matters to God. Everything that God has made is here to stay!

The law of energy conservation stood 50 years before Einstein understood that energy and matter were two forms of the same thing. In *More Than Meets the Eye,* Swenson wrote that now we know "that the total of both energy and matter are conserved. We can't make them; we can't get rid of them. We can move them around, transform them, or convert them from one form to another. But the total amount always stays the same."[132]

Said another way, all of creation brought into time has now become eternal. Nothing is ever destroyed—it only changes in chemical content. The eternal one brought time, as well as all of His creation, out of eternity and now all will remain eternal—including time that relates now to eternity.

Dallas Willard's use of the "eternal kind of life" has never-ending (no pun intended) implications. To think like we are in eternity now, to live like we are in eternity now, to treat others like we are in eternity now would make everything look different, at least to us. It just might look like we were seeing the kingdom Jesus offers.

In the last four centuries, there have been as many awakenings scientifically as there have been spiritually. In fact, there may have been more. Spiritually we have been awakened only to hit the snooze button without ever getting fully awake to the kingdom of God as our home where we adopt His way of life and experience being His family.

Our current culture has made the "kingdom of God" only words we repeat. The kingdom has become like a convenience store where we can run in to get an item we forgot while shopping. Or it is a discount store where we get good buys on big items.

Jesus said the kingdom is to be our point of reference for all of life. We are to live seeing the kingdom. All of life's decisions are to begin by seeking or seeing first the kingdom.

With a kingdom perspective, we can think through all the reigning ways of God in guiding our decisions. The kingdom of God has never been tried in America or much of the world. We have been too busy building the church, which only Jesus can build, instead of receiving a kingdom already built.

What Really Matters?

What really matters to God? Everything that God made matters. That is why it is indestructible! How much matter did He make? Richard Swenson reports:

> The universe contains approximately 100 billion galaxies. In total, this is estimated to equal a trillion, trillion, trillion tons of matter.
>
> Consider how much energy this represents…. To convert mass to energy we multiply the mass by a very large number, namely the speed of light squared (186,000 miles per second—or about 671 million miles per hour)…. The amount of matter God created in the universe is impressive.
>
> But the energy equivalent of this matter is much, much greater. And that is not all. Not all the energy in the universe exists in the form of matter. Much of it exists freely in the energy state rather than the matter state. Adding these two amounts together (the amount of energy existing within matter, plus the amount of energy existing in the energy state) yields an energy figure that is incomprehensibly large.[133]

Everything that God made matters. That is why it is indestructible!

The "incomprehensible" energy or activity of God in creation must register in our consciousness. More than the energy in matter, both known and still unknown, across the 100 billion galaxies is the energy not found in the form of matter. God is not limited to His creation. Why have we developed a view of God that He may be able to cure a common cold, but is helpless in healing cancer or Ebola? Or is so limiting that we embrace Him having "all power and authority," but He cannot use doctors and medicine in healing as well as prayer and supernatural manifestations. He may want to share with us ways to heal cancer or Ebola medically on a regular basis.

Richard Swenson offers bullet points of what God is saying in creation:

- That He is powerful at a level beyond human comprehension.

- That He alone has the ability to create mass energy out of nothing.

- That He formed us with the ability to observe mass-energy—not to create it.

- That if we need a source of energy, it is better to connect to God's energy source (infinite) than to humanity's energy source (nonexistent).[134]

We can learn from the awakenings in science to pay attention to every dimension of life. Science keeps looking at smaller and smaller evidences of reality. From massive amounts of matter, to electrons, to neurons, to quarks, to strings, to neutrinos, the search continues.

In the study of matter, physics, an awakening occurred that rocked science labs. Einstein was among the scientists who pushed back against the findings. A new look at what God made is called quantum physics or quantum mechanics.

Quantum comes from the Latin word *quantus*, which means "how much." So the question of *how much* caused people to keep probing smaller and smaller particles that comprise all things.

We see objects as predictable. The desk I am writing at was custom made for me by a special friend. I can count on it to be in this place every time I sit here composing thoughts, as I am now. The desk, however, is made up of atoms and subatomic particles that like to move, and do so continuously. "Atoms and subatomic particles are unpredictable. They will not stay put," Swenson writes.[135]

So my desk is ever-moving—I just can't see it move. I am not concerned about the unpredictability of these subatomic particles, because I know additional information about creation and its coherence.

Scripture makes it clear that God made all things through Christ. *"He is the image of the invisible God, the firstborn over all creation. For by him all things were created: things in heaven and on earth, visible and invisible, whether thrones or powers or rulers or authorities; all things were created by him and for him. He is before all things, and in him all things hold together"* (Colossians 1:15-17, NIV).

He created all the things that need to be held together. With His attending presence "all things hold together." From His power comes creation's masterpiece. Through His power it coheres and is held together.

With His attending presence "all things

hold together." From His power comes creation's masterpiece.

Classical physics, however, preferred precision over probabilities…. Einstein, for one, was appalled at the finding that "atoms and subatomic particles are unpredictable. They will not stay put." His initial unwillingness to accept this finding led to the quip that God does not play dice with the universe. (To which his friend Niels Bohr retorted: "Einstein, stop telling God what to do.") In disgust, he said he would rather be a cobbler, or even an employee in a gambling house, than a physicist.[136]

God's Attention to Details: Small Details

But "how much" was still not answered in the probing process. The discovery of smaller and smaller elements of God's creation led to yet another theory, called "superstrings." Though the theory is still not proven, it is generally accepted. Swenson writes:

> If superstrings exist—and there is strong evidence they do—they are very, very small.

> A superstring loop is a hundred million billion times smaller than the nucleus of an atom…. "Imagine, if you can, four things that have very different sizes," explains Freeman Dyson. "First, the entire visible universe. Second, the planet earth. Third, the nucleus of an atom. Fourth, a superstring. The step in size from each of these things to the next is roughly the same…. To experimentally probe the domain of the superstrings, engineers would have to construct a particle accelerator measuring one thousand light-years around."

> Strings are like ultra-thin vibrating rubber bands. It seems the entire universe is one huge disco, filled with infinitely tiny elastic filaments twisting and vibrating rhythmically. To better visualize what we are talking about, let's zoom the microscopic camera down past the electrons, neutrons, protons, and quarks. By now, we have entered infinitesimal space, descending smaller, smaller, smaller … until finally,

we arrive at what first looks like a point. But as we approach closer, we see that this is not a point but a wiggling string. According to this theory the whole universe is made up of such strings.

The vibrating string has a surprise for us—extra dimensions. The visible world we inhabit seems to be made up of three spatial dimensions plus time. String theory, however, requires at least nine spatial dimensions, possibly more. These additional dimensions are tightly rolled up and thus perceptibly applicable in the functioning of the universe.[137]

Why all this time devoted to the issue of the particles of God's creation? Because in this understanding of the quantum, the "how much" of God's intricate details, is found an understanding of God we desperately need in this love-starved and anxious time in history.

The quantum of physics can lead us to see quantum love. The "how much" of God's love continually reveals there is more. You are loved. I am loved. Everyone you now know and will know is loved. God does not offer generalized, group love, but very personal and detailed love.

Neither does He make mass mailings, hoping that a few will learn He loves them. He writes us personal letters found in many forms and wordings. You are reading one now. These smallest particles that make up something as vast as this far-flung universe indicates there is more of God to experience, just as there is more of His creation to see.

The "how much" of God's love continually reveals there is more. You are loved. I am loved.

Think of it this way: The vibrating strings contained throughout all of creation are like a great symphony being played that we are being prepared to hear. These vibrating rhythmical strings are playing a love song of God to you. God loves his universe. He loves you!

But he also takes time to love and tune his strings that are contained in the minutia of his masterpiece. They reflect His love for you. Only wrongly organized thoughts in the amazing mind He gave you can miss this!

"How much" of quantum reality teaches us to know how much God loves us. Science desires truth. But science cannot lead you to love. It is the truth of God that leads to love. Without love from God we are still left without being at ease with God.

In *The Divine Conspiracy,* Dallas Willard writes:

Before the laws of science can explain anything—these laws must have something from which to start. Science, then, may explain many interesting things, but it does not explain existence. Nor does it explain why the laws of science are the laws of nature. And it does not explain science itself.[138]

God Is More Real Than Any Other Reality

God's nearness to you now is more real than any reality you can experience outside of Him. His presence and activity in microscopic—and beyond microscopic—reality should make us aware that God is looking at us!

Let's take another step toward learning how interactive the presence of God is found in all of His creation. We have followed the progression from atoms to electrons to protons to neutrons to quarks and then to strings. There is yet another visitor from the invisible world near you—right this second.

Your Body Is Invaded Each Second

In fact, there are sixty billion of them passing through your body each second. These are neutrinos. Let's let Dr. Swenson describe them:

Neutrinos were discovered in 1956. Historically their name … is an offshoot of a neutron. Neutrinos are even more ghostly than the elusive electron. "Every second, sixty billion of them, mostly for the sun, pass through each square centimeter of your bodies (and everything else)," explain researchers at the giant neutrino detector site in Japan. "But because they seldom interact with other particles, generally all sixty billion go through you without so much as nudging a single atom."

A beam of neutrinos can pass through a trillion miles of solid lead and emerge totally unscathed. Produced in large numbers by nuclear reactions in stars, these numberless neutrinos—so vacuous that almost nothing can stop them—stream constantly across the universe at the speed of light. (May I remind you, that is how fast God travels, since He is light? .. My comment, Jim Hylton)

Even though such a mass seems almost too small to bother with, it is nevertheless of great interest to scientists. For decades, astrophysicists have been looking for the missing mass of the universe predicted by their calculations. Neutrinos have infinitesimally small mass but exist in infinitely high numbers. When you do the math, it might indeed be the case that neutrinos are the answer to the "missing mass" puzzle.

The trillions of neutrinos that pass through our bodies every second come mostly from our own sun. After dashing through our anatomy, the landscape, and the earth itself, they streak out into space for a long, lonely journey to nowhere but the doorstep of God.[139]

When I first learned of neutrinos, I began wondering if I should feel 60 billion, or at least some number, of their sneaky, streaking presence. Of course, I don't feel anything. But I do believe they are there. Science practitioners have no reason to lie to me.

God is equally present whether we feel Him or not. He has said so, and we can believe Him. His love convinces me, as does His truth. In fact, He is either love and truth, or He is a lie.

He has said He is both love and truth. I believe Him! Through believing Him, He has become more real to me than the line of print I am composing now.

Knowing tiny neutrinos inhabit your body should not make you uncomfortable. They have not come to harm you. Knowing that God wants to inhabit your body, which He made to co-manage with you, should not make you uncomfortable either. He will not live there to make you uncomfortable. He will come and make you at ease!

God is equally present whether we feel Him or not. His love convinces me, as does His truth. In fact, He is either love and truth, or He is a lie.

Loving God with our minds is a major part of being at ease. The disconnect between God and our minds causes our entire consciousness to be void of an important awareness.

The greatest thing that can occur in your life is to love the Lord your God with all your heart, all your soul, and all your mind (Matthew 22:37)! This was the answer Jesus gave to a lawyer asking about the most important commandment in the law. He said this as He shared what God most wants us to experience.

But when the Pharisees heard that Jesus had silenced the
Sadducees, they gathered themselves together. One of them, a

lawyer, asked Him a question, testing Him. "Teacher, which is the
great commandment in the Law?" And He said to him, "'YOU
SHALL LOVE THE LORD YOUR GOD WITH ALL YOUR
HEART, AND WITH ALL YOUR SOUL, AND WITH ALL
YOUR MIND.' This is the great and foremost commandment.
The second is like it, 'YOU SHALL LOVE YOUR NEIGHBOR AS
YOURSELF.'" On these two commandments depend the whole
Law and the Prophets
(Matthew 22:34-40, NASU) (emphasis is mine—JH).

The mind, as well as heart and soul, is intended to experience the realization of life's purpose. We are to love God, who already loves us. Without the mind loving God, we never know real love or the real God. Our mind must be engaged in an interface with God.

A Godless Mind Does Not Come from a Mindless God

We do not have a mindless God. But we can have a godless mind—a mind with a god less than He really is. All creation, including our bodies, reflects the brilliance of God's mind. A godless mind develops when our mind contains a self-made or a religion-made image of God instead of His true likeness.

When God is less to us than He really is, we worship a god made by our thoughts instead of God's thoughts. This is why hearing God is essential to our knowing God.

Dallas Willard, in *The Divine Conspiracy*, insightfully described this frequent distortion of God: "I personally have become convinced that many people who believe in Jesus do not actually believe in God. By saying this I do not mean to condemn anyone but to cast light on why the lives of professed believers go as they do, and often quite contrary even to what they sincerely intend."[140]

How we allow the image of God to be restored in our mind is an essential issue in our being at ease. Dallas offers a helpful contrast between the world Jesus offers and our own self-made image.

Jesus, by contrast, brings us to a world without fear. In His world, astonishingly, there is nothing evil we must do in order to thrive. He lived, and invites us to live, in a world where it is safe to do and be good. He was understood by his first friends to have "abolished death and brought life and immortality to light through the gospel"

(2 Timothy 1:10). Thus our posture of confident reliance upon him in all we do allows us to make our life undying, have eternal worth, integrated into the eternal vistas and movements of the Spirit.[141]

A life of purpose has been presented clearly, and received with unprecedented appreciation, by Rick Warren in his classic *The Purpose Driven Life*. God is purpose driven also. When we know who He is, when we understand how He is driven by love for each person, we know that *"God is love"* (1 John 4:16). Dallas Willard continues to teach us:

> The purpose of God with human history is nothing less than to bring out of it … an eternal community of those who were thought to be just "ordinary human beings." Because of God's purposes for it, the community will, in its way, pervade the entire created realm and share in the government of it. God's precreation intention to have that community as a special dwelling place or home will be realized. He will be its prime sustainer and most glorious habitant.

> But why? What is the point of it? The purpose is to meet what can only be described as a need of God's nature as totally competent love. It is the same purpose that manifests itself in his creation of the world. Only in the light of such a creation and such a redeemed community is it possible for God to be known in his deepest nature. They make it possible for God to be known. And love unknown is love unfulfilled. Moreover, the welfare of every conscious being in existence depends upon their possession of this knowledge of God.[142]

The grandeur of creation speaks of God's love with might and power. The microscopic content of creation speaks of God's infinite love in small detail.

Science has shown us a planet, a universe with other planets and suns, a galaxy, and then other galaxies—800 billion galaxies, discoveries seemingly with no end. Science also shows us atoms, electrons, protons, neutrons, quarks, strings, even neutrinos. We have moved to smaller and smaller details in God's creative construction. All of God's matter really matters.

Knowing God includes both His size and His invisible details. He is God omnipotent (all power), omniscient (all knowing), and omnipresent (all present). His names connote many splendored characteristics: Elohim, Jehovah Jireh, Nissi, Shalom, Shammah, Emmanuel—to acknowledge only the best-known ones.

The names speak of His activity. All activity comes from who He is— *love*. God's size is big enough to contain all power, yet He is small enough to enter a cell, in order to enter a body, in order to enter life. And from a cross, followed by resurrection, to be proven to be incarnate love.

At Ease with God, Whose Love Never Ceases

Our ability to be at ease does not occur without knowing God. Possessing this knowledge of God allows us to experience Him and His love nature. Love without God is no different than a god without love. Part of our culture would advocate loving love and having faith in faith.

Promises made by people to love forever abound, but the promises of people are without substance. We cannot love forever without God. Love does not need to promise—love needs only *to be*. God's nature of love is *to be*.

He instructed Moses to tell his people: "I Am that I Am" has sent me. God will be what He will be. Love will be, not a promise, but the presence of the God expressing love.

Love never ends because God never ends. He is without a beginning or an end. So is His love.

The Eternal Action of God Is to Love

In his most helpful book, *The God Who Loves You*, Peter Kreeft gives a comprehensive look at God's love in action:

> God cannot fall in love, not because He is less loving than we, but because he is more. He cannot fall in love for the same reason water cannot get wet: it is wet. God is love, and love itself cannot receive love as passivity. It can only spread it as an activity. God is love-in-eternal-action.[143]

Love wants to know, to be known, and to enable others to know. "Love unknown is love unfulfilled," as quoted by Dallas earlier, helps us understand God's desire to make Himself known.

Knowing is one of the amazing gifts granted us in the creation of the brain. From this amazing network of neurons, a guidance system of our spirit develops our mind. Our mind can know both truth and lies. The right to choose what we believe is always ours to exercise.

Truth Is Returned in Christ—We Can Stop Forgetting

When we welcome the Spirit of God to awaken and guide our spirit, we can know truth. Truth is more than a concept. Truth was embodied in a person, Jesus Christ. He declared, *"I am the way and the truth and the life. No one comes to the Father except through me. If you really knew me, you would know my Father as well. From now on, you do know him and have seen him"* (John 14:6, 7, NIV).

The Greek word for truth has significant implications. Randy Alcorn, in *Fifty Days of Heaven,* recognizes the meaning of truth as remembering God. "The Greek word for truth, *aletheia*, is a negated form of the verb 'to forget,' so that knowing the truth means to stop forgetting."[144]

Our mind can know both truth and lies. The right to choose what we believe is always ours to exercise.

Not remembering, or not knowing, started early in man's history in the garden, as we have seen. The first family quickly forgot truth. Truth, then, is a return to the reality of God Himself.

Peter Kreeft helpfully expands this understanding of truth:

> The Greek word for truth, *aletheia*, contains the word *Lethe,* the river of forgetfulness in Greek mythology. *Alethea* means literally "not-forgetfulness," and it connotes the idea that truth is a knowledge that is innate in us. And what we need to do is remember it.[145]

Innate awareness of God as truth is easier to comprehend knowing that there is encoded memory in all cells. It is quite probable that even the cells in our brain remember a day when truth was found in God.

Our issue now is to align the memory in our cells with God's way of speaking to us. This intuitive or innate record in cells can partly explain how people in other cultures have found the reality of certain aspects of God's mind and ways.

The Greek thinkers—Socrates, Plato, and Aristotle—saw into the invisible world and recognized the existence of God. Plato gave us the word for righteousness. While only seeing parts of God's invisible world and only part of Him, they knew God was good and that goodness, or righteousness, was an important quality in life. While they believed in God, they missed the greatest characteristic of God—that He is love.

How we see God is how we see life. If an image of God is created in our thinking capacity without the reality of God's presence to give clarity, we have a distorted image. That is why many in our culture live with an image of God who bears no likeness to the God who met Moses on a mountain. Nor to the likeness of an image of God, who accepted incarnation in a body like ours, dressed Himself as a man, and sat down on a lofty slope to talk to a vast crowd about a kingdom being theirs as a gift.

That is why many in our culture live with an image of God who bears no likeness to the God who met Moses on a mountain.

He is the Son of God, who exchanged His life with us at the cross.

"Now the eternal truth of God's nature—which is love—is expressed, revealed, and played out like a movie onto the screen of time in the historical truth of God's fidelity to His people and to His promises.... Trace the word "true" through scripture with a concordance. You will be surprised how often the word refers to something that comes true in time, especially a promise made by God. Count the promises of Scripture. You will find hundreds of them, and all are guaranteed to come true. This is a dramatic, dynamic conception of truth. Truth is not something static but something that happens in history. It is something that you can see! ... But before you see it you must believe it.[146]

The process of learning to know God was carefully thought out by God. His infinite provision to let us know His reality is as ingenious as His creative language inscribed in our cellular codes. Peter Kreeft, whose writings I have come to enjoy in this recent part of my journey, says some unique and helpful things. Let's allow his insights to become part of our spiritual sight.

A Book About the Word of God—Not the Words of God

Kreeft refers us to a book that will let us know God.

But the Bible lets us know. It is the only book that can tell us ... because it is the only book that has been written not just by the human characters inside the story but also the divine author of the story. Its perspective is double, that of the characters and that of the author, or that of the human authors and that of the divine author. Christ is the

Word of God in person. The Bible is the Word of God in writing. Both are the Word of God in words of men. Both have a human nature and divine nature.

And we are still in the story! The divinely guaranteed interpretation of the story is complete, and the canon of Scripture is closed. But we carry on the story itself....What kind of story are we in? … The Bible's answer is that *we are in a love story*. We are notes in a love song. Every movement of every molecule is a vibration of the universal lyre of love.

Christians call the Bible the *Word of God*. Why not call it the "words of God?" It has millions of words in it. It contains many books and many authors. How is it *one word*?

The whole point of Scripture is to give us eternal life by pointing to the Savior, the Life-giver. Yet many know the words but not the Word, the many signs but not the One signified, the pointing fingers but not the person they all point to. That is like preferring a photo album to a person. Old Testament Scripture is Christ's photo album, and those who refused Him had their noses in the pictures and could not see the person. They were eating the written prescription from the druggist instead of taking the medicine it prescribed. Life Himself was standing before them, and they kept spelling it out "L … I … F … E."

The analogy of the portrait works nicely. As a physical entity, a portrait is many things.… But the person is what makes the portrait one—the portrait gets its unity from the person it portrays, rather than the molecules that make it up. Similarly, the Bible gets its unity from Jesus, not from the books that make it up. Scripture is not just the words of God, but the Word of God because its unity is Christ the Word of God.

And Christ is love incarnate. He is incarnate because He is love. The Incarnation happened only because of love, both His and His Father's love (John 3:16). He came out of love, He shows love, teaches love, exemplifies love, lives love, and finally dies for love. He is the point of the Bible and He is pure love, that is why the Bible is a love story.[147]

Who would not want to know God once they *know God*? A self-crafted image of God, created by wrong teaching or any wrongful distortion, causes many to hide from God.

Some may hide Him in their file of thoughts instead of hiding from Him. He keeps reaching out to anyone who will pause to consider Him. Regardless of what we have offered Him, God offers us His love.

God Blesses Even When His Name Is Used to Curse

The militant language of an atheist will not repel God's offer of Himself. Profane language that pronounces a curse, using the name of God, does not change God's desire to bless. His desire is to bless both, the one being cursed, and the one who spoke the curse.

Our behavior does not change God's behavior. He is love.

Atheism contains a two-edged sword of sadness. One edge contains disappointment for a person who is missing the reality of a living God. The second edge reveals a disregard for the appearance of God and, many times, a denial of His speaking to them.

Atheism contains a two-edged sword of sadness.

Those who give voice to their thoughts that there is no God are not sharing all of their thoughts. Francis Bacon said, "An atheist is only an atheist from the teeth out."

One atheist, who wrote of God's visit to him, is more honest than some. Jean-Paul Sartre was an avowed atheist. Sartre had a cousin as famous for knowing God as Sartre was for denying God existed. Albert Schweitzer—Nobel Prize winner, Christian doctor, theologian, musician, and missionary to Africa—came from the same family tree as Sartre. My compounded sadness comes from there being no connection between them and God's family tree.

Francis Bacon said, "An atheist is only an atheist from the teeth out."

These amazing words shared by Kreeft, in his book *Heaven*, broke my heart:

Sartre . . in his autobiography, *The Words*, tells how he became an atheist: "Only once did I have the feeling he existed. I had been playing with matches and burned a small rug. I was in the process of covering up my crime when God saw me. I felt his gaze inside my head and my hands. I whirled about in the bathroom, horribly visible, a live target. Indignation saved me. I flew into a rage…. I blasphemed, I muttered like my grandfather: 'God damn it, God damn it, God damn it.' He never looked at me again."[148]

While Sartre concluded that God never looked at him again, that is highly unlikely. It is more likely he never looked at God again. God never stops looking at us any more than He stops loving us.

God's love is not repelled by our behavior. Only the hardness of the heart, the evil of the heart of unbelief, keeps a person from knowing His presence. If Sartre's account was the time when the line was forever drawn between God and him, it was Sartre who drew it.

The image of God is created in our mind. That image, reached without God, is always a misshapen image. People reach many tragic conclusions. Sartre may have reached one of them.

Disappointment with God Comes from Our Misshapen Image

Misshapen images of God can be found in most mental files. Even committed Christians carry erroneous distortions. That is why Dallas Willard carefully took time to help us across bridges to better understanding.

If Sartre's account was the time when the line was forever drawn between God and him, it was Sartre who drew it.

One distortion of concern for Dallas was the idea some people develop that we never face discomfort or risk in our walk with God. Because of wrong viewpoints, he explains: "Such a response partly explains why God remains humanity's greatest disappointment."[149]

When God is "humanity's greatest disappointment," something is either terribly wrong with our method of comprehending God, or something is wrong with God. Obviously we are the issue, not God. So our comprehension needs revision.

Our unhealthy thoughts and conclusions about God lead to our being ill at ease and to our body being potentially unhealthy. Where do we get a look at God that is authentic? Paul knew where to get a full view of God!

For God, who said, "Let light shine out of darkness," made his light shine in our hearts to give us the light of the knowledge of the glory of God in the face of Christ (2 Corinthians 4:6, NIV).

The light of the knowledge of the glory of God, shining from the face of Christ, filled Paul's life. What he experienced, he wanted all to experience with him.

Paul prayed, "… *that you, being rooted and established in love, may have power, together with all the saints, to grasp how wide and long and high and deep is the love of Christ, and to know this love that surpasses knowledge—that you may be filled to the measure of all the fullness of God*" (Ephesians 3:17-19, NIV).

Healthy Thoughts from a Once Twisted Mind

Some of the healthiest thoughts about God ever written can be found in the writings of this man Paul, who once loathed the God that he had heard could be found in Christ. Here is but a part of the masterpiece of his knowledge of God.

> *Love is patient, love is kind. It does not envy, it does not boast, it is not proud. It is not rude, it is not self-seeking, it is not easily angered, and it keeps no record of wrongs. Love does not delight in evil but rejoices with the truth. It always protects, always trusts, always hopes, and always perseveres. Love never fails* (1 Corinthians 13:4-8, NIV*)*.

Paul knew that God is love. He was telling us how God acts because He is love. He is telling us how we can act when God's love enables us. I will paraphrase this reality of God's nature and His ways:

God is patient. God is kind. God does not envy. God does not boast. God is not proud. God is not rude. God is not self-seeking. God is not easily angered. God keeps no record of wrongs. God does not delight in evil but rejoices with the truth. God always protects, always trusts, always hopes, and always perseveres. God never fails.

Right about now, you understandably may be asking, "Why are you taking so much time with an issue I have known about since childhood?" Because God has become a theory, not a reality, to many. We have a culture that knows a concept—"God is love"—without knowing the *God* who loves. We may even know an "edited" version of this concept: "God so loved the world He gave His only son so that whosoever believes in love will not perish." The best-known Scripture in the Bible that reads "whoever believes in Him" has been edited in many minds to read: "believes in love."

Believing in Love or Believing in the God Who Loves

To believe in love without knowing God is to miss both love and God. Believing God comes from knowing He loves us.

Many can say, "Jesus loves me, this I know, because the Bible tells me so." Though that statement is correct, it is incomplete. God's desire is to tell us personally. He may use the Bible. He may use other people. He may use the Holy Spirit speaking to us. But He wants us to experience His love as part of His presence with us. We are to live by every word coming from the mouth of God, not just words coming from a printed page or heard spoken about God.

God's presence known and experienced makes the Bible a Living Word, not just a printed word. God wants to speak of His love in a personal way as we experience Him. Believing Him leads to experiencing Him. Experiencing Him leads to knowing the limitlessness of His love. That is why God likes to speak to us. Just as importantly, that is why we must learn to hear Him speak.

Experiencing Him leads to knowing the limitlessness of His love.

In the validating experience of God telling us He loves us, we know love as God's nature, His love shared by His Holy Spirit. *"God has poured out his love into our hearts by the Holy Spirit, whom he has given us"* (Romans 5:5, NIV). In love's infusion love's power as God's nature *"bears all things, believes all things, hopes all things, endures all things"* and never ends (1 Corinthians 13:7). Love released in us by the Holy Spirit enables us to bear all things, believe all things, hope all things, and endure all things through the unending supply. The Bible tells us so; God's Spirit makes it so.

The Bible Is God's Love Story

Letting God define Himself means we are spared the erroneous pursuit of creating another misshapen image such as Paul encountered in the forest of man-made gods on Mars Hill. The disciple who best knew God's true character in Christ was John.

He came to know he was seeing God in action in the exhibit of Christ's love.

Reading John's gospel, and later his letters, makes the love story of the Bible very clear. He was equally aware, as was Paul, that many gods were offered in the marketplace of thought in the world. He took time to warn everyone with instructions to test the spirit behind words because of false prophets (1 John 4:1). Then, he gave the test standard.

Dear friends, let us love one another, for love comes from God. Everyone who loves has been born of God and knows God. Whoever does not love does not know God, because God is love. This is how God showed his love among us: He sent his one and only Son into the world that we might live through him. This is love: not that we loved God, but that he loved us and sent his Son as an atoning sacrifice for our sins. Dear friends, since God so loved us, we also ought to love one another (1 John 4:7-12, NIV).

His epistle is filled with the love language of God. His life was filled with the love of God. No wonder he wrote what is called the smallest Bible: *"For God so loved the world that he gave his one and only Son, that whoever believes in him shall not perish but have eternal life"* (John 3:16, NIV).

As a young man, John attended the school of Christ. He was in class the day Jesus taught on the hillside, where we have spent much time. He never left the class, though the method of teaching changed after the resurrection of Christ and His ascension. The Holy Spirit became the resident teacher. The class was relocated many times, but John remained a student, ever learning.

John was the last of Jesus' disciples to die. With advanced age, wisdom abounded and his focus narrowed. As if his supply of bullets was more limited, he carefully saved each bullet of truth.

So the bullet point of truth most used was God's love. Tradition has it that one of John's disciples complained about John's redundancy of talking about love. "Why don't you talk about anything else?" the disciple asked. And tradition has it that John answered: "Because there isn't anything else."

Our proper response to the fact that nothing is more important than the reality of God's love, God's enabling, and God's unending supply is …

THANK YOU!

CHAPTER TWENTY-THREE

Food for Thought – from Bone to Brain

Food and thought were the two major issues of choice in the garden of beginnings. Our human parents thought what God thought and ate what God said. A first-ever experience came when they thought without regard to God.

Adam and Eve's independence led them to consume information that contained death. Their next steps led to consuming forbidden food. Thought for food instead of food for thought changed the order of life. Jesus lived knowing that food for thought came from His Father. When asked by His disciples why He had neglected eating, He indicated He was eating the best food. *"I have food to eat you know nothing about…. My food,"* said Jesus, *"is to do the will of him who sent me and to finish his work"* (John 4:32, 34, NIV).

This presentation of the poles of life cannot be considered mere allegory. It is not a fable akin to a nursery rhyme or children's story meant to entertain.

This visit to the garden is like a visit to a medical clinic to get a report on the basic status of our health and eternal destiny. It is our annual check-up times ten, with every issue of life involved.

Two trees—the tree of life, or tree of knowledge of good and evil.
Two offers—life or death.
Two sources of thought—love or fear.
Two responses—belief or unbelief.
Two experiences—ease or dis-ease.

—J.H.

We have seen in past chapters that science has found new food for thought. Gerald Schroeder wrote: "Science has discovered a reality it had previously relegated strictly to the mystical. It has discovered the presence of the spiritual, for that is really what the mystical is, within the land of the living."[150]

The acknowledgment from an acclaimed thinker and professor of physics like Schroeder that science has found the presence of the spiritual is no small breakthrough. Science has indeed made a discovery.

But discovery is not enough without entering and enjoying the reality. Spiritual food for thought is our most important source to sustain life. The food we eat, both physically and spiritually, affects our health.

Physical food is an essential for maintaining life. Let's invite Dr. Swenson to resume a short tour of some of the essentials of our biological clinic.

All human activities, even rest, require energy. To provide this needed energy, our bodies require the periodic intake of nutrition…. The body takes this raw "fuel" in the form of food, processes it, and sends it to the cells, where biochemical processes convert it into usable fuel for the tiny cellular biofires.[151]

Dr. Swenson has a chart that indicates how our organs consume this energy supply while we are resting:

Liver and spleen—27%
Skeletal muscles and heart—25%
Brain—19%
Kidneys—10%
Others, including the digestive system—19%

The average stomach has about one-quart capacity. Throughout the day, however, it produces over three quarts of gastric fluid, including hydrochloric acid in a concentration strong enough to cause tissue damage. That the muscular stomach does not digest itself is remarkable.

As the food passes through the pylorus of the stomach, it enters the twenty-two-foot-long small intestine…. The overall absorptive surface area of a small intestine equals that of a tennis court.

The small intestines contain not only chemical enzymes and large surface areas, but also what has been called a *second brain*. "Structurally and neurochemically, the enteric nervous system (ENS) is a brain in itself," explains cell biologist Michael D. Gershone. The nutrition-to-energy process is so essential to our survival that God apparently did not trust it to the simple principles of mechanics."[152]

This lesson from biology makes a profound statement. God did provide the food supply essential to life with a second brain. For emphasis sake, I quote again biologist Gershone's statement: "Structurally and neurochemically, the entire nervous system (ENS) is a brain in itself." God wanted food assimilated to benefit every cell.

"Food for thought" was probably not a term coined from that function, but it could have been. That second brain with God's encoded cells reveals how God thinks. With skills on loan from God, the digestive system functions as designed.

A second brain or mind for spiritually correct thinking is just as important. God provided that brain to guide our ability to sustain life. A mind of the spirit, or the mind of Christ, was provided in creation's planning.

It is this mind developed in Christ that returns us to normal correct thinking. We will do well to reacquaint the brain cells located in our head with His offer to guide our receiving and digesting spiritual food.

A Liver to De-Liver

Soon after entering the small intestine, food passes the sphincter where the liver and gall bladder add their contributions. Next to the skin, the football-sized, three-pound liver is the largest organ in the body. Its 300 billion cells perform over 500 functions. The gall bladder, tucked under the liver almost as if it were hiding from the chest cavity—is surgically expendable, the presence of a healthy liver is not optional.

All of the blood flowing away from the stomach and intestines must first pass through the liver before reaching the rest of the body. The liver is thus situated at the crucial crossroads, entailing countless responsibilities. It detoxifies substances, guards vitamin and mineral supplies, stockpiles sugar, produces quick energy, maintains new proteins, regulates clotting factors, controls cholesterol, makes bile, maintains hormones balance, stores iron, assists immune functions, and is even responsible for making fetal blood cells in the womb. One thing it does not do is complain. It will work and work without protest, even under enormous abuse.

More than any other organ in the body, the liver has tremendous regenerative properties. Actually, liver cells rarely reproduce themselves in a healthy body—all their attention is given to the myriad of tasks that cannot be performed by any other tissue. However, when a part of the liver is injured or destroyed, the remaining healthy cells go into Amish barn-building mode.

In such a crisis, "virtually all of the surviving hepatocytes leave their normal, growth-arrested state and proliferate until the destroyed part of the liver is replaced," explain hepatologists Anna Mae Diehl, MD, and Clifford Steer, MD, of the American Liver Foundation. "Amazingly, the liver is generally able to perform its usual functions, even when large fractions of hepatocytes are actively replicating."[153]

Food for thought is as essential as food to supply our body. We will not live as God intended without food for *both* mind and body.

Physical Food Is a Parallel to Spiritual Food

Our physical nutrition, or food, is a parallel to spiritual nutrition found in God's thoughts. Moses understood this parallel. He saw a replay of the event in the Garden of Eden when the switch occurred from eating the food of God's thoughts to eating the food of deceptive, deadly thoughts.

From that understanding, he wrote what is essential for everyone to know and thus to live. God changed the diet of His people to teach them what to eat. "Manna," or the wafers of food He gave them in the desert, changed their diet to teach them to *"know that man does not live by bread alone, but man lives by every word that comes from the mouth of the Lord"* (Deuteronomy 8:3, ESV).

A word coming from God has no benefit to us unless it is believed. We are to live by every word that comes from God's mouth. Selecting only certain words indicates we do not believe God. Eve knew and quoted words from God, but she had ceased to believe them. God's people heard God's words in the desert, but they did not believe them.

We are to live by every word that comes from God's mouth. Selecting only certain words indicates we do not believe God.

The writer of Hebrews confirms this truth: *"For we also have had the gospel preached to us, just as they did; but the message they heard was of no value to them, because those who heard did not combine it with faith. Now we who have believed enter that rest, just as God has said"* (Hebrews 4:2, 3, NIV).

The Thoughts from God Are Like Food Necessary for Life

Attractive food on the table, however well prepared, will not keep us from starving to death. It must be eaten. Until it is received and started through the digestive process, it cannot reach the liver to allow the delivery of life in the blood to occur.

Going to buffets or cafeterias and perusing the excellent presentations of attractive food leaves those walking by—perhaps even lingering to admire the quality—no better off. Until the reality of Jesus' offer to *"take and eat, this is my body given for you"* occurs, we will die. We must open our mouths wide and let God fill them. We must taste and see that God is good. *"Taste and see that the Lord is good; blessed is the man who takes refuge in him"* (Psalm 34:8, NIV).

This disclosure in Hebrews centers on God's word, or God's thoughts. That word is God coming to us through His Son and the Holy Spirit. The issue is clearly declared: *"So, as the Holy Spirit says: 'Today, if you hear his voice, do not harden your hearts'"* (Hebrews 3:8, NIV).

This *is* today and the issue is clear: God is speaking. Everyone hears God's voice whether they recognize God as the speaker or not. A crowd with Jesus heard God speak and later said it thundered (John 12:29). God wants us to hear Him, know God has spoken, and just as importantly, believe Him.

Here is God's description of why hardness of the heart must not occur: *"Take care, brothers, lest there be in any of you an evil, unbelieving heart, leading you to fall away from the living God"* (Hebrews 3:12, ESV).

At issue is the believing or the unbelieving heart. Falling away from the living God starts with one step—unbelief. It usually leads to many more steps. If continued, it will lead to a hard heart of rebellion.

God Rested Because He Believed

God rested in the completion of creation because He believed. He believed it was finished. He believed all of the Trinitarian oneness of Himself would complete their covenant assignment. The Trinitarian oneness—Father, Son, Holy Spirit—caused Him to believe Himself. Thus He asks us to embrace the same belief.

There Is No Opposite of God: No Equal Exists

The devil is not the opposite of God. There is no opposite of God. No other one exists who has all power, all attending presence, and all knowledge. The devil is a fallen angel, not a fallen God.

Evil cannot gain ground in our lives except through unbelief. When the devil sought to deceive Jesus in temptation, he started with the same tactic as he used in the garden. "If *you are the son of God …* " the devil said, tempting Jesus to make a stone, which looked like a smooth loaf of bread, into bread to eat.

Jesus took the bread from His Father by believing Him instead of the bait of the devil's questioning. No evil could touch Him. Later, Jesus said the devil "comes to me and there is nothing in me that is in common with him or belongs to him" (John 14:30; this is my paraphrase—J.H.).

Spiritual warfare is won or lost on the battlefield of believing God. That is why Adam and Eve were not trained in spiritual warfare in the garden. They were taught to make the right choice, not engage in spiritual warfare. This issue of protection was within them; they were to believe what God said.

Winning the battle that was lost in Eden starts at the same place the loss occurred by believing God. There is a battle. There is a victory already won offered to us in Jesus if we believe Him.

Controlled Thoughts from God Are Smart Weapons

Our weapons of warfare are smart weapons that are ours if we believe God. In my earlier book, *The Supernatural Skyline*, I devoted space to discuss the devil, the demonic, and our victory in Christ. I won't take time to review that here, because the ground of the enemy's activity, the mind, is taken from him when we hear and believe God's living Word.

> *For the weapons of our warfare are not of the flesh but have divine power to destroy strongholds. We destroy arguments and every lofty opinion raised against the knowledge of God, and take every thought captive to obey Christ (2 Corinthians 10:4-6, ESV).*

Every Thought Is a Potential Mine Field

Every thought is a potential minefield in this war. Whenever opposition to the knowledge of God is offered as an opinion, it has deadly potential. Before the thoughts designed to destroy us can germinate, we are to "destroy arguments and every lofty opinion" seeking to gain ground in our mind. Every thought is to be reviewed. Our reality/truth detector needs to stay on all the time.

Every thought is a potential minefield in this war.

Life and death are set before us. That is the picture of a battlefield complete with sound effects. We hear the sounds of life in the joy God gives with accompanying thanksgiving. We hear the sounds of death in the cries of anguish and fear with the accompanying ingratitude.

A Second Brain–Both Need Proper Uses

The second brain of the digestive tract should help us understand our body knows that food is essential. The second brain oversees its travel to the liver for needed additives and then delivery through the blood to every cell in our body.

The liver is well named, probably by Greek physicians. We live as this organ supplies its 500-plus functions that come from 300 billion cells. This vital organ is there to de-liver. When the many deliveries do not occur, disease or death may occur. We *live* because of the faithful duty of the liver.

Believing God is spiritually akin to the liver's biological delivery system. When we do not believe God, the supply of God's provision is stopped at the gateway of our choice.

Let's review Dr. Swenson's remarks: "The liver is situated at a crucial crossroads, entailing countless responsibilities…. All the blood from the stomach and intestines must pass through the liver before reaching the rest of the body."

The liver is a distribution center of life to the body. Our belief is the key to the release of God's life to our entire being. We eat from His tree of life by believing.

We are actually taking His life, knowing His life, tasting His life-giving love by believing Him. *"Open your mouth and taste, open your eyes and see … how good God is. Blessed are you who run to him"* (Psalm 34:8, *The Message*).

Until we open our minds in belief in the way we open our mouths to welcome food, we have not believed. Believing God is tasting God for ourselves. He offers us Himself. His Word, when believed, is life-giving.

The Word of God is life when we believe God and allow the sustaining factors of life guide our thoughts. God's Word is inspirational, compelling, challenging, puzzling, seemingly contradictory to some, and it is countless other descriptions! Until we believe God, His Word is a concept standing as a possible choice among many alternatives.

When God is believed the Word comes alive—just as Jesus was alive in the flesh as both God and man. The Living Word is not a theory of concepts in a book about religion, but it is God speaking here now to me as I write—and in another installment, with you where you are, as you read and hear Him.

This point is vital in understanding the integration of God's thoughts to our being at ease and to our health. Our spirit, soul, and body are nurtured by the believed, living Word of God.

> For the word of God is living and active and sharper than any two-edged sword, and piercing as far as the division of soul and spirit, of both joints and marrow, and able to judge the thoughts and intentions of the heart. And there is no creature hidden from His sight, but all things are open and laid bare to the eyes of Him with whom we have to do (Hebrews 4:12, 13, NASU).

Getting to the Bare Bones of Health

Another look at our organic medical clinic will give further understanding to this important relationship between God's thoughts and our health. Now Dr. Swenson will help us look at our foundation.

> The adult human body has 206 bones, a number 40 percent decreased since infancy, due to the fusion of adjacent bones. Bones are the composition of mineral crystals (mostly calcium and phosphorus), collagen, and cells. The resultant material is as strong as granite in compression and twenty-five times stronger than granite under tension.

> People are routinely shocked to discover the pressure bones must withstand. Considering the twenty-six bones in each foot, orthopedist

Dr. Brand observes that "a soccer player subjects these small bones to a cumulative force of over one thousand tons per foot over the course of a match." The femur is stronger than reinforced concrete and must bear an average of 1,200 pounds of pressure per square inch with every step. The mid-shaft of the femur is capable of supporting a force of six tons before it fractures

The core of many bones contains marrow, a remarkable blood cell factory that turns out a trillion cells daily. It produces red blood cells [RBC] (with a life span of 20 days), platelets (with a life span of six days), and white blood cells [WBC] (with a life span of one day or less). If blood loss occurs in the body, the marrow can dramatically increase the RBCs and platelets according to need. If infection threatens, the WBC numbers surge. Cells of [the] immune system also are initially derived from the bone marrow. In addition, the marrow contains a small number of invaluable stem cells that assure the continuation of future generations of marrow cells.[154]

Life Is in the Blood

Throughout the Bible, God pictured spiritual reality with symbols. Following Eden, pictures were planted in minds through the shedding of blood of animals on altars. This important symbol was explained to Moses and then described in his five books. Blood was a symbol of life.

> *"For the life of the flesh is in the blood, and I have given it to you on the altar to make atonement for your souls; for it is the blood by reason of the life that makes atonement"* (Leviticus 17:11, 12, NASU).

"Life is in the blood" was a truth known to God's people. Again, Moses was the author chosen to share this truth. Sacrifices and blood placed on altars were indelible imprints in their understanding.

God's Word Goes to the Source of Our Blood

God's Word believed becomes part of us. As noted a few paragraphs earlier, God's living Word pierces us as a knife in order to be part of us *"sharper than any two-edged sword, and piercing as far as the division of soul and spirit, of both joints and marrow."*

Like a surgeon's scalpel, the piercing, penetrating, and participating activity of God's thoughts engage our basic make-up. Our body experiences this penetration of God's life-invading power in the bone structure.

The purpose of the invasion is to reach the bone marrow contained in many bones. Why is that important? What does God have in mind to send His living Word to the marrow of our bones? Dr. Swenson highlights why: "Many bones contain marrow, a remarkable blood cell factory that turns out trillions of cells daily." God wants His living Word present to guide the quality control of the making of trillions of cells daily. His encoded word in all our cells is being serviced with the refreshing memory of God's language.

At the most basic level of our biological life—the making of blood cells—God again participates in the making of healthy blood. Those whose lives are filled with God's living Word often experience healing. *"He sent His word and healed them, and delivered them from their destructions"* (Psalm 107:20, NASU).

A Healing Bible is a Bible Believed

A friend of mine, Tom Davis, grew up in greater Los Angeles. He met Christ dramatically in a church building during an earthquake. He moved from a church with much symbolism to a church of teaching and ministry, joining John Wimber. John, whom I also was privileged to know, believed Jesus is still doing all that He once did. John called this: "Doing the stuff—the stuff Jesus did!"

Healing was a large part of what Jesus did. As a gifted musician, Tom served with John Wimber in the Vineyard Church in Anaheim and in conferences where he witnessed countless people being healed.

From this understanding of God's desire to heal, Tom developed what he calls *The Healing Bible*. This Bible has highlighted passages of examples and promises for healing.

As part of Tom's aid to help a reader focus on the many promises of God for healing, he developed a quality CD. It is a classic combination of music that highlights God's love, His promises to heal, and His commitment to care for us. Interspersed with music is the reading of God's Word.

Countless people have listened to this recording, believed what God was saying, and been healed. Miracles have occurred in some lives. The recording was played in one hospital room, with hospital approval, 24/7. Though unconscious, a patient awoke and recovered from a tragic automobile accident.

An outstanding local educator was being treated for leukemia. At first, she faced the diagnoses calmly. In her own words, a "meltdown occurred later on." Barely able to talk, she called her friend Rusty Mayeux, who also is one of my friends.

He quickly responded to her anguish. "Here is an important tool for you," he said as he gave her *The Healing Bible*. Having no background of Bible knowledge, she was somewhat skeptical. But her respect for Rusty caused her to begin listening to the CD and reading selected verses. As she listened she began hearing God and later said, "God was always talking, but I wasn't hearing." Hearing God led to experiencing His presence. When she returned to the doctor they found no sign o leukemia.[155]

Though this is a book about health, not healing, healing is necessary for some to return to health. I say this because it illustrates the power of God's Word engaging our bodies' needs whether the need is healing or health. The second reason is to make you aware of the recording and the Bible. You will find information about obtaining the Healing Bible and the CD by going to: http://amberroseministries.com/healing-bible-cd/.

What God Thinks, What We Think, What Our Cells Think

God's language in our cells is a scientific fact. God's language in our soul is a spiritual fact. God's language in our spirit is a supernatural fact.

Our cells do not question what God knows or what God wants to do. Neither does the rest of creation. In fact, all of creation eagerly waits for God's family to resume management and complete the development of planet earth (Romans 8:21, 22).

God's language in our cells is a scientific fact. God's language in our soul is a spiritual fact. God's language in our spirit is a supernatural fact.

The gap that disconnects us from God occurs specifically in the space between our soul and spirit. Evidence of that is found in our thoughts and in the desires of the heart. God's remedy is sharing His life-embodied Word, His thoughts, to separate, or coordinate, our soul and spirit.

A coordinated leadership starting with the spirit gives us a renewed mind. In this spirit-led, soul-guided forum of thought, our bodies are glad to have thoughts in agreement with God's language in our cells.

Let's remember that we are not bodies, though we occupy one, or souls, though we function with one. Instead, we are a spirit made in God's likeness. God comes to our aide by dividing soul and spirit.

The two need dividing, since the soul is dominant while the spirit is basically dormant. We must be born spiritually, Jesus said. Spiritual birth activates God's family likeness and returns us again to God's residence—the kingdom of Heaven!

The amplified Bible enlarges this meaning by saying: "*The word that God speaks is alive and full of power … penetrating to the dividing line of the breath of life (soul) and [the immortal] spirit*" (Hebrews 4:12, AMP).

God's Word penetrates to the "dividing line" of soul life and spirit life. They are no longer enemies, but one, through both hearing God and knowing His thoughts. With a spiritual birth, we are as awake in our spirits as we are in our souls.

> We are awake to "*things which eye has not seen and ear has not heard, and which have not entered the heart of man, all that God has prepared for those who love Him*" (1 Corinthians 2:9, NASB).

> For to us God revealed them through the Spirit; for the Spirit searches all things, even the depths of God. For who among men knows the thoughts of a man except the spirit of the man which is in him? Even so the thoughts of God no one knows except the Spirit of God. Now we have received, not the spirit of the world, but the Spirit who is from God, so that we may know the things freely given to us by God (1 Corinthians 2:10-13, NASB).

Our Source of Mind Power Is the Spirit of God

We know the thoughts of God as revealed by the Spirit of God, which are revealed to the spirit of man that is in us. This is the way we *know from God* the things freely *given to us by God*. High IQs do not have an edge when knowing and hearing God. It is not brainpower. It is mind power, and mind power involves the spirit of man joining the Spirit of God.

Science knows we have a mind created in part by our brain, as Gerald Schroeder acknowledges, but it cannot explain how the mind is developed. Our spirit's access of our soul or brain results in our mind developing to think forever.

We can do that without God—but we can't do it right. We never get it right without His guidance. That is in part the source of restlessness, or being ill at ease.

Our spirit awakening and actively engaging in the management of our life results in the restoration of eternal life lost in the miscarriage of Eden. Our spirit is not a "whimsy wisp" but the substance of life itself.

Dallas Willard nailed it, in *The Divine Conspiracy*:

> We pull all these thoughts together by saying that spirit is *unbodily personal power*. It is primarily a *substance*, and it is above all God, who is both spirit and substance.

> To understand spirit as "substance" is of utmost importance…. It means that spirit is something that exists in its own right—to some degree in the human case, and absolutely so with God. Thoughts, feelings, willings, and their development are so many dimensions of the spiritual substance, which exercises a power that is outside the physical. Space is occupied by it, and it may manifest itself there as it chooses. This is how Jesus sees our world.[156]

The Call to Spirituality: Awakening to the Thoughts of God

> This is how the call to spirituality comes to us. We ought to be spiritual in every aspect of our lives because *our* world is the spiritual one. It is what we are suited to. Thus Paul, from his profound grasp of human existence counsels us, "To fill your mind with the visible, the flesh is death, but to fill your mind with the spirit is life and peace" (Romans 8:6).[157]

"Our world," or spirit, as described by Dallas, includes "thoughts, feelings, willings"—our right to think and choose. God gave it to us. God will not take it from us, nor can any other power. Nothing can separate us from this love-endowed right, the right of choice.

When our spirit is awakened to life, the death that occurred in the garden is reversed. We awaken immediately in our spirit. Then our soul awakens to new thoughts and our body begins to realize new management has occurred.

An Offering God Desires–One We Need to Give

Good reasoning or thinking follows as thoughts now taken captive align with God's thoughts. Paul's remarkable insights from the spirit conclude that the most reasonable or wise thing we can do is give our bodies to the Lord as a living museum of His workmanship.

God is not calling on us to do a self-directed, self-made home makeover. He is calling on us to give back to Him all He has given to us—our body, mind/soul, and spirit.

> *Therefore I urge you, brethren, by the mercies of God, to present your bodies a living and holy sacrifice, acceptable to God, which is your spiritual service of worship. And do not be conformed to this world, but be transformed by the renewing of your mind, so that you may prove what the will of God is, that which is good and acceptable and perfect (Romans 12:1, 2, NASU).*

Giving our bodies as a living sacrifice makes us what God intended, a temple where God lives with us. He does not live in buildings made with human hands. He lives in the creation made by His hands, especially our bodies.

In the giving of our bodies, we now accept a teaching doctor as the primary care physician of our clinic. In the giving of our bodies, we begin to experience the renewal of our minds. With that renewal, we will know and want the will of God. His will is good, acceptable, and perfect.

By transferring ownership—the title you hold on your body—to God, you will discover the truth of God's love, God's wisdom, and God's provision as never before. Take time to sign it over now. In addition to you being the most responsible physician giving care to your body, you now have a new resident physician who is also a teaching doctor.

Your mind will experience the difference over the days that follow. Your body will know that the care you are getting is the best of all choices. Look carefully at the decision to have a resident teaching doctor to act with you in the management of your clinic. Reading about this from Eugene Peterson's excellent paraphrase may help.

> *So here's what I want you to do, God helping you: Take your everyday, ordinary life—your sleeping, eating, going-to-work, and walking-around life—and place it before God as an offering. Embracing what God does for you is the best thing you can do for*

*him. Don't become so well adjusted to your culture that you fit into it without even thinking. Instead, fix your attention on God. You'll be changed from the inside out. Readily recognize what he wants from you, and quickly respond to it. Unlike the culture around you, always dragging you down to its level of immaturity, God brings the best out of you, develops well-formed maturity in you (*Romans 12:1, 2, *THE MESSAGE).*

God Was with You in Your Mother's Womb

Here's a summary of the decision: Your body has always been a gift from God. He was with you in your mother's womb. He encoded your cells as they developed. David the psalmist declared this amazing truth: *"For You formed my inward parts; You wove me in my mother's womb. I will give thanks to You, for I am fearfully and wonderfully made; Wonderful are Your works, And my soul knows it very well"* (Psalm 139:13, 14, NASU).

Recognizing that God was in your mother's womb in the development of your body has enormous implications. In part it explains the encoding of our cells.

Giving your body to God is part of giving your life to Him. Since you are temporarily housed there, present your house along with yourself. With the signing over of your body, you are offering a living dedication.

Giving your body to God is part of giving your life to Him. Since you are temporarily housed there, present your house along with yourself.

Dedications or sacrifices that live are irrevocable. Awaken every day as a co-director with God, in Christ, of your medical clinic/body.

Now your body is a living museum of God's creative wonder; both you and God in Christ live there. Remember: *"Christ in you is the hope"* (Colossians 1:27). Hope is now as limitless as God's supply of Himself, His glory.

This is the best decision you have ever made. *The Amplified Bible* calls this *"your reasonable (rational, intelligent) service."* If this were a business deal, you would now have a joint management plan with a partner of unlimited resources, knowledge, and power. (You might wonder why I am suggesting it is a co-management plan. In giving everything to God, He gives it back in co-management as He did in the Garden. What is God's becomes what is ours as His heirs. We are co-managers.)

Remodeling the clinic's physical needs follows a renewal of how the management is thinking. Our new partner has far more experience than we have. Learning from Him how to think, how to organize, how to react to issues, how to eat, how to relax—all of how to conduct life—is only part of the benefit we receive when we give our life and have it returned again.

The returned life is beyond comparison. We get a renewed mind. That process takes time, and the timeline varies from person to person, as we will see in the next chapter.

A Houseless Man's Amazing Home on an Unlikely Corner

A man thought by most people to be homeless said, "I am not a homeless man—I am a houseless man. I have a home with God." The man became an icon of downtown Fort Worth, Texas for 39 years. From an electric wheelchair, Charlie Joyner's life impacted people from every walk of life. They found in him encouragement, wisdom, faith, and hope.

Waving from his chair as cars drove past his prominent corner at Houston and Third streets, he pronounced blessings—unheard by those in vehicles, but not devalued. Some bus drivers making their scheduled rounds drew from his example and returned his blessings with a horn honk. Those walking by him or conversing with him heard his blessings: "God loves you … have a blessed day … don't worry God, is for you … have hope … have courage … God is here with you!"

Every city is either occupied with blessings or curses or combinations of both. Charlie Joyner was a living fountain from whom flowed the blessings he had found in his home with God. This living icon of blessings had far more impact on Fort Worth than most people ever imagined. One life on one corner offering blessings created an atmosphere impacting lives that came into focus as his life here came to a close.

The *Fort Worth Star-Telegram* began covering his story when it became known that doctors had done all for him that their medical skills could. Four articles and some pictures of him offering blessings followed in the daily newspaper, including the account of his memorial service. Following his memorial service, attended by more than 450 people in a ballroom of the Worthington Hotel near his "Corner of Blessing," a video documentary of his life went on Facebook. In less than a week 40,000 hits occurred as people reviewed a life of blessing. By now the viewers are multiplied thousands.

Before leaving his body in death he had already lost part of his body. As a double amputee, Charlie knew our body is not the source of our life. His wheelchair became his leg's partial replacement. Near downtown in 1988, he tried to hop on a moving train. In his fall he lost his legs. With the positive perspective faith gives, he was famous for saying: "Next time I will get a ticket."

Charlie remembered crying out "Oh God, help me!" when he was falling under the train. Then when he awakened in the hospital after a miraculous series of events—being discovered by a couple walking the tracks, being airlifted to the hospital, getting needed blood to live—his first conversation after regaining consciousness was with Jesus Christ. He gave Christ his life as a home. In turn Christ shared with Charlie His home with God. It was that home which Charlie knew, enjoyed, and lived in and from while pronouncing blessings to a countless host of people.

In his fall he lost his legs. With the positive perspective faith gives, he was famous for saying: "Next time I will get a ticket."

One who knew him well said, "He did not come to us, we all went to him. We were draw by a magnetism attracting us." That magnetism of God's call to us was not because of his physical appearance. For most, it took more than one look at Charlie to see a treasure in an unlikely vessel. The cheerful smile coming from Charlie revealed missing teeth that were seen through his scraggly beard, but these missing areas were mere companions to the gleam of joy found in his bright, shining eyes. With a slight lisp in his speech, probably created from his tongue not using the missing front teeth for enunciation, he spoke words that built up faith, that broke down racial prejudice, and that brought God's love for everyone willing to receive.

Following the memorial service, I was able to do something I had long wanted to do. I thanked the man who gave Charlie his right to stake out the busy corner of Third and Houston. As part of the executive ownership of Sundance Square, he had found in Charlie a needed presence, one who was positively influencing the downtown. With wisdom humbly received, Ed Bass realized that Fort Worth would be the better for blessings being spoken by the houseless man.

I thanked Mr. Bass for all of us who benefited from God's wisdom found in his decision to let Charlie occupy his corner. Recognizing Charlie as a person of great worth in a city using the name of "Worth"—this has eternal significance.

Sundance Square Security has made downtown Fort Worth one of the safest of any major city. Part of their codes call for keeping people, who are potentially begging or who create an unfavorable image, away from the pristine zone of "Sundance Square".

Charlie told me he was given the right to be there by one who owned real estate valued in the billions. The ultimate right to be there came from the one whose home Charlie occupied. "When I got to that corner those many years ago, I knew God was telling me this was my place," Charlie said.

A man of great wealth and a man of abject poverty both knew the real worth of God's home. Charlie found and lived in God's home here as all of us can with the attending ease evidenced in his life.

Included in my expressed gratitude was the part the Bass family played in the renewal of downtown with twin Bass Towers of corporate office space and the world class Bass Hall for performing arts. Ed Bass's reply to me was reflective of his gentle, humble reputation known throughout the city. "It takes all of us to build a great city. Every person can make a significant contribution. Charlie was one of the very significant people I came to know. He has left a lasting deposit of blessings in my life as well as our city."

Charlie's change from living in his body to living without it did not require a change in his residence; he is still in his home with God. Jesus described this reality when His own body was facing death, a death like none other. He said to his troubled disciples: "Don't let your heart be troubled. In my Father's house are many dwelling places. I am preparing a place for you." (This is my paraphrase of John 14:2, 3.)

Those troubled disciples moved into that place He prepared when they followed His instructions following His resurrection. Suddenly a sound came from Heaven as they began hearing God. God's presence came in illumining fire and communications from God so they could understand God and each other (see Acts 2:2-4).

The disciples had found the home that Christ prepared. Charlie found the same home while living in Fort Worth. In the Father's dwelling place, God's home, Charlie found the meaning of life, the supplies needed from God for living as a houseless man, and the sound of God's voice teaching and guiding him.

A part of the American Dream has been defined as everyone being able to own a house. God has something better than the American Dream—a conscious, eternal desire for everyone to have a home. Many who own a house have never experienced this home. Without a house, Charlie knew the abiding rest and peace of a home. He was offered a house several times. While grateful for generosity, he preferred living a lifestyle most of us can never imagine. All can afford the home Charlie enjoyed. God spoke through Isaiah of this affordable home with all its provisions:

> *And you who have no money come, buy and eat, come, buy wine and milk without money and without cost. Why do you spend money for what is not bread, and your wages for what does not satisfy? Listen carefully to Me, and eat what is good, and delight yourself in abundance (Isaiah 55:1, 2, NASU).*

Two men of conspicuous contrast met on a corner in Fort Worth. An icon of wealth learned from a houseless man rich in eternal worth. Value properly assessed by Ed Bass as found in Charlie impacted countless people. Many shared with me they came to know God as their companion in life through knowing Charlie. God's love reaches to the heights of office towers, where the wealthy can afford their own convenient apartments as well as their other houses, to the streets, where the houseless live in cardboard boxes. Love does not know price, but instead knows worth—eternal worth.

The Greatest Compliment Ever Paid You

Many homes are awaiting occupancy, which Christ has prepared as He promised. One is prepared for you. Charlie Joyner learned of that home and moved in. In that home he found himself at ease. So do all who move there to live knowing "all things are theirs" in the kingdom of God's conscious presence.

The greatest compliment ever paid you is this: "God wants you part of His family—actually part of Him." He wants you in Christ. He wants Christ in you. You can't get closer to God than that.

I hear Christians talk about getting closer to God. If you are in Christ and He is in you, you can't get closer than Him in you and you in Him! As you go forward, you are not getting closer—you are getting clearer, clearer in your consciousness of His presence, His love for you, His life lived again in you.

Our response when we believe God has given us Himself in Christ, who shares His mind filled with the Father's thoughts, is …

THANK YOU!

CHAPTER TWENTY-FOUR

Health Assurance: A Love-Filled Life

A teaching doctor now practicing in our medical clinic is undoubtedly our greatest assurance of health. Health assurance is found in our teacher's word to us: *"Give attention to my words; Incline your ear to my sayings. Do not let them depart from your sight; Keep them in the midst of your heart. For they are life to those who find them, And health to all their body"* (Prov. 4:20-23, NASU).

Our teacher's list of recommendations: Give full attention to God's words! Listen attentively to what God thinks! Concentrate as they resonate in the heart! Let them live, really live, for they carry life and health to your body!

Jesus gave this same priority for focusing our attention: *"But seek first His kingdom and His righteousness, and all these things will be added to you"* (Matthew 6:33, NASU).

Eugene Peterson assists in giving meaning to this: *"Steep your life in God-reality, God-initiative, God-provisions. Don't worry about missing out. You'll find all your everyday human concerns will be met. Give your entire attention to what God is doing right now, and don't get worked up about what may or may not happen tomorrow. God will help you deal with whatever hard things come up when the time comes"* (Matt. 6:33, 34, *THE MESSAGE*).

He who gets our attention gets our heart. Seeking health or healing is not our first priority. Seeking God with His many expressions of love and acceptance is our first priority. Seeking first His kingdom is an acknowledgment that we believe He is all and He is in all (1 Corinthians 15:28).

We are seeking Him for who He is, not for what He has for us.

What He has for us is already ours because of who He is. His testimony, which we reviewed in Chapter Six, made it very clear. His testimony says, *"All things are yours…. For all things belong to you, whether the world or life or death or things present or things to come; all things belong to you"* (1 Corinthians 3:21-23, NASU).

The Best Health Care Plan Ever Devised

The most comprehensive health care plan ever devised is found in the kingdom of God. Finding the kingdom benefits of health assurance rarely occurs by stumbling into them. We find them by seeking, or prioritizing our thoughts. Governance of the kingdom includes all of life, thoughts, actions, marriage, home, work, play, words, attitudes, friendships, and finances—full coverage.

God's Grand Creation: The Kingdom of God

The kingdom of God is not a small, remote, insignificant island to be visited occasionally during vacation time. It is the centerpiece of God's grandeur, both in Heaven and earth as well as in time and eternity.

America's Grand Canyon never ceases to create unequaled awe in those seeing it for the first time. The kingdom of God is God's Grand Canyon of eternal grandeur.

Legend has it that an American Indian seeing the Canyon for the first time tied himself to a tree. He was apparently fearful that the vast expanse opening before him would swallow him up. God's grand reality, His kingdom reality, offers a view of life without parallel. We have dominion or management engagements as vast as His creation. But the size and scope, the beauty of ever-changing colors, and the satisfaction of being part of His eternal plan must be seen as part of Him.

Apart from Him, the kingdom-sized view could intimidate us. But seeing Him expressed in every aspect of His kingdom brings love's embrace, which leaves no room for fear.

Our gift of the kingdom of God is a home with a vista of beauty ever unfolding. Seeing the kingdom is seeing time in eternity, microscopic intricacy in gargantuan size, love's tenderness in limitless power, and a man named Jesus of Nazareth as God Almighty! With a God view, we see man returned to be one with God, and man then returned to be one with each other, just as Jesus and His Father are one (John 17:21).

America's Grand Canyon never ceases to create unequaled awe in those seeing it for the first time. The kingdom of God is God's Grand Canyon of eternal grandeur.

The size of this canyon of reality is so encompassing it makes the Grand Canyon appear as a pebble at the beach. But most amazing of all, it will fit in us. Just as I have used lots of ink to describe the quantum aspect of going from galaxies to atoms to neutrinos, God found a way to give the kingdom back to us.

The Kingdom Fits in You

His kingdom comes, starting inside and working out. For the kingdom is not the big canyon of the universe or the biggest canyon of the galaxies. Though it is all that and more, it is the substance of life, designed to fit *in you* as *part of you*.

Just as God made atoms you can't see and did not stop but kept making smaller components, including neutrinos, He makes His kingdom fit in us. Remember, Jesus said, "Fear not little flock," for the Father *wants you* to have the kingdom. He was not addressing the big flock, but the little me and the little you. We feel little, but the big kingdom still fits in the little space His love arranged for occupancy.

Our Teacher Calls Us to Our Destiny– The Eternal Kind of Life

Our teaching doctor, who comes to guide our tour of self-discovery, will guide our potential. Leaf Hetland shares a classic illustration of a teacher calling a student to their destiny. Our resident teacher is calling us to our destiny, the eternal kind of life.

Mr. Holland's Opus, a movie, provides the illustration. *Opus*, a word from Latin, means work. The life work of Mr. Holland, played by Richard Dreyfuss in the movie, was his desire to compose music. His dream went unfulfilled. Teaching high school music became his career.

Leif shares his own good vision of *Seeing Through Heaven's Eyes*, which is the title of his book, when he comments:

> When he retires from teaching, the school hosts a surprise assembly in his honor. On stage are his students, sitting with instruments in hand, waiting for him to conduct the work that he had labored in obscurity to create? It is then we realize—and perhaps he realizes, too—that the great American symphony he would be remembered for was not the one on the music stand, but the one written in the minds and lives of his students.
>
> One of those students—now governor of the state—is a woman he once had in his class.[158]

This movie is one of my favorites, probably in part because I once taught high school English and speech. While a pastor in Marionville, Missouri, I was virtually voted into the school system to meet their high standards for a credentialed secondary English teacher. Many flashbacks occurred for me, both from teaching as well as relating to so many people across the years.

Mr. Holland's first day of teaching is marked by sounds not intended to ever come from the instruments being played. That is not unlike the sounds that come from our lives as potential instruments of God.

> As he listens, Mr. Holland spots a girl who is failing at the clarinet, a fact not only noticed by him but everyone. He waves his baton for the students to stop.

My comments: May I make this point? He is not stopping the music. He is stopping the sounds that are *not* music. Music would have come from the notes found in the composition, but the notes weren't being played. As our conductor, God guides in stopping our sounds so His music can be heard.

> "OK. OK. That wasn't bad. That wasn't bad at all." He looks over his glasses at the gangly girl slumping in her seat. "Ah … Ms.? … I'm sorry," he points to her, apologizing for not knowing her name.
>
> "Lang," she says sheepishly. "Lang. Gertrude Lang."

My comments: His wisdom and tolerance abound in his teaching skills. He commends, yet corrects with equal skill. In an after-class interview he gets to know Gertrude Lang.

> "How long have you been playing?"

"Three years," she says matter-of-factly.

Mr. Holland is taken aback. "*Really?*" He pauses, searching for words that won't crush her. "And so you find you get all the practice time that you need?"

"I practice constantly."

Mr. Holland pauses, then exhales, again searching for what to say. One well-meaning but ill-chosen word could devastate her. "Well. Then I think … I think maybe … you and I should find some time to work on an *individual* basis."

His words infuse her with life. You can see it in her eyes, hear it in her voice. "That would really be great."

"I don't have a lot of time … "

"That's OK. Whatever time you can give me, it doesn't matter." And by now, she is animated. "I *really, really, really* want to do good at this."

"I bet you do," he responds, suddenly wondering what he has gotten himself into. "Well, why don't you come in a half-hour before first period tomorrow, and we'll just start … and … "

She is beside herself, beaming. "OK. Thank you." And she curtsies almost as a reflex. "Thank you very much."[159]

Insights shared here by Leif are invaluable to us as well as all those whom we influence.

He has made her day and possibly he has saved a part of her from dying.[160]

Those who find and hear God's words find life.

Scenes in the movie show a future governor practicing with diligence. She is alone in a small room after school. Her irritating sounds are just as diligent. With eyes full of tears, she fights to turn sounds into music.

Mr. Holland is leaving for the day, and on his way out he calls to her. "Give it up, Ms. Lang." As he walks away he hears her crying. He stops and pauses, wondering what to tell her. Coming to the doorway, he explains, "School's out, Ms. Lang. I meant, give it up *for the day*."

"I'm terrible," she says, the tears coming stronger now. "I'm terrible. I … I tried, and I just … I just want to be good at something." And a lifetime of pain spills out. She sits straight in a hard, wooden chair, gathering her emotions. "My sister got a ballet scholarship to Julliard. And my brother's going to Notre Dame on a football scholarship. My mother's won the blue ribbon for watercolor so many times they retired the category. And my father's got the most beautiful voice." The next words are so painful to dredge up that she almost can't do it. "I'm the only one in my family who … I, I, just can't … it doesn't make any difference …. anyway … I—" She can't go on. Getting up, she walks out.

At a loss for words, Mr. Holland can only stand there.

When she based her worth on performance and weighed her performance against the performances of others in her family, the scales always tipped in their favor. She felt worth-less because her performance was less.

The next scene we see the young woman coming into the music room, where Mr. Holland is playing the piano softly to himself. She is poised, resolute, her long red hair parted in the middle and flowing down her shoulders.

"Mr. Holland?"

"You're late. And you left your clarinet here the other day."

"Yeah, I … if you know anyone who wants it—"

He stops and turns. "I'm giving up clarinet." A pause, as if she has rehearsed this. "I'm just goofing up everybody else anyway. I just wanted to say thanks, thanks for trying." She turns and walks to the door.

"Isn't it any fun?" His words stop her.

She turns, pausing a moment. "I wanted it to be."

Mr. Holland gets up from the piano bench with a sigh. "You know what we've been doing wrong, Ms. Lang? We've been playing the notes on the page." He puts a record on a nearby phonograph.

"'Well, what else is there to play?"

"Well, there's a lot more to music than playing the notes on the page." The needle makes contact with the vinyl. The song is "Louie, Louie" by the Kingsmen. "These guys, for example. Now, they can't sing. And they have absolutely no harmonics. And they're playing the same three chords over and over again." He pauses. "And I *love* it." A smile comes to his face and the beginning of a laugh. "Do *you*?"

She smiles. "Yeah."

"Why?"

And we see life returning to her face. "I don't know."

"Yeah, you do."

She answers sheepishly, "Because it's fun?"

"That's right!" His passion builds. "Because playing music is supposed to be *fun*. It's about *heart*. It's about *feeling* and moving people and something beautiful and being alive, and it's *not* about the notes on a page. I can teach you the notes on a page. I *can't* teach you that other stuff."

Again he pauses, thinking on his feet. "Do me a favor." He stops the phonograph. "Pick up your clarinet—and play with me." She picks up her instrument and sits in the chair. "This time," he says, as he takes away her music stand, "no music."

For a second she resists. "Oh."

"Because you *already* know it. It's already in your head and your fingers and your heart. You just don't trust yourself to know that." He takes his place at the piano next to her. "OK. Here we go. Ready? One, two, three, four."

The clarinet instrumental is Acker Bilk's signature song, "Stranger on the Shore." She follows him, but after a few seconds a squeaky note escapes. She grimaces.

"OK. Do it again. This time, not so much lip on the mouthpiece. One, two, three, four."

But she does it again, this time scolding herself. "Oh!"

"No," he says. "Now don't *do* that."

He pauses. "Let me ask you a question. When you look at yourself in the mirror, what do you like best about yourself?"

Her eyes fall onto the long, red hair, cascading down her shoulders.

"My hair."

He smiles, nodding, as if to agree. "Why?"

"My father always says it remind him of the sunset."

This pleases him. He pauses then says, "Play the sunset." Another pause, and he walks her through it. "Close your eyes." And she closes them. "One, two, three, four."

She follows his accompaniment, surprising herself at how easy it is, how *good* she is, how beautiful the music is that's coming from her instrument. She almost stops in amazement. Mr. Holland smiles, then laughs. "*Don't* stop playing!"

As she continues playing, he stops to watch her, marveling at the transformation taking place before his eyes. How do we explain the miracle that took place in that moment? When the young woman realized she wasn't auditioning—that she already had a place in the family, a secure place where she was unconditionally loved and unimaginably cherished—she could relax.[161]

The Spirit Is the Teacher: The Soul Listens and Learns

Our teaching physician's wisdom also calls from us what He knows is placed within us. This story teaches us the differences between the soul and the spirit in unmistakable sequence.

Our soul wants to learn to play the notes. Our spirit knows to play the music. As we yield to the spirit, the soul gets to enjoy what only the spirit can create from within. The Spirit is our teacher, and our soul listens and learns.

Religion, by whatever brand name it uses, always teaches notes. God comes with His thoughts. He does not teach from the lectern but through the Holy Spirit in us. His first thoughts are always about how much He loves us.

As we yield to the spirit, the soul gets to enjoy what only the spirit can create from within.

His love is not because of what we do but who we are. We are His children, however far from home we have traveled. We are His children, however hard we have worked for Him at home, yet at the same time never allowed

Him to love us.

Mr. Holland wisely instructed Ms. Lang to listen to the teacher *within her*. He relinquished his role so a melody played by both her soul and spirit could occur. As she relaxed and listened, she could hear the music growing louder within her. She no longer followed the cadence of the piano Mr. Holland played. A harmony even more beautiful was occurring inside her.

We Can Be Still and Know as God Knows

The love song of God's created melody plays in all of creation. God is love. That is the song played by the Holy Spirit in us when our Teacher instructs us to "be still and know."

> **We are His children, however hard we have worked for Him at home, yet at the same time never allowed Him to love us.**

"Be still and know that I am God" (Psalm 46:10). Our knowing God leads us to knowing ourselves and knowing as God knows. This is the music of God's love for our need to know the reality of life.

The life of the soul is the spirit. The life of the body is the soul. Alignment of the spirit with the soul results in alignment of the soul with the body. Only God's presence, His Spirit, the Holy Spirit, can achieve this relationship.

Only the living Word, the God-spoken Word, through His presence, brings our spirit to life. Our part is to believe what God has spoken. When our spirit comes alive, our soul comes alive, followed by our body.

Who Switched Off My Spirit?

Through *Who Switched Off My Brain?*, Dr. Caroline Leaf's writings have contributed a great deal to my thinking during the past four years. She has extremely valuable research about our thinking process, and she offers helpful application.

Research indicates we only use about 10 percent of our brain. So, it is not totally switched to an off position. It is more like a rheostat dialed back to a level far below half capacity. But now the real question is: "What if the rheostat is turned to full capacity?" Would we have most of our problems solved? No, because we still need a spirit awakening.

We are more than a brain directing the affairs of our life and our world. We are a spirit with a soul containing both a brain and a body—the brain housed temporarily in that body. "Who Switched Off My Spirit?" could be a title for a helpful book as well.

Neither our spirit nor our brain is switched off totally. Like a rheostat, our spirit is turned to a very low level of function. Responses from our spirit register in our lives whether we know we are a spirit or not.

Our spirit is more like a baby in the mother's womb. The baby in the womb is alive and has some awareness of sounds, nourishment, conditions around it and, probably most importantly, a consciousness of being wanted or not wanted, loved or not loved. Our spirit has similar awareness.

The baby in the womb is waiting for the most important part of his or her life—being born. Our spirit is waiting to be born—to be born again. Being born again is not getting back into our mother's womb. Nicodemus has already had that discussion, and he did it with One who knew birth from a mother as well as birth from a Father.

We are waiting for a birth from a Father. Our spirit knows about a birth from a Father—the God who fathered mankind. Being born again returns us to the Father, the only One who can make us at ease.

The miscarriage of eternal life as described in Genesis calls for a birth to return us to life as God intended. We are not at ease without a birth that releases our spirit from the womb of self control to restore us to God's family.

We are waiting for a birth from a Father. Our spirit knows about a birth from a Father—the God who fathered mankind.

Without our spirit being switched on, our brains cannot be switched to full capacity. Our brains are meant to work under spirit supervision.

All of life was redeemed or brought back to God from the unlikely position of the cross of Christ. There He paid the price to clear the record. Sin cannot separate us from God, only unbelief.

Christ's Most Cherished Possession: His Spirit

From a cruel method of execution—crucifixion—Christ reunited all of life to God. There He highlighted His own consciousness of Himself. He was first and foremost a spirit. It was His spirit that He guarded to the final completion of His role to reconcile all things unto God.

"Father, into your hands I commend my spirit" (Luke 23:46*).*

That He entrusted His spirit to the Father, in a trauma without parallel, must register in our understanding. His spirit alone was unscathed.

His body was emaciated beyond recognition. His soul was filled with the dark dregs of sin from the cup He drank. His spirit remained God's likeness in Him. This was His greatest possession, His eternal identity—God in Him.

Need I mention that he did not call for His body's preservation? Nor did He call for His soul's cleansing from the awful toxin that had drained into His soul, a soul that previously had no sin.

It was His spirit that must bear God's image by believing as God intended. His spirit was placed in the Father's care—complete oneness was secured.

My many references to the garden from these cliff notes of what life is meant to be must be seen alongside this tree where Jesus died. Adam and Eve took their spirits away from God by ceasing to believe Him. Instead, they believed a masquerading father of lies. Their spirits embraced the opposite of truth coming from perfect love.

The Spirit of God was again joined to the spirit of man in the birth of Jesus. With a body like ours, He lived as a Son with a fully activated spirit, just as Adam and Eve initially experienced. In a place totally opposite from the tranquil Garden of Eden, the Son of God—who was equally son of man— joined man's spirit to God as Father again.

The colossal importance of this epic moment must not be measured by the space I am allotting to the discussion. Jesus gave His Spirit to God on the cross so your spirit, and my spirit, can again know and enjoy oneness with God. *"Father, into your hands I commend my spirit,"* was the believing declaration to God for who He is!

Adam and Eve ceased to believe God for this oneness, but Jesus completely believed God, enabling him to regain our source of total restoration to God's family. Never was there less than total oneness with the Father-God and Son of God, Jesus.

Eternal oneness was their bond, and that had never changed as Jesus became flesh like us—with a body. He was unlike us because His spirit remained one with God.

A Separation to Gain Our Restoration

"My God, My God, why have you forsaken me?" were words none could have imagined Him ever speaking. Though never alone and never forsaken before this, Jesus became the most all-alone figure of history. Sin, which never touched His perfect life, now *was* His very life.

All of sin in all of time became His by transfer. Instead of being one with God, He was one with sin. He drank a cup filled with what He had no part in brewing.

Though never alone and never forsaken before this, Jesus became the most all-alone figure of history. Sin, which never touched His perfect life, now *was* His very life.

The greatest suffering of the cross was not the physical torture, but the agony of spiritual identity, of being separated from the Father. No longer experiencing God's presence—no longer buoyed by strength from limitless power—Jesus believed God. Though the conscious bond in His soul with His Father was severed by sin's engulfing presence, His Spirit remained connected.

"Into your hands, I commend my spirit." That act of believing grants us the right to believe God as well. Our believing comes from a gift of faith. Jesus believed for us so we can believe with Him.

His act of believing His Father with the guardianship of His spirit gives us access to the same unity. This is the faith, or believing, that pleases God. Without it we can't please God.

Everything Jesus did for us on the cross, including believing God for us, enables us to believe God with Him. We can rest our case in His provision by believing Him.

An Awakened Spirit Guides Our Mind, Which Thinks Forever

When our spirit awakens in the birth from God, our spirit awakens our brain to new leadership. The brain has already begun developing a mind. With new leadership, both the brain and the mind begin to function as designed in creation.

Our mind is ours—eternally. Our brain will be switched off in death. The mind will think forever, whether it thinks as God thinks or thinks without wanting God's thoughts. That is why getting that right, here and now, has eternal consequences.

This light or understanding shines upon every person. No one is left without the enlightenment needed to illuminate our choosing. *"That was the true light which gives light to every man coming into the world"* (John 1:9, NKJV).

Paul Learned to Know God By Jesus Teaching Him

Paul knew this gift of knowing God. It is not a special gift for certain special people. The manner of His appearance to each person will be as unique as the person.

His knowledge of God was far more than the initial encounter with Jesus on his way to Damascus. For three years, he chose to be isolated in Arabia while learning from Jesus.

> *For I did not receive it from any man, nor was I taught it, but I received it through a revelation of Jesus Christ…. I did not immediately consult with anyone; nor did I go up to Jerusalem to those who were apostles before me, but I went away into Arabia, and returned again to Damascus. Then after three years I went up to Jerusalem to visit Cephas and remained with him fifteen days* (Galatians 1:12-16, 18, ESV*).*

As amazing as it seems when first considered, Paul's teacher is our teacher. We are equipped to hear God and should hear God on a daily basis. God never slumbers nor sleeps, so He does not take time off. He has more effective communication than all of the communications technology of our day.

Developing a Conversational Relationship with God is the subtitle of Dallas Willard's book *Hearing God*. All his books are profound and worth the time to read and even reread.

God never slumbers nor sleeps, so He does not take time off.

If all good writing is rewriting, then all good reading is rereading. Conversation with God is not only possible but is a normal relationship when we are at ease with God.

One of the reasons Dallas's books are so valuable is the volume of quotes from Scripture, God's written Word. In the credits of *Hearing God*, two pages with five columns of Scripture references are found. He used an estimated 470 references!

In his best-known *Divine Conspiracy*, he again quotes more than 400 biblical references. His love for God and knowledge of God was intertwined with his own rereads of the most important book in his life, the Bible.

With a marvelous memory, Dallas could do a reread without opening his favorite book. He dialed up verses, he savored their meaning, and he heard God and shared how we can hear Him also.

> God's impressions *within* and his word *without* are always correlated by his providence *around*, and we should quietly wait until these three focus on one point…. If you do not know what you ought to do, stand still until you do.[162]

He identifies three of the most frequent ways God speaks: Impressions of the Spirit, passages from the Bible, and circumstances in our lives.

Then, with carefully developed illustrations, he teaches us to hear God's still, small voice and recognize His distinct and recognizable voice. His "circumstances of life" include God's voice through other people who hear Him.

Circumstances Shape Our Lives

Knowing that his own life was shaped by circumstances, he shares how God is present in all circumstances. Learning how to accept guidance from events in life is a vital part of hearing God.

After many readings of his book, and after knowing Dallas personally, I was very impacted to consider the following illustration was similar to his own experience in life. As I have shared, his mother died when he was two years old. He would have understood the experiential need of a child without a mother for comforting, assuring love

> A little child's mother died. He could not be adequately consoled and continued to be troubled, especially at night. He would come into the room where his father was and ask to sleep with him. He would never rest until he knew not only that he was with his father but also his father's face was turned toward him. He would ask in the dark, "Dad, is your face turned toward me now?" And when he was at last assured of this, he was at peace and was able to go to sleep.[163]

Circumstantially his tender heart had learned that God's face is always turned toward us. Had Dallas not learned at every stage of life that God's face reveals His love, there is no way to estimate the number of people whose lives would never have learned life changing insights.

Had he chosen to mistrust God from his childhood experience, he could have filled a brilliant mind with fraudulent thoughts. Instead of countless opposites from God's thoughts, his mind was filled with faith, hope, and love because he learned God's love-filled face is always turned toward us.

Children learn at an early age to monitor the face. Smiles, frowns, laughter, concern, or anger are all languages they know before learning verbal language. Detection of spirit reality begins before our birth, and we are born with spiritual discernment. Knowing God as seen in the face of Jesus is knowing God's clearest image.

Children learn at an early age to monitor the face. Smiles, frowns, laughter, concern, or anger are all languages they know before learning verbal language.

"For God, who said, 'Let light shine out of darkness,' has shone in our hearts to give the light of the knowledge of the glory of God in the face of Jesus Christ" (2 Corinthians 4:6, ESV). Dallas often quoted that verse precisely because he learned to see that face as a child!

Flashing Lights Signal Importance

If it were possible to put flashing lights behind the print I am writing, I would urge the publisher to install them. We cannot think correctly until we know what God thinks. We cannot know what God thinks until we hear God.

Instead of doing our own independent thinking or letting other people tell us what we should be thinking, it is time we invite God into the discussion. God enjoys thinking with us. Learning from others, like Dallas, is one of God's ways of speaking to us.

Get the book *Hearing God*! When God speaks, He is not limited to His words in the Bible for us. Though He often speaks to us with a Scripture, He speaks of many things from many sources. He never speaks of things that will contradict His written Word, but He has far more to say than Scripture contains.

Remember, He is not likely to shout you down or turn off whatever program you have chosen for entertainment. You hear by listening. You listen by getting still. Stopping the noise, as Mr. Holland did with his orchestra, leads to hearing the sound of God's voice.

Disciplines are of major importance. We may start with God with few disciplines developed in our lives. Knowing God requires time spent consciously with Him. We learn from Him, and part of our learning is how to make Him part of our conscious day. He can be as real to you in every aspect of life as the consciousness you have now as you read!

He is not likely to shout you down or turn off whatever program you have chosen for entertainment. You hear by listening. You listen by getting still.

Our first thoughts each new day can be His presence and His eagerness to be part of your thinking throughout the day. Your last thoughts of the day can be thinking with Him and thanking Him.

How long does it take to replant the "trees," or dendrites, in our brain, where thoughts occur? That varies with every life. A replant is needed for all of us. But don't assume your schedule will look like anyone else's. Major replants can take place in hours for some. Some people may take weeks, some months, and some years to know a new arrangement of plantings from the Lord.

An Australian Who Learned to Hear God

One of the more interesting people I have met recently is Dr. Peter J. Daniels of Adelaide, Australia. His thinking skills accelerated quickly once he knew God personally. His life story is an example of the ability to think with God.

As he was guided by God's thoughts he learned to think with highly acclaimed people. From obscurity and near poverty he became a man who influenced people all over the world. After amassing wealth that made him a billionaire, he started giving it away to causes that honored God.

His autobiography, *Living on the Edge*, includes this account of encountering God, when he was just 15. (Daniels came to know God at age 26.) When a friend turned back from a 35-mile bike ride into the countryside to hunt rabbits, the teenage Daniels continued to peddle his way alone.

> I continued until I reached our predetermined destination. Something unusual happened during my time away alone, out in the Australia bush. I came across an old derelict church with no front door and broken windows. There were birds nestling in the rafters and weeds growing up through the floor.
>
> At that church, standing all alone, I felt a radiant presence that held me in bondage for at least an hour. The simple fact was that I could not have left if I had wanted to, and yet I really did not want to. Over many years I have tried to analyze what actually took place there and yet to this day I find it quite beyond explanation.[164]

Challenges with thinking in Daniels's early life would not change quickly. His strong will gave him some advantage, but dyslexia left him struggling in most studies. Diphtheria struck his body a blow that almost took his life.

His fight against the odds included growing up in a fairly dysfunctional family. Bricklaying became his skill in making a living for his lovely wife, Robina, and growing family.

A Transforming Choice

At age 26 he made a transforming choice. Billy Graham came to Adelaide for a crusade. Peter and Robina attended. Robina decided to go forward to receive Christ in her life. Peter initially declined to follow Robina—and then raced after her.

> My prayer life and hunger for knowledge developed towards [the] desperation point. I had certainly changed.[165]

This man, whose lengthy shadow of influence has touched countless lives around the world, was virtually illiterate at the time he developed a "hunger for knowledge." Here is the scope of his willpower linking up with God's power in thought.

> Over many years my appetite to study and learn resulted in my reading over 6,000 biographies, plus books on history, economics, theology, and politics. I began to understand that the muscle of the mind can stretch and expand, ever ready to make room for much, much more. I also observed that knowledge becomes useless unless it is put into action with a plan and a timetable, and unless it has a value when measured against the only true moral value of performance.... You and you alone are responsible for your future, and that life is not chances but choices.[166]

Peter Daniels's life-changing choice to know God found in His Son Jesus Christ led to many right choices. We are responsible for our future, as he so clearly summarizes. God's gift of choice is ours to use daily.

The Varied Speed of Transformation

We have already reviewed the amazing three hours Ben Carson spent studying the book of Proverbs. The subject he studied at age 14 was anger. You will remember that anger from being taunted led him to almost drive a knife into the body of an obnoxious youth.

Behind a locked bathroom door he learned what God thought. In prayer He believed God. He has never stopped believing God. With evident gratitude, he now shares that he has never known that anger again. In as short a span as three hours, Ben Carson's thoughts changed from having uncontrolled anger to having self-controlled thoughts from God.

In my earlier book I shared a story from the life of former President George W. Bush. In a neighbor's house near his home in Dallas, he shared with our group his remarkable thinking transition.

Included in the group that evening were recovering drug addicts. It is well known that as a young man George W. Bush was addicted to alcohol. With his usual candor and warmth, he congratulated the group on the members' newfound freedom from drugs.

He shared his own story. Then he said, "While I appreciate the 12-step program taught as a means of recovery, I took only one step. I took a step to Jesus Christ and my life changed from that time to this."

Setting the Mind on Christ
One Second Out of Every Minute

Frank Laubach, known for developing the World Literacy Crusade, wrote of how his life was transformed. He began to cultivate the habit of turning his mind to Christ for one second out of every minute. Out of this practice he reported realizing he was being enabled by God to achieve things he could not have achieved. He found that he would turn around and find what he was needing waiting for him. His work was attended by God working along with him.

A Right Answer in an Unlikely Place

A motel room with a gang of drug addicts is an unlikely place for God to speak up. But speak up He did. The gang found a place to hide when law enforcement was closing in for arrests. Their leader is now a dear friend and spiritual son of mine. On this night, years ago, he had booked three rooms, and he wasn't looking for God to be one of the occupants.

All of the gang was high on drugs, including Kurt Chism, the leader. Days of running and hiding had taken its toll. Drug-induced sleep came to all of them except Kurt. He turned on the television set to pass the time. *Ghost Busters*, popular in that period of time, was on, and it captured his attention.

He heard the ghost leader in the TV drama instructing the ghosts to acknowledge him as their leader, saying, "Tell them who you believe! Tell them who you believe!" The ghost leader was wanting he own name to be the answer. Suddenly, into the mind of Kurt Chism came an answer he would never have imagined.

"Say Jesus! Say Jesus!" was heard in Kurt's mind as clearly as if it had been an audible voice, though it was not audible. Surprised and dismayed that such a thought could occur in his mind, he was shocked into being fully awake.

His shock was many-fold. He knew who Jesus was but had wanted nothing to do with Him since the day he saw a gang kill his brother on his mother's lawn. That day was marked with a totally wrong conclusion about God not caring and thus not acting to save his brother. Since he wanted nothing to do with God, why was God now wanting to have something to do with him?

He knew who Jesus was but had wanted

nothing to do with Him since the day he saw a gang kill his brother on his mother's lawn.

A fictitious ghost was demanding an answer on TV. "Tell them who you believe!" Kurt's mind had an answer he would not have expected before: "Say Jesus!" Twice the demand to declare who he believed was answered as Kurt spoke out loud, "Jesus – Jesus!"

Then, just as clearly, he heard the inner voice in his mind telling him to collect all the guns from the gang while they slept or, he knew, he would be killed. Agreeing with the voice in his mind to say Jesus, he further agreed with the wisdom of the voice to gather up all the guns. He is certain that action saved his life. God's voice was heard in a mind least expecting God to say anything.

Today this former gang leader is a new kind of leader. He leads a family, a church, a neighborhood and is becoming a leader in his city and nation.

The Answer to How Long It Takes to Think with God

Now I am ready to answer the question of how long it takes to change our thought patterns: *It takes as long as it takes to believe God.*

Some may take a longer time to know what God thinks and to believe Him, but the timeline is based on believing Him. Abraham believed God when he knew very little about Him. God counted him righteous from that day forward. He believed what God said (see Romans 4:3).

God believed Abraham also. He told Abraham he would be the father of many nations. They agreed to believe each other and believe together for all nations to be part of God's family. God's family would be made up of all people and all nations. To this day, God and Abraham still believe together (see Genesis 17:3-5).

We do not see in order to believe. We believe in order to see.

Jesus said to her, "Did I not say to you that if you believe, you will see the glory of God?" (John 11:40, NASB).

Believe God now. He believes you. It is important to get this right because whatever you believe shapes your life forever.

You can know—and He will know—you believe Him when you can genuinely say …

THANK YOU!

Why Does Eternity Take So Long?

Jesus lived in two worlds at once. His view of Heaven was as clear as His view of earth. Paul also lived in two worlds at once. His letter to the Ephesians shares how we can access both worlds.

I know of no contemporary who lived in these two worlds as did Dallas Willard. We were the same age. We grew up about 50 miles from each other as the crow flies, but I did not know him until later in life.

I first met him, vicariously, through reading his mind-expanding insights. Both my mind and heart were enlarged. Early in my reading of Dallas's thoughts, my mind was challenged. I put his *The Divine Conspiracy* back on the shelf two or three times before really absorbing life-changing insights.

I later learned others have shared that same experience of difficulty in reading Dallas. Doctors, trained in reading voluminous amounts of complicated material, have shared with me the challenge of reading the latent thoughts of wisdom from this remarkable mind.

I mention this to encourage you not to turn back when reading what seems to require an extra effort. Going the second mile in reading may take you to an essential vista of life, one that God intends for you.

There are times when you read gifted writers and then later meet them; you find they are more gifted at composing words than interacting personally. Not so with Dallas. He was the same in person as in print. But he was even more impacting in person. The warmth of his love, his humility, and his genuineness were evident in a way printed words cannot convey. None of his remarkable insights or mental quickness lessened his warmth of being a person conscious of God's likeness.

Just as God shaped him uniquely to share with thousands about the "eternal kind of life," God took him to the transition of death to teach us to be at ease in taking that transitional step. He was at ease in life knowing God guides us in His ways in the most important issues that we face.

He identified three of these issues: *Who we are, why we are here*, and *what is the good life?* We cannot know any of these three things without knowing God through His Son Jesus Christ and the Holy Spirit, our teacher.

Dallas was equally at ease in facing death. His departure from his body has lessons for all of us. Grace for living is part of our birthright in God's family. Grace for dying is just as much a part of that right.

He identified three of these issues: *Who we are, why we are here*, and *what is the good life?*

We are so often focused on living well and finishing well that we forget to draw from the grace deposits for the transition from our bodies. Or we may not know the deposits exist. Our not knowing or not drawing from grace for dying would be like having millions of free air miles to fly anywhere in the world—and never cashing them.

I am going to take time to review the transition of Dallas Willard to "God's full world," as he often referred to our future home. His departure will serve as a good travel guide. I am certain God arranged his travel to encourage us.

Eternity Lives in Every Heart

Eternity was put in Dallas's heart, as it is in all of God's children. *"He has made everything beautiful in its time. Also, he has put eternity into man's heart"* (Ecclesiastes 3:11, ESV).

Eternity was kept before him beginning from childhood. That was the request of his mother at her departure when he was two: "Keep eternity before the children."

Eternity was known by him as part of life now. "The eternal kind of life" was his description of the life we live according to God's design. The will of God is to be done on earth as it is in Heaven.

Eternity is not to be saved until later. God brought time out of eternity and takes time back into eternity. Christ lived in eternity and time as part of His reconciling or returning all things back to God.

A Doctor's Shocking Report

"Is there a difference in the way Christians face death as compared to non--Christians?" That was my question to an experienced doctor friend. I listened in stunned amazement to his answer, which was the opposite of what I had expected.

"There is virtually no discernible difference that I have observed," he said. Knowing I was hearing from a doctor with more than twenty-five years of hospice practice, my thoughts went from shock to surprise to a search for explanations.

Dr. David Capper continued his observations, with some amplifications.,

"Some Christians do face death confidently. So do those who are not Christians. Many who are Christians face death with apprehension and at times fear, just as non-Christians," Dr. Capper told me.

Several thousand people have taken their last steps with the compassionate, thoughtful care of this Christian doctor and his capable hospice team. I had expected him to tell me that Christians face death with a much greater confidence than others.

While I did not question my friend's unexpected response, I asked the same question of another family practice doctor with whom I serve as a fellow elder. Without hesitation, he gave me the same answer.

My conclusion is this: We haven't taught people the right to experience and enjoy Heaven before going there. Jesus' announcement that the kingdom of Heaven is at hand still stands! Many Christians in our current church culture lack the basic understanding of how eternal life is part of *life now*.

Understanding Heaven Starts Here

Heaven starts here. So does hell. Embracing God or pushing God away starts here. Who we are here and what we think here determines our knowing life or death.

Dallas had learned that the kingdom of Heaven comes here to us. Before we can go to Heaven, Heaven comes to us. We learn to expect Heaven to come. We learn to pray for the will of God to be done here as in Heaven.

"I will probably be dead sometime before I know it," were the words that came from Dallas when the doctor told him he would probably not live much longer. Ease that characterized his thoughts about living enabled him to be at ease with thoughts about dying.

Long before that medical report, he believed the many reports he knew from God's thoughts. He had long chosen to believe God's reports.

We haven't taught people the right to experience and enjoy Heaven before going there.

His consciousness of God's occupying presence in His creation enabled him to enjoy God's presence everywhere, as we have seen. His consciousness of God's presence as a companion in his life was an equal awareness. The reality of God's presence so attended his thoughts that the transition called death would not alter his consciousness. He knew that an interval of time might elapse before he knew death had occurred in the body.

In the Body or Not, We Are Alive

I know of only one other person who said anything comparable. That person was the apostle Paul. He was thought to be dead at Lystra (Acts 14:19). Among his associates was Doctor Luke. It is unlikely they would not have been able to determine if life remained his body.

About fourteen years afterward, Paul said, *"I know a man in Christ who fourteen years ago—whether in the body I do not know, or out of the body I do not know, God knows—such a man was caught up to the third heaven. And I know how such a man—whether in the body or apart from the body I do not know, God knows—was caught up into Paradise and heard inexpressible words, which a man is not permitted to speak"* (2 Corinthians 12:2-5, NASU).

Paul's experience was different from that of Dallas's. The similarity lies in the fact that Paul said some things that were discernible and some that were not. He was conscious of being in the "third heaven," or Paradise with God.

Paul knew that whether in the body or not, we are alive. He did not know whether this trip was with his body or without it. He knew where he went. He knew what he heard. He obviously knew he came back with the instructions not to report the wonder of the words he heard or the glorious grandeur of all he saw.

Dallas' experience in his body ended as no other that I have known personally. Having kept the ability to communicate to the end, he shared going down a hallway conscious of witnesses on both sides. He always valued the witnesses, those already living without bodies, on the other side. Then came his final words, and the refrain of this book: THANK YOU!

The reality of God's presence so attended his thoughts that the transition called death would not alter his consciousness.

Every time I review God's arrangement for Dallas to remain lucid to both see and report the host of Heaven, as well as his final two words, I pause in awe to offer my thank you to our all-wise and loving Father.

A Spiritual IQ for All

Life is not about getting to Heaven. Life is about *getting in on Heaven here* and now. This consciousness of His presence is not for a few with spiritual IQs so high they would rival Einstein's natural IQ. Every member of God's family, through knowing Christ, is intended to experience His presence. Spiritual IQs are for all. Children can have as high a spiritual IQ as an adult. In some cases they may be higher. Jesus honored and affirmed children as having an awareness of God as much as anyone.

Learning What Dallas Learned

Let's again step into Dallas's classroom through his writings, where so many lives found understanding of life.

> The mind or the minding of the spirit is life and peace precisely because it locates us in a world adequate to our nature as ceaselessly creative beings under God. The "mind of the flesh," on the other hand, is a living death. To it the heavens are closed …

> Jesus, by contrast, brings us into a world without fear…. He lived and invites us to live in an undying world where it is safe to do and be good. He was understood by his first friends to have *abolished death and brought life and immortality to light through the gospel*" (2 Timothy 1:10).

Once we have grasped our situation in God's full world, the startling disregard Jesus and the New Testament writers had for "physical death" makes sense. Paul bluntly states, as we have just seen[,] that Jesus abolished death … simply did away with it. Nothing like what is usually understood as death will happen to those who have entered his life.

To one group of his day who believed that "physical death" was the cessation of the individual's existence, Jesus said, "God is not the God of the dead but of the living" (Luke 20:38). His meaning was: those who love God and are loved by God are not allowed to cease to exist, because they are God's treasures. He delights in them and intends to hold onto them. He has even prepared for them an individualized eternal work in his vast universe.

At this present time the eternally creative Christ is preparing places for human sisters and brothers to join him. Some are already there—no doubt busy with him in his great works. We can hardly think they are mere watchers. On the day he died, he covenanted with another man being killed along with him to meet that very day in a place he called Paradise. This carries the suggestion of a lovely garden-like area.

Too many are tempted to dismiss what Jesus says as just "pretty words." But those who think it is unrealistic or impossible are shorter on imagination than long on logic. They should have a close look at the universe that God has *already* brought into being before they decide he could not arrange for the future life of which the Bible speaks.

Anyone who realizes that reality is God's, and has seen a little bit of what God has *already* done, will understand that such a "Paradise" would be no problem at all. And there God will preserve every one of his treasured friends in the wholeness of their personal existence precisely because he treasures them in that form. Could he enjoy their fellowship, could they serve him, if they were "dead"?[167]

Understanding that reality is found in God as evidenced in creation framed the panorama enabling Dallas to see Heaven in the preview of what "God has already done." He knew that "Jesus brings us into a world without fear." That included the fear of death.

He saw God by seeing Jesus, who said, "He that has seen me has seen the Father." He saw God in the grandeur of His creation. He saw God in the lives of God's people. He saw God in the telescope or the microscope. He saw God because the pure in heart see God.

Stepping Into the Shadow While Seeing the Light

Though we walk into the shadow of death, we find beyond the shadow is light. A shadow is actually lessened light. Darkness is not the cause of a shadow.

Death as a transition creates a shadow, leading to the opening of God's illumining vista of Himself, His family, His host of angels, His eternal engagements, and His gift of life as He intended it to be enjoyed.

David knew this reality of death as a shadow created by the light of life. He became aware of God's presence with him as a youth. Probably while being stalked by a deranged King Saul, David lived in the shadow of death. David was already chosen to be Saul's successor. Spears thrown by hit men thudded against cave walls where he hid. He never returned the spears in revenge.

He became aware of God's presence with him as a youth. Probably while being stalked by a deranged King Saul, David lived in the shadow of death.

With the thudding sounds of potential death all around him, David heard from God the sounds of life. Hebrew thought form follows first hearing from God before declaring what is heard. Long before the sounds of death greeted David's awareness, he learned to hear God.

David heard God say:

I am your shepherd, you will not want.
I will make you to lie down in green pastures.
I will lead you lead beside still waters.
I will restore your soul.
I will lead you in paths of righteousness,
For my name's sake.
Though you walk through the valley of the shadow of death,
You will fear no evil.
My rod and staff will comfort you.
I will set a table before you, in the presence of your enemies.
I have anointed your head with oil.
Your cup overflows.

Surely goodness and lovingkindness will follow you all the days of
your life,
And you will dwell in my house forever.
— This is my paraphrase of Psalm 23

As a shepherd knowing love for his sheep, knowing their names, knowing their needs, He came to know God, who knows everyone by name. He repeated what he heard God say to him. This is probably the second-most familiar passage in the Bible.

The Lord is my shepherd,
I shall not want.
He makes me lie down in green pastures;
He leads me beside quiet waters.
He restores my soul;
He guides me in the paths of righteousness
For His name's sake.
Even though I walk through the valley of the shadow of death,
I fear no evil, for You are with me;
Your rod and Your staff, they comfort me.
You prepare a table before me in the presence of my enemies;
You have anointed my head with oil;
My cup overflows.
Surely goodness and lovingkindness will follow me all the days of
my life,
And I will dwell in the house of the Lord forever
(Psalm 23, NASU).

David begins by talking about God.

God is our caring shepherd—even laying down His life for us. No one goes unnoticed.

Then it seems David is talking to us, telling us what God wants to be to us.

Food for thought offers life-filling nutrition—we can lie down in rest.

He takes us to still waters to drink and make us at ease.

Our soul is restored with His energizing provisions.

He walks us along paths of righteousness—the goodness of life.

His name's sake, with His full rights, is ours to use as He directs.

David transitions from talking *about* God to talking *to* God. Hearing and knowing God always leads to a conversation with God. This is the normal order of our thinking with God.

You have prepared a table for fellowship in the presence of enemies.
Your anointing of oil covers my head.
You have filled my life like a cup to running over.
Your goodness and mercy that I know now I will know forever.
Your house is mine forever.

I suggest you listen as David talks with God—and then join him. Say after David what he says. You may do it silently if you are in a place where it is not appropriate. But if you are in a place with only you and God, saying it aloud may be most effective.

Hearing and knowing God always leads to a conversation with God. This is the normal order of our thinking with God.

Here are my thoughts paralleling David's, or even better, you might offer your own:
You are my Lord guiding me as a shepherd.
Guide my thoughts to your quiet thoughts of rest.
Restore my soul's thoughts with yours.
When I walk where I have never walked—into a shadow called death,
Fear will not go with me because you are my companion!
Your loving presence is my rod and staff to comfort and protect!
Your table of food strengthens me, and enemies can only watch.
Oil with your soothing covering upon my head guides my thoughts.
My cup of life's joy is running over instead of running dry.
I will enjoy you now and live and enjoy you in your house forever.

Two Long-Term Friends Stepped Through the Shadow

Two of my long-term friends stepped into that shadow during the writing of this book. Though they were unique, they had one thing as a shared trait: Both knew the presence and fellowship of God as the most important person in their life.

I had the privilege of watching both experience God's life and presence as their own. I experienced Him along with them. Learning to hear God and know God while they were also learning was part of the bond of brothers' friendship.

Such a brothers' friendship will be forever enjoyed. They are a tad ahead of me in the journey. I am still on assignment here, getting this book written, along with several other venues.

Hollis Dain "Doc" Smith

Hollis Dain Smith was the first of the two men I refer to to experience God's enabling presence while in this "shadow land," as C.S. Lewis described it. He experienced that presence beyond the shadow.

Some of the story of our encounter with God's taking up residence in our city I shared in my earlier book, *The Supernatural Skyline*. I mention it only as a reference for filling in blanks if you are interested.

It was in the county seat town of West Plains in South Missouri while I was pastor of the First Baptist Church that a man's man became one of my close friends. Dain Smith earned a walk on position on the University of Missouri Football Team. He played at center as an offensive lineman and developed himself as one of the strongest men, physically, I have ever known. Though an injury cut his football career short his physical strengthening program was a way of life. His major was veterinarian medicine. So, his nickname for many was simply "Doc."

As God's "manifest presence" began showing up in church services in our church as well as events across the city, Dain was ready to know the transformation occurring in me and countless others.

A former medical missionary doctor to China was a member of the church. She knew the spirit-filled life. A young man from the church, Jay Davis, learned of the spirit-filled life through Campus Crusade for Christ.

This was all a wonderful example of God's "divine conspiracy" so well described in Dallas Willard's classic book. (Dallas grew up about fifteen miles from West Plains.) God's conspiracy is a conspiracy of love. This love will not stop at any "keep out, private property" signs.

Dain Smith watched lives changed. He listened to people report the reality of love that cleansed and completed life. One day he took a call to treat a cow that was attempting to give birth. While driving several miles in his state-of-the-art veterinarian's service pickup, he called out to God. God took his call.

Soon Dain was as conscious of God being present in the cab of that pickup as himself. Jesus became as real to him as all the reality around him.

With a gravely deep voice, he said, "I just began singing that 'rinky dink' song, 'Amazing Grace.'" Though not a singer before, he sang the rest of the way to save the life of the cow and her unborn calf. With the completion of his duties, he sang his way back to his office.

Bonds created in God's presence are eternal bonds. Dain and I knew and loved each other from those days forward. Though miles eventually separated us, the bond kept us as close as ever, and when together, it was like we had never been apart.

When he called with the news that a malignant tumor had been diagnosed in his body, I knew sorrow, concern, hope for healing, and confidence that he could not lose.

His journey to "fuller life" was one of quiet preparation. Never in the months that followed did he discuss his departure with anyone. None of his closest spiritual confidants, or even Dorothy Ann, his much-loved wife, heard any thoughts from him about death. Our conversations, mostly by telephone, were about the good times of the past and our looking forward to good times to come.

Preparation and planning were always a part of his life. So he discussed his funeral and his preferences but not once did he speak to anyone about the transition that was about to occur. He lived in confidence and he left his body with the same confidence. God's presence was real to him across the many years—since the days of their pickup truck ride together to the time he left his body.

He lived in confidence and he left his body with the same confidence.

Some refer to deeply spiritual people as those who wear their religion on their sleeve. Dain didn't wear religion on his sleeve. He wore a relationship with God as part of his very life.

Tom Blanton

Only a few months after Dain's transition to enjoy more of life, another friend literally stepped into the limitless expanse of Heaven's grandeur. Tom Blanton, my longtime friend here in Fort Worth, was walking, as he had walked most mornings, with his former next-door neighbor, Bob Cross.

They were probably halfway through their power walk for cardiovascular benefits. Laughter, as usual, was part of their walk and talk. Bob Cross shared with me how Tom was at full stride, laughing about an amusing subject they were enjoying together. Suddenly he gasped, bent forward to catch himself, and crumpled to the street.

With skills in CPR, Bob went to work along with summoning help. Men from a fire station within shouting distance arrived quickly—but Tom was already gone.

Tom and I spent years in an up-close bond of brother's friendship. For eighteen years, I was pastor at Lake Country Baptist Church in Fort Worth. Tom and Jeannie and their family joined during the first year I served.

Soon Tom became an elder of the church. We served together on an important board, developing *Fulness* magazine, a renewal magazine that reported God's manifest presence while bringing awakening across America.

As God's presence brought awakening to our church and many other churches and cities, Tom was one who invested. He was an entrepreneur. Investments were part of his life by that stage of his journey in a kingdom of business activities. Tom's new investment came on the terms Jesus described as relates to the kingdom. Jesus said, "Sell all and buy in with me."

> *"The kingdom of heaven is like a treasure hidden in the field, which a man found and hid again; and from joy over it he goes and sells all that he has and buys that field. Again, the kingdom of heaven is like a merchant seeking fine pearls, and upon finding one pearl of great value, he went and sold all that he had and bought it"* (Matthew 13:44-46, NASU).

Tom bought in with Jesus. He was one of the more unusual men I have known. He and Jeannie came to Fort Worth as a young couple just starting life together. They moved next door to a young couple that became their business partners and close friends.

The neighbor's father owned a small company. Before long, Tom and the neighbor bought out the father. Eventually Tom bought the entire, greatly expanded business. As the years unfolded, many companies were started and run successfully by a man who learned to invest.

But his investment in God's kingdom was the best investment he ever made. Early in Tom's business career he stopped by our home before going to his office. As we sat on the deck overlooking our neighborhood and Eagle Mountain Lake, Tom shared that his main business was failing. A meltdown was occurring.

He sought counsel with a concern for his family and his employees. His buy-in with Jesus was never a question. He was really asking for counsel as to how to maintain that commitment and honor Jesus in a potential bankruptcy.

He went through that storm with Jesus stilling the waves. Other storms came at times, but Tom was one who knew Jesus' presence in his boat.

With little formal education, he trained his mind to understand complicated documents related to business and to read spreadsheets with the skill of the professionally trained. He learned to invest and grow companies.

At the time of his departure, He owned five companies with more than forty entities, or sub-companies. Over the years, millions of dollars for kingdom expansion came from his accounts.

Yet his greatest joy was the pearl he bought, the "pearl of great price."

Where We Go Is More Important Than How We Leave

Dain left this life slowly yet confidently. Tom left this life at full stride.
Of course, I was impacted that two men so close and so meaningful in my life had stepped where I only see partially. The contrast in their departure schedule is impacting as well. Hospice care was part of assisting Dain and Dorothy Ann in those final weeks. Tom was planning and discussing expansions in many venues in his varied duties until the final moments of his thoughts here.

Why the difference? That question, like many we have, is not for us to know. Paul knew that where he was—whether in his body or without it—all that he learned there was classified information. A non-disclosure agreement was enacted. Disclosure will come to all of us when we step through the shadow into the light.

A day is coming to all of us when we will "know as we are known."

So ... Why Does Eternity Take So Long?

Why does eternity take so long? was a question that flashed in my mind one morning a few years ago. It was a thought I had never considered. Whether I was hearing it for the first time or I had heard someone raise the question before was unclear.

Because it seemed urgent, I believed it was from the Lord. I knew He does not ask questions for information but to introduce discussion. I asked for guidance. While I have given much thought to the question, guidance was accelerated as I began writing this book.

My attention focused on a verse memorized years ago: "*For now we see in a mirror dimly, but then face to face; now I know in part, but then I will know fully just as I also have been fully known. But now faith, hope, love, abide these three; but the greatest of these is love*" (1 Corinthians 13:12, 13, NASU).

We are going to know fully, and our knowing is related to God knowing us. We have glimpses of many things now. It is like looking in a smoked-up mirror. But clarity is coming in breathtaking sharpness as we see face-to-face compared to seeing a face in a smoky mirror.

We are now known by God, angels, and the host of witnesses already with the Lord. The ancient Geek admonition "Know Thyself" is never fully realized apart from the eternal perspective. Knowing as we are known includes both knowing ourselves as well as all other needed knowledge. God and His family know us in our developmental stages, our understanding, and our skills here. They know us better than we know ourselves.

They knew Dain and Tom better than I ever did. They knew that Dain was one of the most skilled and innovative veterinarians who ever practiced. He made complicated surgeries on animals seem easy. Crossbreeding highly productive beef cattle in the latter part of his career resulted in a prized, valuable herd. The wisdom and skill he exhibited attracted young men to learn from him.

In one period of his life his own church staff, made up of young pastors, asked him to teach them skills in leadership and management. He did it gladly. They loved it because they knew he loved them as well as the process of equipping them.

Dain's legacy here stretched far beyond his skill in caring for animals, inventing equipment, or developing better genetics in cattle. He cared for people and called them to their destiny.

My son, Randy, was one he called out and up to his potential. Dain was a surrogate father to Randy in years I traveled and spoke across our nation and sometimes in other nations. One more call came as Dain asked Randy to do the eulogy at his memorial service. He responded with his well-chosen words of honor and deep love.

Will Dain be found spending most of his time chatting with friends in Heaven's retirement village? Since there is no retirement plan or even a retirement concept suggested in the Bible, why would there be a retirement village along a gold-paved street? Dain found activity, creativity, and productivity fulfilling here. All those qualities are being developed even more in his expanded knowingness.

Tom had a similar influence on young men as well as young women because of the years of leadership he gave as chairman of the board of Lake Country Christian School. His business also attracted young men with great promise. They wanted to work with him and learn from him.

Since there is no retirement plan or even a retirement concept suggested in the Bible, why would there be a retirement village along a gold-paved street?

He could research trends and then get ahead of the curve. If he wasn't ahead, he quickly adjusted to the track of others. As a developer on several acres of choice property, he wondered why a well-known financial icon was suddenly buying up all the surrounding land.

Research alerted him to the discovery of natural gas in the Barnett Shale. Those reserves stretched through most of the Metroplex. He and his team quickly adjusted to the potential of developing a company that would pull natural gas from the reservoirs under Tarrant and Dallas counties.

Restoring cars was more than a hobby with recreational value. For Tom, it became a small business and led him to winning countless awards in classic car shows. His sixteen-cylinder Cadillac was a project spanning more than eight years with proportionate costs. He heard the car run for the first time only days before his departure.

Would Tom become skilled in the restoration of cars and the development of natural resources and then be called to sit in the shade of a lovely tree for eternity? Would a man with the ability to develop large tracts of land and start companies want to spend eternity merely remembering? I think not!

Restoration of broken things and the development of the resources that creation contains is a project he is already skilled to accomplish. He is probably already engaged in Heaven's new city, engaged in development that will come here as a new Heaven and earth community.

Neither of these remarkable friends had taken voice lessons so they could join Heaven's longest-ever choir performance. Praise was part of their life, but not particularly through music. Work was a form of praise for them. They are not likely sitting in the choir loft. They are working on projects to prepare for Heaven and earth to merge.

They are not likely sitting in the choir loft. They are working on projects to prepare for Heaven and earth to merge.

Planets need developing around us. Infrastructure of all aspects will be required. On some planets, drilling for water will probably precede drilling for oil and gas or substances yet to be discovered. But we won't know what all that will call for until we know as we are known.

Knowing in Time and Eternity

If everybody knew what he or she most needed to know, what would that be? I think we can learn that by listening to God. He gives the basis for that discovery—we "will know as we are known." While writing this, I saw a connection between knowing in both time and eternity, one I had never considered. Look at this truth with me.

> *For now we see in a mirror dimly, but then face to face; now I know in part, but then I will know fully just as I also have been fully known. But now faith, hope, love abide, these three; but the greatest of these is love* (1 Corinthians 13:12, 13, NASU*).*

Faith, hope, and love are connected to our knowing in time and eternity. We know faith, hope, and love here and now by knowing God. Amplified knowledge will continue with "face to face" clarity. Faith, hope, and love are eternal attributes of God. We get them from Him, enjoy them with Him, and share them with others.

We know *real* love by knowing God, who is love. We have faith by knowing God's love also. Hope becomes ours as well through experiencing God's love connecting us in faith.

Love's greatness among the three comes from love being the source of both faith and hope. With love comes faith's awareness of substance and evidence. Faith activated by love gives us hope's assurance.

Both Dain and Tom faced issues that were not easy to face several times through the years. Both knew the supply of love with faith's substance and hope's assurance of things seen by God and shown to them.

Faith is part of hearing God or knowing God (Romans 10:17). The gift of faith is one of the spiritual gifts (1 Corinthians 12:9). Faith is a noun *and* a verb, a quality and an action. Faith is a "title deed" and "proof of things not seen," as the Amplified Bible says (Hebrews 11:1).

Faith as Currency to Use for Life's Needs

God gives faith—we use it as currency for the needs of life. All of the heroes in the faith hall of fame in Hebrews 11 used God's gift of faith to do the exploits described. The measure of faith has been given to everyone for guided thinking (Romans 12:3).

Peter gives a classic summary of faith as currency in his second Epistle: *"Make every effort to add to your faith goodness; and to goodness, knowledge"* (2 Peter 1:5, 6, NIV). Faith already belongs to us. "Now use it!" Peter instructs us. This gift from God is the means of the list of add-ons to God's character development in us. We use the currency of faith for all that is needed in life.

Then Peter lets us know God's thoughts: "If you don't have these things you are either blind or forgetful" (verse 9; this is my paraphrase). All these things are ours if we only stay awake and pay attention in God's class.

Hope is part of awakening to God's glorious presence. Paul's experience in God's gift of hope can be seen Romans 5. This is to be our experience as well. He is rejoicing in the hope of God's glory.

Then he follows a cycle of hope as part of God's presence as He accompanies us through a series of experiences. These are experiences we won't sign up for. Hope is found in glory, then hope is found in suffering, hope is part of being steadfast, hope continues in proven character, and hope emerges even stronger as God's love is poured out by the Holy Spirit in our heart (Romans 5:1-5).

These three gifts from God are always found in company together. The greatest is love because God's nature of love provides faith and hope as part of His eternal fellowship with us.

Both Dain and Tom knew these gifts. Faith as currency was used in all they did. With that currency at work, hope existed for things not yet seen except in their own minds. Hope existed when challenges faced them.

Both lived with three companions: Faith, hope, and love. Both stepped through the shadows to the light with all three companions accompanying them because they abide forever.

The Massive New Development: Our Universe

That is why the continuum and linkage of what we know here will be part of our knowing in eternity. The mass of creation that science discovered, and is still discovering, is undeveloped.

The newly created earth was undeveloped except for a garden seen by Moses. God's "press release" contained a selected disclosure of creation's beginning. The dialogue reviewed was obviously selected. We know those salient parts, which give us a picture as a starting point for future completion, the completion or development of all of remaining creation.

The undeveloped earth awaiting the expansion of a garden for Adam and Eve suggests the same scenario for us. It is pretty easy to conclude that God's wisdom included Adam being part of the creation of the garden, where he and Eve would be co-managers with God.

Adam may have been allowed to observe Eden's creation, at the least, or he may have even participated, at the most. He certainly participated with God in creation by naming the animals. Even so, our dominion management role with God will not be a short-term project. Eternity will take as long God lives, works, creates, and develops all of His family estate.

His family members will probably be planners with Him. Creativity is part of His DNA. Our spiritual DNA contains the same creative capacities. His language found in all of creation is found in us.

Allow me one more quote from Dallas:

> We will not sit around looking at one another or at God for eternity but will join the eternal Logos, "reign with him," in the endlessly ongoing creative work of God. It is for this that we were each individually intended, as both kings and priests (Exodus 19:6, Revelation 5:10).[168]

How long it will take to develop trillions of galaxies will be known in the doing of it! Time will merge back into eternity, from which it came. Eternity will afford the full energy of living in the present as if it just began.

God Works from Rest–And the Rest of God Becomes Ours

God's rest was not the rest of inactivity, but the rest of completion providing a foundation for continued work. Jesus made it clear His Father was working (John 14:10, 11). Jesus worked with His Father, just as we work with Him. That relationship of co-labor will be forever.

Rest is ours because God's rest is shared with us. God works from rest. We can rest with Him and work from His rest. Creativity requires rest.

Meeting "The You" That You Barely Know

You are going to know as you are known. I am going to know as I am known. God is the only One who fully knows us. God is the only One who knows fully and also knows Himself —"I Am Who I Am" (Exodus 3:14). My continued emphasis on knowing who we are will be fully answered in the graduation to life's full measure.

> # You are going to know as you are known. I am going to know as I am known. God is the only One who fully knows us.

The you that you may barely know, maybe only briefly met, is going to be known. God already knows you. The one who declares "I Am Who I Am" will let you say with Him: "I am who I am." In honor of God's workmanship, we can say, "I am who I am"—God's created child.

Our brain/mind computes voluminous amounts of information about us without ever consulting us with the process by which it gains the message it sends. Physicist Gerald Schroeder refers to this being performed by "the other you, the you you never ever meet."[169]

Using the example of a child crying in the night and our being awakened, he describes, neurologically, how we awaken. We know our child cried. But, Schroeder writes, the "other you" is "there housed in the head that lets 'you' hear, see a rose, or smell a fragrance."[170]

Then he describes the voluminous process "the you" our brain supplies. The cry is heard in the ear and sent through a long neurological route, which includes the thalamus, the temporal cortex, the amygdala's subconscious, the hypothalamus, and the cerebellum where "the you" we know is awakened.

> In that remarkable "you" we do not know is housed a wonderful capacity for calculations which God created to work without our supervision or even knowing their existence. This housing is held by what seems to be nothing other than a hundred thousand million axons, each having thousands of terminals, connecting and interconnecting with a million billion (1,000,000,000,000,000)

dendrites. To get an inkling of what that number, and hence your brain[,] is all about, I urge you to count to a billion, a million times. After all, in some sense, the part of you that you have not met has done it, so why don't you do it also? At one number each second, with no breaks for resting, that task will occupy you for the next thirty million years.

The brain has space for two versions of you; the you you never meet but that meets with you every moment of your life as it regulates all the automatic functions of your body; and the you you know so well, the one that feels as if it is just above the bridge of your nose within your forehead. The one you know is also a composite of two: the analog emotions whose source we often cannot even identify, and the particulate sensory data of sight, sound, touch, taste, and smell.[171]

You are probably wondering why I am relating this complicated information when you know you are at the end of the book and I am about to close this writing? Because knowing "the you" of God's masterful spiritual workmanship is far more profound than our physiological self we do not know. If it would take the next thirty million years to count the components of our brain's circuitry in one application, as Dr. Schroeder has calculated, how much longer will it take to know all the facets of being one of God's masterpieces, a new creation?

That being true, it may be part of the reason eternity will take so long. We will be learning the marvels of who we are as well as managing the marvels of His creation. One of the marvels will be our knowing—knowing as we are known. Accessing knowledge just out of our reach now will be an endless delight.

> How great is the love the Father has lavished on us, that we
> should be called children of God! And that is what we are!
> The reason the world does not know us is that it did not know
> him. Dear friends, now we are children of God, and what we
> will be has not yet been made known. But we know that when
> he appears, we shall be like him, for we shall see him as he is.
> Everyone who has this hope in him purifies himself, just as he is
> pure (1 John 3:1-3, NIV).

Meantime, in the reality of His love-filled presence, we are learning to think and to know. Our dendrite/trees of thought are being replanted, straightened from life's storms, and nurtured with life from His words being heard now (Matthew 4:4).

For myself, months of time spent thinking through implications from countless sources has led to some important conclusions. There is probably an important connection between the naming of two trees in the garden and now having verification from physics of the presence of tree-shaped dendrites in our mind. These are trees of thought we constantly use to guide our choices each day.

The choice is the same as in the garden: we either use God's thoughts—or thoughts from another source. From our choice, we live either in the garden of God's reigning presence, His kingdom, or a location of self-directed engagement. Our location, without knowing God's presence, is less than God intended or we will ultimately desire. The result is our being ill at ease. In the kingdom of the heavens where God shares Himself, His love, His power, and His provision, we can be *at ease*.

Near the Trees of Thought There Is a Cross

Our anatomy, now well known from scientific evidence, not only includes the likeness of trees in our brain, but the shape of a cross.

Optic nerves traveling in route from the eyes to the brain intersect with one another on their journey in an area called the chiasm. The chiasm is located in the bottom of the brain. *Chiasm* is the Greek word for cross.

I was first made aware of this from an esteemed friend, R. Michael Siatkowski, MD, whose specialty in medicine is ophthalmology. Here are the insights he shared with me:

> The anatomy of the visual system is such that the optic nerves, traveling en route from the eyes to the brain, intersect with one another on their journey in an area called the chiasm. The chiasm is located at the bottom of the brain. Chiasm is, of course, the Greek word for the cross. Thus, the structure responsible for all our thinking is supported from below by the cross—we are truly made in God's image! J. Lawton Smith, MD (neuro-ophthalmologist) writes in *A Physicians Faith* (2007 edition): "the human brain receives no visual information that does not go by way of the cross (chiasm)." … This was foreordained before the foundation of the world, and has been anatomically imprinted in every mortal who has lived since Adam was created! No visual input can be

received by the human brain that does not go by way of an anatomical structure we all possess, which is truly a CROSS!

From the research of physicist Gerald Schroeder this same formation of visual circuitry is described, in *The Hidden Face of God*: "In point-by-point transmission from each retina, a ganglion of a million or so nerves carries the image aft into the brain where the two optic nerves—one from each eye—meet and divide."[172]

His book also carries an artist's drawing illustrating the eyes being connected to the brain with the optic nerves from each eye meeting in the frontal area of the brain. Approximately half of the nerves cross from each eye to the other side of the brain while the other half move to the same corresponding side of the brain. The drawing clearly depicts the crossing of visual information in every brain.

It is documented in Scripture that God can be seen and recognized from His created order. Just as thoughts form the shape of trees—dendrites—sight forms the likeness of a cross at the intersection of the retinal signals. The most recognized symbol in our world today, the cross, has a neurological likeness in our visual system. No case can be proven that God knew that in this day of evidence from physics and science we would know that visual awareness involves a cross. Yet the fact exists that everything we see passes through a cross for recognition in our brain.

Here is what Scripture says about creation revealing God. The epistle of Paul to the Christians of Rome is known as a distillation of God making Himself known to all mankind. In the first chapter of the letter Paul makes an unmistakable statement about the role creation plays. Paul says God has made Himself plain to everyone!

*For what can be known about God is plain to them, because
God has shown it to them. For his invisible attributes, namely,
his eternal power and divine nature, have been clearly perceived,
ever since the creation of the world, in the things that have been
made. So they are without excuse. For although they knew God,
they did not honor him as God or give thanks to him, but they
became futile in their thinking, and their foolish hearts were
darkened* (Romans 1:19-21, ESV).

Where Do You Find God Looking Back at You?

Creation is evidence of God looking back at us as much as the evidence Francis Collins found in the profound insight of C.S. Lewis. Lewis described Moral Law, evidenced in all people, as God's evidence of His own existence as well as presence. Though a self-developed atheist, Collins knew that law as part of his life experience. From this insight Francis Collins was honest enough to ask the question quoted many pages ago: "Was this God looking back at me?" He found his conclusion to be: YES!

Jean-Paul Sartre found God's presence made known to him. His response was the opposite of Francis Collins. He flew into a rage, profaning God's name. Instead of a blessing he offered a curse, calling for God to damn. But that is the opposite of God's nature.

God is not limited as to how He is seen or how He is heard. Our response to seeing God or hearing God then becomes the issue of choosing life or death.

Paul states that case unmistakably in this epic disclosure of God being seen by every person through creation.

> … *his eternal power and divine nature, have been clearly*
> *perceived, ever since the creation of the world, in the things that*
> *have been made (Romans 1:20).*

All the things that God has made bear evidence of Him. How He is seen is determined by the comprehension that occurs within our brain, our mind, and our spirit. Perhaps the most important evidence of Him in creation is when we look in a mirror, knowing now that "there is more than meets the eye."

Most important of all is how we respond! Paul announces,

> *So they are without excuse. For although they knew God, they*
> *did not honor him as God or give thanks to him … (Romans*
> *1:21).*

The evidence of God calls for a response. Those left without an excuse did so because they did not believe God. Honor to Him was due. Giving thanks to Him was due. Francis Collins turned with honor and gave thanks to God. He turned from atheism to God in belief. Jean-Paul Satre turned in rage against God. He believed God was there but dishonored His name and turned away in unbelief, which led to his announced atheism.

Giving thanks that flows from our life comes from being thankful in all things (1 Thessalonians 5:19). Giving thanks or not giving thanks is the measurement by which we know we believe God or refuse to acknowledge Him as God, with the accompanying confidence of His love resulting in confidence to believe.

Every experience in seeing God calls for the giving of thanks in honor due to One who honors us with His presence. We are seeing God whether we know it is God or not. We see because we are willing to look. We look because we are willing to believe. We believe because we are willing to honor Him and give thanks to Him.

Giving thanks or not giving thanks is the measurement by which we know we believe God or refuse to acknowledge Him as God,

The opening thought of this book was to look in the mirror and see yourself. Now there is the reality that eternity includes seeing ourselves, or knowing ourselves, in a new image finder. It is not a mirror but the face of God. In the face of God we find our true identify. We know ourselves because God introduces us. Already known by Him, we begin to know the person we are to become and have become in Christ.

Being at ease is God's provision for every person. Everything we face can be faced at ease. All things are ours: *"the world, life, death, things present, things to come—all are ours"* (1 Corinthians 3:22). *"For I am convinced that neither death, nor life, nor angels, nor principalities, nor things present, nor things to come, nor powers, nor height, nor depth, nor any other created thing, will be able to separate us from the love of God, which is in Christ Jesus our Lord"* (Romans 8:38, 39, NASU).

Nothing can separate us from the love of God—except our thoughts! God's love-filled presence is only forfeited when our thoughts will not welcome His being Emmanuel—God with us!

In Every Garden God Is with Us

A hymn I grew up enjoying shares the account of Jesus being in a garden but not recognized. "In the Garden" was written by C. Austin Miles after his devotional time spent reading John's account of the resurrection of Jesus.

Though I will paraphrase the account, you may want to read it for yourself. You will probably remember the first words of the hymn are:

"I come to the garden alone, While the dew is still on the roses."

Austin Miles is reliving Mary Magdalene arriving at a garden where Jesus was buried. He is giving her a voice to describe coming alone to a garden containing a grave.

It was a grave like no other. For John's gospel links the account of the death of Jesus to a garden and to the presence of a grave surrounded by beauty. *"At the place where Jesus was crucified, there was a garden, and in the garden a new tomb, in which no one had ever been laid"* (John 19:41, NIV).

I believe it is more than significant, even monumental, that John describes the death of Jesus in the presence of a garden. Further, he describes the garden offering a grave where the body exhibiting God in human flesh was laid. In that garden, and from that grave, a resurrected body was raised, declaring the defeat of death, as Jesus promised. John's carefully worded description of the life of Jesus being given on a cross near a garden and returned from a grave in the garden has a direct link to the eternal life God first shared with Adam and Even in a garden. Adam and Eve did not carry eternal life to full term. But Jesus bought it back! Then from the tomb he brought it back to personally give to everyone who will receive by believing Him in resurrected reality now.

Now let me paraphrase John's equally careful detail of the first appearance of the resurrected eternal Christ. Early in the morning before light pushed darkness away, Mary came to the garden. She knew Jesus as few others knew His life-giving ways. Yet the last time she saw Him, there was no life left.

The garden was the same, but the grave was different. A grave as empty as Mary's own once-hope-void heart was all she found. She ran to tell the disciples. Then she returned after them. But the garden now contained more than before. Two angels were there at the grave. They asked her why she wept. Then the wonder of it all was that Jesus was there. Mary turned and saw Him. Yet one who had seen Him countless times did not know the One she had braved the darkness and potential danger to be near. He was hidden from her in plain sight.

Yet one who had seen Him countless times did not know the One she had braved the darkness and potential danger to be near.

She talked—to the one she most wanted to see—about what she could do to find the body of Jesus. Looking straight at Him, she assumed she was looking at a mere garden attendant. Then Jesus spoke: "Mary." Her name, coming from His voice— was a sound Mary knew. Her heart heard again His words of life, hope, peace, joy, and love.

The timelessness of God's presence greeted C. Austin Miles in April 1912. He chose to read the account I just paraphrased. He read of a garden with a grave that was empty and a life like no other ready to share His resurrected reality.

A song was born from what Austin Miles describes as his becoming part of the story John was telling. "Under the inspiration of the vision I wrote as quickly as the words could be formed the poem exactly as it has since appeared. That same evening I wrote the music."[173]

> *I come to the garden alone, While the dew is still on the roses,*
> *And the voice I hear, falling on my ear, The Son of God discloses.*
> *And He walks with me, and He talks with me,*
> *And He tells me I am His own,*
> *And the joy we share as we tarry there,*
> *None other has ever known.*

Mary came to a garden alone—yet she was not alone. She needed only to look with eyes of understanding.

That understanding came in the words Jesus spoke to her.

We too live by every word that comes from the mouth of God.

Whatever the garden, we are not alone.

In the garden of wrong thoughts we are not alone.
In the garden of deep despair we are not forsaken.
In the garden of every sort His voice can be heard.
In the sound of His voice we hear a call to walk with Him.
In the sound of His voice we know we are His own.
In the sound of His voice we share in His joy.
—J.H.

In the garden of the reality of the kingdom of the heavens, we join Dallas and all the host of Heaven in saying to our Father …
THANK YOU!
THANK YOU FOR SHARING YOUR LIFE!
THANK YOU FOR SHARING YOUR PEACE!
THANK YOU FOR SHARING YOUR LOVE!
THANK YOU FOR SHARING YOUR CREATION!
THANK YOU FOR SHARING YOUR ETERNITY!

Notes

Introduction: Thinking with God

1. www.brainyquote.com

2. C. S. Lewis, *The Weight of Glory and Other Addresses* (Grand Rapids, MI: Erdmans, 1973), p. 58.

3. James P. Gills, MD, *God's Prescription for Healing* (Lake Mary, FL: Siloam, a Strang Company, 2004). p.3

4. Ibid, 9.

5. Richard A. Swenson, *More Than Meets the Eye* (Colorado Springs: NavPress), p. 17.

6. Colossians 1:26, 27, *THE MESSAGE: The Bible in Contemporary Language* © 2002 by Eugene H. Peterson. All rights reserved.

Chapter One: The Most Advanced Medical Clinic You Can Visit

7. Richard A. Swenson, *More Than Meets the Eye* (Colorado Springs: NavPress, 2000), p. 80.

8. Ibid, 79, 80.

9.   Gills, p. 66

10.   Swenson, 39, 40.

11.   Ibid, 56.

12.   Ibid, 57.

13.   Ibid, 59, 60.

14.   Ibid, 48, 49.

15.   From Swenson, paraphrased. Page 66.

16.   Francis Collins, *The Language of God* (New York, NY: Free Press, Simon & Schuster), pp. 2, 3.

17.   Swenson, 61-63.

18.   Ibid, 64,65.

19.   Ibid, 66.

20.   Ibid, 66.

Chapter Two: We See with Our Brain, Not Our Eyes

21.   Swenson, 32.

22.   Robert Kurson, *Crashing Through* (New York, NY: Random House Publishing Group, 2007), p. 3.

23.   Ibid, 18,19.

24.   Ibid, 21, 22.

25.   Ibid, 28.

26.   Ibid, 125.

27.   Ibid, 127.

28.   Ibid, 126.

29.   Ibid, 126-128.

30.   Ibid, 129, 131.

31.   Ibid, 174.

32.   Ibid, 234, 255.

33.   Ibid, 259.

34.   Ibid, 265.

35.   Ibid, 272.

Chapter Three: God's Visit to a Doctor's Brain

36.   Personal paper written, and shared with the author, by Dr. Russell Lambert.

37.   Ibid.

38.   Ibid.

Chapter Four: Thank You–The Fitting Response of a Thinker

39.   John Ortberg, www.christianitytoday.com/ct/2013/may-web-only/man-from-another-planet

40.   Dallas Willard, *Hearing God* (Downers Grove, IL: Intervarsity Press, 1984, 1993, 1999, 2012), p. 18.

41.   John Ortberg, www.christianitytoday.com/ct/2013/may-web-only/man-from-another-planet

42.   Willard, *Hearing God,* pp. 37, 38.

43.   Ibid, 64.

44.   Ibid, 145, 146.

Chapter Five: A Gifted Mind Guides Gifted Hands

45.   Ben Carson, *America the Beautiful* (Grand Rapids, MI: Zondervan, 2012), p. 54.

46.   Ibid.

47.   Ibid, p. 114.

48.   Ibid, p. 115.

49.   Ibid, 111, 112.

Chapter Six: God's Testimony Includes … You

50.   E. Stanley Jones, *The Unshakeable Kingdom and the Unchanging Person* (Bellingham, WA: McNet Press, 1972), p. 79. Reprinted with permission from Abingdon Press, USA.

Chapter Seven: A Garden with God's Presence

51. Jean Delumeau, *History of Paradise: The Garden of Eden in Myth and Tradition* (Urbana, IL: University of Illinois Press, 1995), p. 8.

52. Ibid, 6.

53. Ibid, 11.

54. Swenson, 174.

Chapter Eight: The Temporary Closing of the Garden

55. Peter Kreeft, *The God Who Loves You* (San Francisco, CA: Ignatius Press, 2004), pp. 166.

56. Craig Groeschel, *The Christian Atheist* (Grand Rapids, MI: Zondervan, 2010)

57. Gerald Schroeder, *The Hidden Face of God*, (New York, NY: TOUCHSTONES, 2001) p. 108.

58. Ibid, 113.

59. Caroline Leaf, *The Gift in You* (Southlake, TX: Improv, Ltd., 2009) p. 31.

60. Ibid, 153, 154.

Chapter Nine: Back to School: God's Kindergarten

61. Robert Fulghum, *All I Really Need to Know I Learned in Kindergarten*, (New York, NY: Random House Publishing Group, a Ballantine Book, 2003), p. vii.

62. Ibid, vii.

Chapter Ten: Replacing Thoughts and Replacing Cells

63. Schroeder, 146, 147.

64. Ibid, 152.

65. Peter Kreeft, *Heaven: The Heart's Deepest Longing (Expanded Editon)* (San Francisco, CA: Harper & Row Publishers, Ignatius Press, 1989) p. 130.

66. Ibid, 130.

67. C.S. Lewis as quoted by Peter Kreeft in *Heaven,* 131.

68. Dallas Willard, *The Allure of Gentleness* (San Francisco, CA: HarperOne Publishing, 2015), p.xiii

69. Ibid, 67.

70. Swenson, 17.

71. Swenson, 17, 18, 19.

Chapter Eleven: Getting Around to Thinking Straight

72. Caroline Leaf, *Who Switched Off My Brain?* (Nashville: Thomas Nelson Publishers, 2009), pp. 14, 15.

73. Ibid, 16.

74. Ibid, 17.

75. Ibid, 13, 14.

76. Dallas Willard, *The Divine Conspiracy* (New York, NY: Harper One, 1997), p. 79

77. Ibid, 76, 77.

78. Ibid, 76.

79. Leif Hetland, *Seeing Through Heaven's Eyes* (Shippensburg, PA: Destiny Image Publishers, 2011), pp. 21, 22.

80. Willard, *The Divine Conspiracy,* p. 63.

Chapter Twelve: The Friend of Thinkers, Good and Bad

81. Willard, *The Divine Conspiracy,* 105, 106.

Chapter Thirteen: God-Shaped Thoughts

82. Willard, *The Divine Conspiracy,* 93.

83. Ibid.

84. Ibid, 94.

Chapter Fourteen: Selecting Plants for the Garden of Thoughts

85. Leaf, *Who Switched Off My Brain?*, p. 49.

86. Ibid, 51.

87. M. Scott Peck, *The People of the Lie* (New York, NY: Simon and Schuster, 1983), p. 83.

88. Ibid, 206, 207.

Chapter Fifteen: Paying Off or Paying Back

89. NET Bible, copyright © 1996-2006 by Biblical Studies Press, L.L.C., Dallas, Texas, www.bible.org. All rights reserved. Used by permission.

90. Brian Zhand, *Unconditional?* (Lake Mary, FL: Charisma House, 2010). p.103.

91. Brian Zhand, *Unconditional?* (Lake Mary, FL: Charisma House, 2010). pp.31-34

Chapter Seventeen: The Power of Endless Life: What to Do with It

92. Swenson, *More Than Meets the Eye*, 95, 96.

93. Willard, *The Divine Conspiracy*, 302.

94. Ibid. 302

Chapter Eighteen: Don't Save Eternity Until Later

95. Swenson, 144, 145.

96. Willard, *The Divine Conspiracy*, 391.

Chapter Nineteen: The Lord's Prayer Becomes Our Prayer

97. John Piper, www.desiringGod.org, Resource Library, November 4, 1984.

Chapter Twenty: Replanting Thoughts: Repentance

98.   Willard, *The Divine Conspiracy*, 80.

99.   Ibid, 79.

100. Ibid, 80.

101. Leaf, *Who Switched Off My Brain?*, 19, 20.

102. Ibid, 21.

103. Ibid, 22, 23.

104. Ibid, 24.

105. Ibid, 39, 40.

106. Ibid. See this list on pp. 162-175.

107. Ibid, 39.

108. Ibid, 87.

109. Ibid, 36, 37.

110. Ibid, 88.

111. Leaf, *The Gift in You,* 149.

112. Ibid, 150, 151.

113. Holy Bible, New Living Translation®, copyright © 1996, 2004 by Tyndale Charitable Trust. Used by permission of Tyndale House Publishers. All rights reserved.

Chapter Twenty-One: If You Tell God to Leave, Where Will He Go?

114. Gerald L. Schroeder, *The Science of God* (New York, NY: Free Press—Simon & Schuster, Inc, 1997), p. 166.

115. Ibid, 168, 169.

116. Ibid, 171.

117. Willard, *The Divine Conspiracy*, 67, 68.

118. Ibid, 68.

119. Ibid, 79.

120. Ibid, 76.

121. Schroeder, 75.

122. Willard, *The Divine Conspiracy*, 144.

123. Ibid, 145.

Chapter Twenty-Two: What's the Matter with God?

124. Willard, *Hearing God,* 274.

125. Kurson, *Crashing Through,* 174.

126. Kreeft, *Heaven,* quoting Augustine in *Confessions I*, 64, 65. This is paraphrased from: "Thou has made us for thyself, our hearts are restless until they rest in thee."

127. Francis Collins, *The Language of God* (New York, NY: Free Press, Simon & Schuster, Inc., 2006), p. 16.

128. Ibid, 19.

129. Ibid, 29.

130. Ibid, 224, quoting C.S. Lewis from *Mere Christianity.*

131. Ibid, 225.

132. Swenson, 123.

133. Ibid, 124.

134. Ibid, 125, 126.

135. Ibid, 134.

136. Ibid, 136.

137. Ibid, 138.

138. Willard, *The Divine Conspiracy,* 384.

139. Swenson, 109, 110.

140. Willard, *The Divine Conspiracy,* 91.

141. Ibid, 84.

142. Ibid, 385, 386.

143. Kreeft, *The God Who Loves You,* 53.

144. Randy Alcorn, *Fifty Days of Heaven* (Carol Stream, IL: Tyndale House Publishers, 2006), p. 197.

145. Kreeft, 108.

146. Ibid, 109, 110.

147. Ibid, 111-114.

148. Kreeft, *Heaven*, 191.

149. Willard, *Hearing God*, 274.

Chapter Twenty-Three: Food for Thought– from Bone to Brain

150. Schroeder, *The Hidden Face of God,* 171.

151. Swenson, *More Than Meets the Eye*, 84.

152. Swenson, 85.

153. Swenson, 85, 86.

154. Swenson, 87, 89.

155. www.amberroseministries.com/miracle-stories-2/

156. Willard, *The Divine Conspiracy,* 81, 82.

157. Ibid, 82.

Chapter Twenty-Four: Health Assurance– A Love-Filled Life

158. Leif Hetland, *Seeing Through Heaven's Eyes,* 129.

159. Ibid, 130.

160. Ibid, 131.

161. Ibid, 131-134.

162. Willard, *Hearing God*, 221.

163. Ibid, p 241.

164. Peter J. Daniels, *Living on the Edge* (Strathalbyn, South Australia: World Center for Entrepreneurial Studies, 2004), p. 43.

165. Ibid, 67.

166. Ibid, 25, 26.

Chapter Twenty-Five: Why Does Eternity Take So Long?

167. Willard, *The Divine Conspiracy*, 83-85.

168. bid, 378.

169. Schroeder, *The Hidden Face of God*, 126.

170. Ibid.

171. Ibid, 127.

172. Ibid, 115.

173. www.songfacts.com, "In the Garden"

A previous book by Jim Hylton:

beingateasebook.com

At beingateasebook.com, you may order the folowing:

- The Supernatural Skyline
  $12.00 plus postage

- Additional copies of Being at Ease
  (autographed by request)
  $15.00 plus postage

You may also use the site to contact Jim Hylton with
questions and to inquire about speaking engagements.
Please know that Jim will do his best
to respond to you personally.